AF887241

GLOBAL ECONOMIC STUDIES

THE GLOBAL FINANCIAL CRISIS: POLICIES AND IMPLICATIONS

Global Economic Studies

Additional books in this series can be found on Nova's website under the Series tab.

Additional E-books in this series can be found on Nova's website under the E-books tab.

Financial Institutions and Services

Additional books in this series can be found on Nova's website under the Series tab.

Additional E-books in this series can be found on Nova's website under the E-books tab.

GLOBAL ECONOMIC STUDIES

THE GLOBAL FINANCIAL CRISIS: POLICIES AND IMPLICATIONS

JOHN P. GALLAGHER
AND
EMMETT C. WILKINS
EDITORS

Nova Science Publishers, Inc.
New York

Copyright © 2012 by Nova Science Publishers, Inc.

All rights reserved. No part of this book may be reproduced, stored in a retrieval system or transmitted in any form or by any means: electronic, electrostatic, magnetic, tape, mechanical photocopying, recording or otherwise without the written permission of the Publisher.

For permission to use material from this book please contact us:
Telephone 631-231-7269; Fax 631-231-8175
Web Site: http://www.novapublishers.com

NOTICE TO THE READER

The Publisher has taken reasonable care in the preparation of this book, but makes no expressed or implied warranty of any kind and assumes no responsibility for any errors or omissions. No liability is assumed for incidental or consequential damages in connection with or arising out of information contained in this book. The Publisher shall not be liable for any special, consequential, or exemplary damages resulting, in whole or in part, from the readers' use of, or reliance upon, this material. Any parts of this book based on government reports are so indicated and copyright is claimed for those parts to the extent applicable to compilations of such works.

Independent verification should be sought for any data, advice or recommendations contained in this book. In addition, no responsibility is assumed by the publisher for any injury and/or damage to persons or property arising from any methods, products, instructions, ideas or otherwise contained in this publication.

This publication is designed to provide accurate and authoritative information with regard to the subject matter covered herein. It is sold with the clear understanding that the Publisher is not engaged in rendering legal or any other professional services. If legal or any other expert assistance is required, the services of a competent person should be sought. FROM A DECLARATION OF PARTICIPANTS JOINTLY ADOPTED BY A COMMITTEE OF THE AMERICAN BAR ASSOCIATION AND A COMMITTEE OF PUBLISHERS.

Additional color graphics may be available in the e-book version of this book.

Library of Congress Cataloging-in-Publication Data

The global financial crisis : policies and implications / editors, John P. Gallagher and Emmett C. Wilkins.
p. cm.
Includes index. ISBN 978-1-61470-317-4 (hbk.)
1. Financial crises--United States. 2. Global Financial Crisis, 2008-2009. 3. Finance--United States. 4. Financial institutions--United States. 5. United States--Economic policy--2009- I. Gallagher, John P. II. Wilkins, Emmett C.
HB3722.G5956 2011
330.9'0511--dc23

2011022490

Published by Nova Science Publishers, Inc. †New York

CONTENTS

PREFACE

This book presents current research in the study of the global financial crisis. Topics discussed include banking and financial infrastructure continuity; increasing IMF resources and the role of Congress; analysis and policy implication of the global financial crisis; implications for the United States and foreign and trade policy effects.

Chapter 1 - The Treasury Department and other agencies have long had the responsibility to ensure that the financial sectors of the economy are able to continue operations after physical and economic disruptions. This report outlines the financial sector's recovery plans for two kinds of disasters: the inability to conduct transactions and large losses of asset value. The basic function of the payment system is carried out by banks, and monetary policy affects banks immediately. Because brokers, exchanges, secondary market facilities, and insurance companies carry out crucial financial functions, their regulators and trade associations are involved in continuity of operations planning for contingencies ranging from pandemic flu to terrorist attacks.

Chapter 2 - The current global financial crisis is testing the ability of the International Monetary Fund (IMF), and other international financial institutions (IFIs) to provide sufficient assistance to affected countries. It has also enhanced the IMF's role in crisis management and given it a key place in current efforts to reform the world financial system. During the past half-year, many countries have come to the IMF for assistance and more are likely to apply. Several steps have been taken to expand the IMF 's financial resources and to otherwise augment the funds available to help vulnerable countries weather the present crisis.

Chapter 3 - What began as a bursting of the U.S. housing market bubble and a rise in foreclosures has ballooned into a global financial and economic crisis. The world now appears to have entered a global recession that is causing widespread business contraction, increases in unemployment, and shrinking government revenues. Some of the largest and most venerable banks, investment houses, and insurance companies have either declared bankruptcy or have had to be rescued financially. The world is facing the worst economic conditions since the great depression. Nearly all industrialized countries and many emerging and developing nations have announced economic stimulus and/or financial sector rescue packages, such as the American Recovery and Reinvestment Act of 2009 (H.R. 1, P.L. 111-5). Several countries have resorted to borrowing from the International Monetary Fund as a last resort. The crisis has exposed fundamental weaknesses in financial systems worldwide, demonstrated how interconnected and interdependent economies are today, and has posed vexing policy dilemmas for governments.

Chapter 4 - Over the past several years, China has enjoyed one of the world's fastest growing economies and has been a major contributor to world economic growth. However, the current global financial crisis threatens to significantly slow China's economy. Several Chinese industries, particularly the export sector, have been hit hard by crisis, and millions of workers have reportedly been laid off. This situation is of great concern to the Chinese government, which views rapid economic growth as critical to maintaining social stability. China is a major economic power and holds huge amounts of foreign exchange reserves, and thus its policies could have a major impact on the global economy. For example, the Chinese government in November 2008 announced plans to implement a $586 billion package to help stimulate the domestic economy. If successful, this plan could also boost Chinese demand for imports. In addition, in an effort to help stabilize the U.S. economy, China might boost its holdings of U.S. Treasury securities, which would help fund the Federal Government's borrowing needs to purchase troubled U.S. assets and to finance economic stimulus packages. However, some U.S. policymakers have expressed concerns over the potential political and economic implications of China's large and growing holdings of U.S. Government debt securities. This report will be updated as events warrant.

Chapter 5 - The global financial and economic crisis affects all three of the essential national interests of the United States: national security, economic well being, and value projection. Only occasionally does an event of this magnitude occur that generates such daunting challenges yet also opportunities for U.S. policy. The effects of the crisis on foreign policy, trade, and security are so diverse and widespread that, out of necessity, policy responses must range from the highly specific to the broad and ethereal.

Versions of these Chapters were also published in *Journal of Current Issues in Finance, Business and Economics, Volume 4, Issue 1-2,* published by Nova Science Publishers, Inc. They were submitted for appropriate modifications in an effort to encourage wider dissemination of research.

In: The Global Financial Crisis: Policies and Implications
Editor: J. P. Gallagher and E. C. Wilkins
ISBN 978-1-61470-317-4
© 2012 Nova Science Publishers, Inc.

Chapter 1

BANKING AND FINANCIAL INFRASTRUCTURE CONTINUITY: PANDEMIC FLU, TERRORISM, AND OTHER CHALLENGES*

N. Eric Weiss

ABSTRACT

The Treasury Department and other agencies have long had the responsibility to ensure that the financial sectors of the economy are able to continue operations after physical and economic disruptions. This report outlines the financial sector's recovery plans for two kinds of disasters: the inability to conduct transactions and large losses of asset value. The basic function of the payment system is carried out by banks, and monetary policy affects banks immediately. Because brokers, exchanges, secondary market facilities, and insurance companies carry out crucial financial functions, their regulators and trade associations are involved in continuity of operations planning for contingencies ranging from pandemic flu to terrorist attacks.

Regulators of financial entities have developed guidelines for regulatees to follow to cushion physical and economic shocks. There are procedures to protect business information technology, physical security, and for the continuity of markets critical for the nation's transactions. Government and private sector initiatives seek cost-effective ways to strengthen the resiliency of the financial system's computers against cyber attacks. Many of these arrangements protecting financial institutions against attacks are also part of the national effort to prevent terrorist financing from within the financial system. (See CRS Report RL33020, Terrorist Financing: U.S. Agency Efforts and Inter-Agency Coordination, by Martin A. Weiss et al.) Defense of financial businesses' information systems also helps to deter national threats.

Following September 11, 2001, the nation became concerned with physical security. The anthrax attack in October 2001 heightened worries about biological terrorism. In 2004, the possibility of an avian flu pandemic concentrated continuity concerns on natural occurring challenges to the smooth functioning of the nation's financial system. More recently in 2009, concerns have arisen related to A/H1N1

* This is an edited, reformatted and augmented version of CRS Report RL31873, dated May 4, 2009.

("swine") flu. Congress, regulators, and executive branch agencies have responded to each of these threats. This report will be updated as events warrant.

Banking and Financial Institutions Form a Critical Infrastructure

Financial institutions, including banks, other depositories, securities dealers, insurers, and investment companies are part of the nation's critical infrastructure required for the nation's minimum economic operations [1]. Financial institutions accept funds from various sources and make them available as loans or investments to those who need them. America has vulnerabilities because its financial records are on computers and paper.

Financial institutions face two categories of emergencies that could impair their functioning. The first is directly financial: a sudden drop in the value of financial assets, whether originating domestically or elsewhere in the world, that could cause a national or even global financial crisis. The second is operational: the failure of the support structures that underlie the financial system. Either could disrupt the nation's ability to supply goods and services. They could reduce the pace of economic activity, or at an extreme, cause an actual contraction of economic activity.

It is often argued that the collapse of one prominent entity or interconnected company (such as AIG, Merrill Lynch, or Bear Stearns) could evoke a contagion effect, in which sound financial institutions become viewed as weak, and panicked customers withdraw funds from sound entities, causing sound businesses to fail. Regulators generally address financial problems through deposit insurance and other sources of liquidity (such as emergency loans) for distressed institutions, through safety and soundness regulation, and via direct intervention. One approach is to create special purpose responses to financial stress, such as the Troubled Asset Relief Program (TARP) and Term Asset-Backed Securities Loan Fund (TALF) [2]. They address operational risks through corrective actions (as with the Y2K problem), redundancy, regulation, auditing, and other physical security. Under the worst case scenarios, the Federal Reserve (Fed) attempts to limit economic damage by supplying liquidity to the financial system and employing monetary policy to expand domestic demand (as it did following the 2001 terrorist attacks). In the Terrorism Risk Insurance Act of 2002 (TRIA), Congress expanded the Fed's ability to act as lender of last resort to the financial and real economies [3]. Congress may also legislate direct federal assistance to protect the financial infrastructure as it did in the cases of Chrysler, the Farm Credit System, and New York City to prevent them from defaulting, potentially causing failure in major parts of the financial system and the economy [4]. In 2009, TARP was used to provide relief for General Motors and Chrysler [5].

Pandemic Flu

Recently, the nation has become concerned about the possibility of a pandemic flu outbreak. Large scale illness and quarantines could disrupt the nation's financial system. Proposals have been made to increase teleworking and alternative work locations. The

Department of Health and Human Services (HHS) is the lead agency for government planning. It has created a special website that includes a check list for business planning, at http://www.pandemicflu.gov. In addition, the Department of Homeland Security (DHS) has held regional meetings around the nation to encourage businesses and governments to develop contingency plans for possible future disruptions.

Most of the same public and private groups that have worked to develop continuity of operations plans to recover after a terrorist attack have also worked together to plan for a pandemic. There is a consensus that although a pandemic would cause many of the same problems as a terrorist attack, it could be different. A pandemic could be worldwide, but have local concentrations requiring unprecedented coordination and communication between financial regulators, the private sector, public health officials, school officials, public transportation, mass transit, the communications sector, and police.

Financial organizations such as the American Bankers Association and the New York Stock Exchange have created the Financial Services Sector Coordinating Council for Critical Infrastructure Protection and Homeland Security (FSSCC), which has examined this problem from the perspective of banks and bank regulators, including compliance with the new proposed risk-based capital standards known as Basel II [6]. Their report emphasizes the need to minimize physical contact among employees, customers, and the supply chain; being able to operate with key staff incapacitated; and to have contingency plans if suppliers cannot deliver goods and services.

In October 2007, FSSCC, Treasury, DHS, and the Securities Industry and Financial Management Association (SIFMA) simulated an influenza pandemic with absenteeism rates reaching 49%. [7]. The goals of the exercise were to (1) enhance industry understanding of system risks from flu; (2) provide an opportunity to test plans for a flu pandemic; and (3) study how a flu pandemic would affect the financial structure. Over 98% of the 2,550 participating organizations said it helped them in their continuity planning.

A Government Accountability Office (GAO) study found that many government agencies would have essential team members telecommute during a pandemic, but that very few had tested their plans [8].

A flu pandemic is not just a concern of the United States. The International Monetary Fund published a report in 2006 that, in part, addresses the problems that could confront financial institutions [9]. These include continuity of operations, increased delinquency and default on loans due to illness at borrowers' business, and business disruption. The IMF recommended that financial businesses plan for a contagious outbreak, including provisions in case key staff become ill and for working from multiple locations. Other suggestions included finding ways for staff to commute without using mass transit.

The Role of DHS

The Department of Homeland Security (DHS) is the government agency responsible for communications security oversight.10 Financial institutions and their regulators operate in a different environment from nonfinancial ones. Financial intermediaries' most valuable assets are frequently business records that exist either as intangible computer records or as fragile paper documents. The financial sector rarely owns the external communications systems on which they depend. This lack of ownership limits the sector's ability to protect directly their vital communications. Protecting financial and banking computer hardware and software may require outside support.

DHS works with Treasury Department bodies concerned with financial security. Treasury assigns an expert in financial services matters on a rotating basis to DHS [11]. Following its move into DHS, the Secret Service, in cooperation with the Carnegie Mellon Software Institute, reviewed threats to information systems in critical financial infrastructures [12]. DHS has issued financial institution- specific alerts based on intelligence reports [13]

SAFETY NET MEASURES IN PLACE

This section offers a high level review of the powers of various financial regulators to intervene to prevent financial problems from spreading throughout the economy. It looks at both financial risks (those from a sudden decrease in value or a threat that financial intermediaries might not be able to honor their obligations to depositors) and physical risks (also known as operational and security risks).

Financial Risks

Financial regulation includes deposit insurance, safety and soundness oversight, and the Fed as lender of last resort and ultimate protector of the financial system. Many arrangements protect financial institutions and their customers from different kinds of risk [14]

The Fed has long stood ready to provide liquidity in the form of emergency loans to the banking system. The Federal Deposit Insurance Corporation (FDIC) protects depositors against failure of a bank or savings association. This insurance helps to prevent depositor panics that could drain banks of their funds, and in turn could lead to curtailed lending and calling in loans. Even healthy banks, otherwise untouched by any cause of failure, are vulnerable to runs in which many depositors seek to withdraw their funds.

The FDIC brings order to the process of resolving insolvent banks. This agency has long had authority to prevent the failure of a bank it deems essential, which Congress supplemented in the 1980s and 1990s to allow even greater flexibility. The FDIC may borrow up to $30 billion from the U.S. Treasury for rescue operations. Credit unions have similar arrangements with their Central Liquidity Facility and Share Insurance Fund. The Pension Benefit Guaranty Corporation (PBGC) guarantees pension funds with defined benefits.

The securities industry lacks a pool of emergency liquidity, but the Fed may, if it chooses, lend directly to securities firms. The federal government protects individual securities accounts against operational losses—although not against collapses of market value—through the Securities Investor Protection Corporation [15].

Each state has a guaranty fund to make good the obligations of insolvent state-regulated insurance companies, although there is no national liquidity pool. TRIA provides a federal backstop for insurers willing to provide terrorism insurance. This law is designed to ensure that such insurance remains available by protecting providers against catastrophic losses in the event of terrorist attacks.

Other agencies bolster the national financial safety net maintaining confidence in many other ways. Not all of these entities provide liquidity or rescue in the case of financial failure. For many years, the securities industry and issuers have had overseers and programs designed to prevent a collapse in confidence originating within the system. The Securities and Exchange Commission (SEC) has sought transparency (disclosure) in the financial practices of businesses whose securities are traded in public markets. The Sarbanes-Oxley Act of 2002 sought to restore investor confidence by strengthening the regulation of independent auditors and by increasing the accountability of corporate executives and directors [16]. The Federal Housing Finance Agency regulates safety and transparency of important non-depository housing finance institutions [17]. The Commodity Futures Trading Commission (CFTC) oversees organized markets on futures and similar contracts through self-regulatory organizations.

Every state regulates its state-chartered banks, credit unions, thrift institutions, and companies engaged in securities and futures operations. Although state-chartered depository institutions are subject to federal regulation, the states are the primary regulators for insurance companies, finance companies, mortgage bankers, and the like. All 50 states oversee industry-funded guaranty funds to cover insolvencies in insurance companies, and some sponsor insurance for credit unions. State regulatory bodies for their respective industries are linked through the Conference of State Bank Supervisors, National Association of Insurance Commissioners, and North American Securities Administrators Association.

Most important for the worst cases of financial disruption, the Fed can inject funds into the economy to maintain liquidity in the financial system. Its authority to lend to individual institutions allows it to support institutions that analysts characterize as "too big to fail" because their collapse would pose a systemic risk to the economy. With TRIA, Congress strengthened the Fed's authority to lend to businesses directly in "unusual or exigent circumstances" [18].

Operational and Security Risks

Safety and soundness regulators issue guidelines and specific regulations for redundancy and security in physical and financial systems. They have long required banking institutions to consider operating (security) risks in contingency planning, and now include risk of catastrophic disruptions such as occurred on September 11, 2001. The securities industry is refining its procedures along similar lines. Insurance and other non-depository, non-securities financial businesses have not revealed their continuity plans. Although vital, they are not considered as critical. Few would consider the inability to process car loans, for example, to be as serious a problem as the inability to process checks and securities.

Safety and Continuity in Recent Experience

This section reviews the major financial disruptions since the September 11, 2001 terrorist attacks and how the government responded to reduce the chance that the disruption would spread and cause severe finance and economic problems.

Hurricane Katrina

Almost all of the financial sector's protections put in place in recent years had to be activated regionally due to the hurricanes of 2005. Hurricane Katrina disrupted power and communications in parts of Mississippi, Alabama, and Louisiana. Cash could not be withdrawn, checks could not be cashed, and debit and credit card networks (including ATMs) were down. In addition, facilities of a number of financial institutions were destroyed by wind or made inaccessible by water. Continuity of operations procedures, which are required of all but the smallest depository institutions, include maintaining critical personnel and data storage (with daily backups) at sites located at least 20 miles from a bank's headquarters. In almost every case, data backups worked despite loss of electricity. Joint guidance provided by the four federal bank regulators, and independently by the National Credit Union Administration, advised a temporary easing of regulations, facilitating recovery [19]

Insurance claims did not threaten the industry. Insured losses from Hurricane Katrina were estimated at $40.6 billion [20]. Nevertheless, the U.S. property-casualty insurance industry's net income after taxes rose by more than 4% during that time [21]. Increasing premiums seem inevitable in affected areas, thereby strengthening industry surpluses and viability.

Blackout of August 14, 2003

Emergency response measures noted above helped reduce the financial market damages from the August 14, 2003 power blackout in the northeastern United States and Canada. Treasury received no reports of major disruptions or losses of financial data, in large part because of steps taken to make systems resilient and redundant. Although there were isolated problems, the majority of stock, options, commodities, futures, and bond markets soon returned to normal operation. Banks closed affected offices in New York and Detroit; elsewhere, financial systems operated normally. The Fed's payments and emergency lending systems operated well. Banks borrowed and repaid $785 million from the Fed after the blackout, the most since the week after September 11. Applications for new mortgages fell temporarily because of the blackout. Contrary to initial fears, terrorists had not caused the blackout, and the blackout did not severely stress the nation's financial economy [22]

September 11, 2001

With the September 11, 2001 destruction of the World Trade Center, both problems—financial loss of asset values, and operational interruption—occurred simultaneously. The financial side of the response worked well, as the Fed provided liquidity to prevent panic. It injected more than $100 billion into the banking system. It arranged international facilities to keep the global financial system operating. The Fed and central banks around the world cut interest rates and lent money to banks to ease pressures on borrowers. The SEC issued emergency rules encouraging buying when the stock markets reopened. Trading recommenced rapidly, as the U.S. Treasury security market reopened on September 13, and the equities market was in full operation on September 17. Physical infrastructure recovery required a few days of heroic efforts (e.g., running new connections into Manhattan). Off-site record keeping, sharing of working space with displaced competitors, and increasing reliance on electronic records and communications systems by institutions outside the attack area allowed quick resumption of near-normal operations. Regulators and industry groups made it known that financial firms would need new contingency plans and stress tests to protect against more extreme situations in the future. Many insurance companies stopped writing insurance covering terrorist- related claims. Congress passed the Terrorism Risk Insurance Act (TRIA), at least in part, to encourage insurers to write terrorism risk insurance. Nevertheless, some high-profile commercial properties lack terrorism insurance because of the high cost of such protection in spite of TRIA. The government also provides insurance to domestic airlines under the Air Transportation Safety and System Stabilization Act [23].

Financial Business Continuity Initiatives

The September 11, 2001 attacks on the World Trade Center temporarily disrupted the nation's financial markets, including the New York Stock Exchange and Cantor Fitzgerald, the company responsible for most of the market for government bonds. This section examines the changes that financial regulators have made to improve the resilience of the nation's financial system since September 11, 2001, and plans for future changes.

Government Securities Clearing

Regulators are concerned about the U.S. government securities market, in view of its critical role for conducting monetary policy operations, financing government activities, and providing benchmark prices and hedging opportunities for other securities markets. The Securities Industry and Financial Markets Association (SIFMA) has created NewBank as a standby to settle Treasury securities trades if one of the two dominant clearing banks were to be unable to perform [24].

Communications

The Fed, Treasury, and other banking agencies have strengthened their programs for giving financial firms access to priority emergency communications. In the event of a disruption in normal communications, these programs would give priority services to large-value interbank funds transfer, securities pricing and transfer, and payment-related services.

Sound Practices Paper

The Fed, the OCC, and the SEC have issued an Interagency *Paper on Sound Practices to Strengthen the Resilience of the U.S. Financial System* [25]. The Sound Practices paper covers the largest wholesale financial sector businesses. It does not address retail or trading operations, nor the insurance sector. In April 2006, the three regulatory agencies reported to Congress that the recommendations were substantially in place [26]

Federal Financial Institutions Examination Council

The Federal Financial Institutions Examination Council (FFIEC) coordinates the examinations by FFIEC's four bank and one credit union regulatory agencies. It has published a public booklet on business continuity planning to assist examiners in evaluation a financial institution's risk management.27 The booklet provides guidance to the institutions being regulated.

Basel II

For the largest U.S. commercial banking organizations, the Fed has proposed additional mandates in its planned regulation known as the "Basel II Capital Accord." Among the issues raised by Basel II is a controversial requirement for covered firms to carry more capital for operational risk [28]. Basel II is likely to be revised in light of the financial turmoil that started in 2008.

Executive Branch Initiatives

This section reports on the actions of executive branch agencies to improve their ability to function financially following a catastrophic event. Public-private groups are also discussed.

Government's Own Financing

The E-Government Act of 2002 requires financial offices within the federal government to develop, document, and carry out agency-wide information security programs [29]. Treasury and other agencies have taken steps to protect the government's critical financial functions, including borrowing, making payments (including Social Security), and collecting taxes. Should the threat level rise, agencies will work with state and local governments to increase physical and cyber security measures, disperse individuals critical to operations, and activate backup facilities [30].

Presidential

The President appoints executives from the banking and securities industries to the National Infrastructure Advisory Council (NIAC). The panel advises the White House on cyber security and information security of critical economic infrastructure, including financial ones. Members of NIAC represent major sectors of the economy: banking and finance, transportation, energy, information technology, and manufacturing. It includes representatives from academia, state and local government, and law enforcement. NIAC works closely with the President's National Security and Telecommunications Advisory Committee.

Financial and Banking Information Infrastructure Committee

Treasury's Office of Critical Infrastructure Protection, formed after September 11, staffs the Financial and Banking Information Infrastructure Committee (FBIIC). Its chair is Treasury's Assistant Secretary for Financial Institutions [31].

Its mission is to coordinate federal and state efforts to improve the reliability and security of the financial system [32]. A public sector group, FBIIC was created by executive order in 2001 and includes representatives of state and national financial and banking regulators. FBIIC conducts vulnerability assessments of the retail payments system, government-sponsored enterprises (such as Fannie Mae, Freddie Mac, and the Federal Home Loan Banks), and the insurance industry—none directly addressed in the Structural Change report—and other improvements to financial resiliency [33].

Public-Private Treasury Efforts

Treasury has created a public-private partnership to ally with FBIIC, drawing together industry initiatives and coordinating private sector outreach for critical infrastructure protection and homeland security [34]. Treasury efforts to reduce vulnerabilities include providing alternative lines of communication for market participants. The department provides secret physical security measures to key financial institutions requesting them.

Treasury has a four-pronged overall approach to promoting continuity in the financial system and preventing interruption in case of a catastrophe. The focus first is on people. The second critical element is maintaining a high level of confidence in the functioning of the financial system.

The third element is making sure that markets remain open—or, if they do close, that they reopen as quickly as possible. The final element is that resilience requires diversification in case the primary place of business is nonfunctional [35]

Department of Justice

Independent of other efforts, the Department of Justice has developed a set of Suggested *Best Practices on Computer and Internet Security for Financial Institutions* [36]. The document informs financial firms of national resources available to them.

Private Sector Initiatives

This section summarizes the actions of businesses to improve their ability to survive major economic and financial disruptions. It also reports on public-private collaboration.

FS-ISAC and Payments Networks

The Financial Services-Information Sharing and Analysis Center (FS-ISAC) has approximately 1,000 members in banking, securities, insurance, and investment. It maintains a database of security threats and system vulnerabilities, which they tie in with the previously noted Treasury bodies [37].

Prominent funds transfer networks and securities exchanges have strengthened their continuity plans both independently and in conjunction with FS-ISAC. Through the private sector Partnership for Critical Infrastructure Security, FS-ISAC meets quarterly with sector coordinators for each of the critical national infrastructure sectors. It continues to function actively in public- private partnership and outreach modes, including making defenses available against "phishing" (criminal cyber activity seeking to steal financial data by sending out fraudulent emails) [38].

Securities Industry

The Securities Industry Association (SIA) has released disaster recovery best practices for its members. SIA is working with utility companies in New York to improve physical recovery measures. Although the September 11 terror attacks did not damage its facilities, the New York Stock Exchange (NYSE) has developed backup and redundancy facilities. The NYSE and NASDAQ have agreed to trade each others' stocks if either were to become incapacitated. The NYSE and National Association of Securities Dealers (NASD) have mandated business continuity plans. Measures revealed by the industry require that most securities firms have backup sites far from New York, as the Sound Practices paper suggested, and a wired network to the stock exchange through Consolidated Edison's underground pipes [39]

Banking Industry

Extensive regulatory and supervisory procedures apply to banks as businesses. The potential for targeted cyber disruption exists even for single banking firms. Organizations such as the Banking Industry Technology Secretariat (BITS), the technology arm of the Financial Services Roundtable trade group, focus on industry defenses. It is a nonprofit consortium of the largest 100 financial institutions in the country dealing with strategic approaches to crisis management and payments systems.

Financial Services Sector Coordinating Council for Critical Infrastructure Protection and Homeland Security

Organizations representing financial entities have created the Financial Services Sector Coordinating Council for Critical Infrastructure Protection and Homeland Security, called FSSCC for short. It is essentially a private-sector counterpart to FBIIC. Its members are banking and financial organizations, some of whom have self-regulatory oversight of their groups, and it covers most of America's finance. Its mission is to identify opportunities for coordination, improve knowledge and information sharing, and improve public confidence in sectoral recovery from terrorist attacks and other illegal activities. FSSCC holds meetings with FBIIC [40].

Another example of the multiplicity of connections to strengthen financial industry resiliency is ChicagoFIRST, a regional coalition augmenting nationwide information sharing and policy initiatives. Formed in 2003 when Chicago's financial institutions decided that after September 11 they were as vulnerable as those in New York, it includes many members of FSSCC listed above and Illinois governments. A limited liability company funded by its for-profit members, it has developed defensive capabilities that are recognized as a model for other regional arrangements to fortify specific areas [41]

In the communications arena, FSSCC member organizations have developed contact procedures to coordinate industry members and governmental bodies during emergencies, and merged these connections into a common database.

Legislation and Oversight

This section reports on congressional action in response to disruption to the nation's economy.

Department of Homeland Security

Following the attacks of September 11, 2001, Congress created DHS by combining all or part of 22 different agencies [42]. DHS has responsibilities previously assigned to 22 agencies to protect communications, transportation, and computer networks. These networks are critical to the financial sector's ability to transform data into useful forms of information such as bank account balances, securities prices, orders to buy and sell financial assets, and payments on contractual obligations such as loans.

Intelligence Reform and Terrorism Prevention Act of 2004

Beyond anti-terrorist tactics and financing legislative recommendations, the September 11 Commission's findings led to major financial preparedness legislation. The resulting Intelligence Reform and Terrorism Prevention Act of 2004, P.L. 108-458, requires DHS to report on vulnerability and risk assessments and the government's plans to protect infrastructures, including financial institutions.

Treasury is required to report on "the effectiveness and efficiency of efforts to protect the critical infrastructure of the United States financial system.... " Treasury is to report on its efforts to encourage public-private partnerships to protect critical financial infrastructure. Treasury also has authority for government securities market disturbances parallel to the SEC's authority. After consulting with Treasury, the Fed, and the Commodity Futures

Trading Commission, the SEC is authorized to issue orders and take other emergency actions to address extraordinary private securities market disturbances.

The Fed, the OCC, and the SEC are to report on private sector financial business continuity plans, including more financial services entities than are under existing regulation. The agencies published their guidance in the Sound Practices noted above.

The law urges insurance and credit rating companies to consider businesses' compliance with private sector standards in assessing insurability and creditworthiness, to encourage private investment in disaster and emergency preparedness.

Conclusion: Convergence of Public-Private Practices for Financial Continuity

The private and public sectors have worked together to document and build on the lessons learned from the terrorist attacks of September 11 and other disruptions. Regulators and special purpose groups have monitored the implementation of best practices to the common goal of minimizing future disruptions. This has been done by persuasion, regulation, rule, and law. Although much of the original impetus was a terrorist attack, the new policies have worked well during natural disasters such as hurricanes since Katrina and have been the basis for planning to mitigate the disruption of a flu pandemic.

Acknowledgments

This report depends greatly on previous versions that were written and updated by William D. Jackson, who has retired from the Congressional Research Service.

Appendix: Major Acronyms

BITS	Banking Industry Technology Secretariat
CFTC	Commodity Futures Trading Commission
DHS	Department of Homeland Security
FBIIC	Financial and Banking Information Infrastructure Committee
FDIC	Federal Deposit Insurance Corporation
Fed	Federal Reserve System
FSISAC	Financial Services-Information Sharing and Analysis Center
FSSCC	Financial Services Sector Coordinating Council for Critical Infrastructure Protection and Homeland Security
GAO	Government Accountability Office
NIAC	National Infrastructure Advisory Council
OCC	Office of the Comptroller of the Currency
PBGC	Pension Benefit Guaranty Corporation
SEC	Securities and Exchange Commission
SIFMA	Securities Industry and Financial Management Association
TRIA	Terrorism Risk Insurance Act of 2002

REFERENCES

[1] CRS Report RL32631, *Critical Infrastructure and Key Assets: Definition and Identification*, by John D. Moteff and Paul W. Parfomak. Congress specified financial services as critical physical and information infrastructure in P.L. 107- 56, Section 1016, Oct. 26, 2001. Banking and finance are critical infrastructure similar to telecommunications, water, etc. in U.S. Department of Homeland Security, The Physical Protection of Critical Infrastructure and Key Assets, at http://www.dhs.gov/ xlibrary/assets/Physical_Strategy.pdf; U.S. Department of Homeland Security, The National Strategy to Secure Cyberspace, at http://www.dhs.gov/ xlibrary/ assets/ National_Cyberspace_Strategy.pdf; "Homeland Security Presidential Directive/HSPD-7," at http:// www.whitehouse.gov/ omb/memoranda/fy04/m-04-15.pdf; U.S. Department of Homeland Security, Critical Infrastructure and Key Resources Sector-Specific Plan as Input to the National Infrastructure Protection Plan: Banking and Finance,athttp://www.dhs.gov/xlibrary/assets/nipp-sspbanking.pdf, and U.S. Deptf Homeland Security, National Infrastructure Protection Plan: 2009, at http://www. dhs.gov/ xprevprot/programs/editorial_0827.shtm.

[2] TARP was authorized by the Emergency Economic Stabilization Act of 2008, P.L. 110-343, and TALF was authorized by the Federal Reserve Act, P.L. 63-43, Section 13(3), as amended.

[3] P.L. 109-144, which expired December 31, 2007, extended P.L. 107-297. For a history and other information about TRIA, see CRS Report RS21979, Terrorism Risk Insurance: An Overview, and CRS Report RL34219, *Terrorism Risk Insurance Legislation in 2007: Issue Summary and Side-by-Side*, both by Baird Webel

[4] CRS Report RL34423, *Government Interventions in Financial Markets: Economic and Historic Analysis of Subprime Mortgage Options*, by N. Eric Weiss.

[5] CRS Report R40003, *U.S. Motor Vehicle Industry: Federal Financial Assistance and Restructuring*, coordinated by Glennon J. Harrison.

[6] FSSCC is discussed in "Financial Services Sector Coordinating Council for Critical Infrastructure Protection and Homeland Security," below. Patrick McConnell, *Banks and Avian Flu: Planning for a Possible Pandemic*, undated, at https://www.fsscc.org/ influenza/banks_and_avian_flu_planning.pdf.

[7] Financial Banking Information Infrastructure Committee and Financial Services Sector Coordinating Council, *FBIIC/FSSCC Pandemic Flu Exercise: Media Briefing*, October 24, 2007. Available at http://www.treasury.gov/press/ releases/reports/ panfluhand out.pdf.

[8] Statement of David M. Walker, "Continuity of Operations: Agencies Could Improve Planning for Telework during Disruptions," before the House Committee on Government Reform, May 11, 2006, at http://www.gao.gov/new.items/ d06740t.pdf.

[9] International Monetary Fund, *The Global Economic and Financial Impact of an Avian Flu Pandemic and the Role of the IMF,* Feb. 28, 2006 at http://www.imf.org/external/ pubs/ft/afp/2006/eng/022806.pdf.

[10] U.S. Department of Homeland Security, *Critical Infrastructure and Key Resources Sector-Specific Plan as Input to the National Infrastructure Protection Plan: Communications*, at http://www.dhs.gov/xlibrary/assets/nipp-sspcommunications.pdf.

[11] "Treasury Introduces Upgrades Designed To Help Safeguard Financial Service System," *BNA's Banking Report*, Dec. 8, 2003, p. 836.
[12] U.S. Secret Service, "Secret Service and CERT Coordination Center Release Comprehensive Report Analyzing Insider Threats to Banking and Finance Sector," press release, at http://www.secretservice.gov/press/pub1804.pdf.
[13] Derrick Cain, "Nation's Banks Conduct 'Business as Usual' After Specific Threats to Certain Institutions," *BNA 's Banking Report*, Aug. 9, 2004, p. 221.
[14] CRS Report RS2 1987, *When Financial Businesses Fail: Protection for Account Holders*, by Walter W. Eubanks.
[15] CRS Report RS21741, *Securities Investor Protection Corporation*, by Gary Shorter.
[16] P.L. 107-204, July 30, 2002.
[17] CRS Report R40249, *Who Regulates Whom? An Overview of U.S. Financial Supervision*, by Mark Jickling and Edward V. Murphy.
[18] CRS Report RL34427, *Financial Turmoil: Federal Reserve Policy Responses*, by Marc Labonte.
[19] CRS Report RS22263, *Katrina's Wake: Restoring Financial Services*, by William D. Jackson and Barbara Miles.
[20] Insurance Information Institute, "Nearly 95 Percent of Homeowners Claims from Hurricane Katrina Settled and Tens of Billions of Dollars Paid to Affected Communities in Louisiana and Mississippi, Insurance Information Institute Reports," Aug. 22, 2006, at http://www.iii.org/media/updates/press.760032/.
[21] "In Brief: Despite Storms, P/C Profits Grew 4.4%," *American Banker Online,* Dec. 29, 2005.
[22] "Measures Prompted by Sept. 11 Helped Banks Weather Electrical Outage, Snow Says," *BNA's Banking Report*, Aug. 25, 2003, p.254; Todd Davenport, "In Brief: Outage Sparked $785M of Fed Lending," *American Banker Online*, Aug. 22, 2003; and Rob Blackwell, "Backup Site Questions, Utility Loan Prospects," *American Banker Online*, Aug. 18, 2003. (Hereafter cited as Blackwell, *Backup Site Questions*.)
[23] P.L. 107-42, Sept. 22, 2001.
[24] Shane Kite, "Bond-Clearing Business Gets Its Backstop," *Securities Industry News*, March 6, 2006.
[25] *Federal Register*, vol. 68, no. 70, Apr. 11, 2003, pp. 17809-17814.
[26] Board of Governors of the Federal Reserve System, Office of the Comptroller of the Currency, and Securities and Exchange Commission, *Joint Report on Efforts of the Private Sector to Implement the Interagency Paper on Sound Practices to Strengthen the Resilience of the U.S. Financial System, April 2006*, at https://www.fsscc.org/fsscc/reports/2006/avian_flu.jsp.
[27] Federal Financial Institutions Examination Council, *Business Continuity Planning*, at http://www.ffiec.gov/ffiecinfobase/html_pages/bcp_book_frame.htm.
[28] CRS Report RL34485, *Basel II in the United States: Progress Toward a Workable Framework*, by Walter W. Eubanks.
[29] P.L. 107-347, Dec. 17, 2002.
[30] Department of the Treasury, "Treasury Statement on Measures to Protect the Financial Markets during Hostilities with Iraq," press release, Mar. 17, 2003, at http://www.treas.gov/press/releases/js114.htm.
[31] It was the Office of Homeland Security's Financial Markets Work Group.

[32] Financial and Banking Information Infrastructure Committee (FBIIC), at http://www.fbiic.gov.
[33] Government officials describe initiatives in U.S. Department of the Treasury, *Briefing Book on the Financial and Banking Information Infrastructure Committee and U.S. Department of the Treasury Critical Infrastructure Protection and Homeland Security Initiatives*, Nov. 14, 2002, at http://www.fbiic.gov.
[34] Department of the Treasury, "Treasury Names Private Sector Coordinator for Critical Infrastructure Protection Partnership Effort," press release, May 14, 2002, at http://www.treas.gov/press/releases/po3100.htm?IMAGE.X=35 \&IMAGE.Y=10.
[35] Kip Betz, "Treasury Official Sees Progress in Crisis Preparedness Efforts," *Daily Report for Executives*, Mar. 21, 2003, p.18.
[36] At https://www.fsscc.org/fsscc/reports/2004/FBIIC_Network_Security.pdf.
[37] "About FS-ISAC," at http://www.fsisac.com/about/.
[38] Financial Services Sector Coordinating Council, Financial Services Crises Manual of Procedures, May 3, 2008, at https://www.fsscc.org/fsscc/reports/2008/ FS_Crisis_ Manual_of_Procedures_ver_1.1.pdf.
[39] "After Sept. 11, the U.S. Learned About Its Economic Resilience," *Wall Street Journal*, Mar. 16, 2004, p. A15.
[40] Financial Services Sector Coordinating Council for Critical Infrastructure, *Sector Specific Plan,* Chapter 5 at https://www.fsscc.org/fsscc/publications/ssp/ssp_5_3.jsp.
[41] ChicagoFIRST, 2008 Annual Report, at https://www.chicagofirst.org/resources/ 2008_annual_report.pdf.
[42] P.L. 107-296.

In: The Global Financial Crisis: Policies and Implications ISBN 978-1-61470-317-4
Editor: J. P. Gallagher and E. C. Wilkins © 2012 Nova Science Publishers, Inc.

Chapter 2

THE GLOBAL FINANCIAL CRISIS: INCREASING IMF RESOURCES AND THE ROLE OF CONGRESS*

Jonathan E. Sanford and Martin A. Weiss

ABSTRACT

The current global financial crisis is testing the ability of the International Monetary Fund (IMF), and other international financial institutions (IFIs) to provide sufficient assistance to affected countries. It has also enhanced the IMF's role in crisis management and given it a key place in current efforts to reform the world financial system.

During the past half-year, many countries have come to the IMF for assistance and more are likely to apply. Several steps have been taken to expand the IMF 's financial resources and to otherwise augment the funds available to help vulnerable countries weather the present crisis.

At their meeting in London on April 2, 2009, the leaders of the 20 systemically important industrialized and developing countries (G-20) agreed on several initiatives affecting the IMF and other international organizations. They agreed that the New Arrangements to Borrow (NAB), a supplemental fund to bolster IMF resources, should be increased by up to $500 billion from its present level of $50 billion. The Obama Administration has proposed a U.S. contribution of up to $100 billion. Pledges totaling $255 billion have been received from several countries and others are considering additional contributions. The G-20 also agreed that the IMF should create new Special Drawing Rights (SDRs) to a value of $250 billion and to allocate them to its members through its SDR Department. These new resources would expand world foreign exchange reserves by about 4% and provide needed resources to countries in crisis. The G-20 said in addition that $250 billion would be provided, through their bilateral agencies and through the multilateral development banks (MDBs), for new trade finance, and they said the MDBs should increase their level of assistance by $100 billion to meet crisis needs. They also agreed that poor countries should be aided with some of the gold the IMF is planning to sell. Details of the plans for new trade finance and aid to poor countries have not yet been released. Already pending at the time of the G-20 meeting was a proposal

* This is an edited, reformatted and augmented version of CRS Report R40578, dated May 14, 2009.

for a new increase in IMF quota resources. Negotiations on a package of reforms and a new quota increase had been completed in April 2008 and submitted to the House and Senate leadership by the Bush Administration last November. The U.S. share would be SDR 4.97 billion (about $8 billion). The package includes reforms in the IMF governance process, finances, and procedures. It also includes a proposal that the IMF sell 403 metric tons of gold to create a facility that would cover the costs of its country and global surveillance, technical assistance, research, and other non-lending operations. Also pending in 2008 was a proposed Fourth Amendment to the IMF Articles, originally proposed in 1997, that would create a new allocation of about SDR 21.4 billion.

Some elements of the above require congressional approval and some do not. U.S. participation in the new IMF quota increase and a U.S. subscription of $100 billion for the NAB would require congressional approval. Likewise, amendments to the IMF Articles—including the prospective Fourth Amendment for a new SDR allocation—would require congressional approval. On the other hand, the proposed $250 billion allocation of SDRs (which is being made under a different provision of the IMF Articles) is too small to trigger the legal requirement that Congress give its assent. Any contributions to the IMF, to fund increases in the U.S. quota or to subscribe new resources to the NAB, must be authorized by Congress. In 1967, a Presidential Commission on Budget Concepts recommended that U.S. payments to the IMF should not be treated as budget outlay but rather they should be counted as an exchange of assets which is matched by transfers of equivalent value to the United States from the IMF. Since that time, payments to the IMF have been deemed to have no impact on the Federal budget or on the Federal budget deficit.

On April 2, 2009, leaders from 20 of the world's largest economies—the Group of 20 (or G-20)—met in London, U.K., to discuss measures that might be taken to address the current global economic crisis [1]. They reached agreement in general terms on some steps they might take to (1) help stimulate consumption and recovery in their countries as well as the world economy and (2) help coordinate and strengthen regulation of world financial markets, although they did not commit to any specific steps they should take to address these problems. The area of clearest and most specific agreement among the G-20, however, involved expanding the stock of financial resources available to the IMF (Box 1) by an additional $500 billion to enhance its capacity to assist troubled countries requesting its aid [2]. G-20 members also agreed to create an additional $250 billion in IMF Special Drawing Rights (SDRs). The G-20 agreement to increase the resources of the IMF was approved at the April 2009 spring meeting of the IMF Board of Governors' International Monetary and Financial Committee (IMFC) [3]

This report provides information on (1) the role the IMF has played in the financial crisis, (2) international agreement to increase the financial resources of the IMF, and (3) the role of Congress in increasing the Fund's resources. As will be discussed in detail at the end of the report, congressional authorization, and perhaps appropriation, would be required to increase U.S. contributions to the IMF.

BACKGROUND: ECONOMIC IMPACT OF THE FINANCIAL CRISIS

What began as a bursting of the U.S. housing market bubble and a rise in foreclosures has ballooned into a global financial and economic crisis. The crisis has exposed fundamental weaknesses in financial systems worldwide. Despite coordinated easing of monetary policy and trillions of dollars in intervention by central banks and governments, economies continue to decline into what is turning out to be the most severe global recession since the Great Depression of the 1930s.

Box 1. The International Monetary Fund

The IMF was created in 1946, a result of the 1944 international financial conference at Bretton Woods, New Hampshire. It was created in order to prevent a return of the international financial chaos that preceded -- and in some ways precipitated -- World War II. During the 1 930s, many countries pursued "beggar-thy-neighbor" economic policies -- restricting purchases from abroad in order to save scarce foreign exchange, cutting the value of their currencies in order to underprice foreign competitors, and hampering international financial flows -- in ways that deepened the world depression and accelerated the decline in economic activity.

The IMF was designed to limit or prevent this kind of economic behavior. Technically, the IMF is a specialized agency of the United Nations, but it functions virtually independently of UN control. The IMF must obey directives of the U.N. Security Council, but it need not comply with directives from the U.N. General Assembly or other U.N. agencies. Rather than being organized on a one-country, one-vote basis, as is the United Nations, it has weighted voting. The IMF has 185 member countries, whose voting share depends on the size of their quota or financial commitment to the organization. A country's quota is determined by its GDP size, its openness to international trade and other factors. The amount a country can borrow is determined by the size of its quota. The United States is the largest single shareholder, with a 16.77% voting share. The nine Executive Directors (EDs) representing the G-7 countries and other advanced countries in Europe share nearly 56% of the vote. Most decisions are reached by simple majority, though this is generally expressed by consensus. Some special matters (changes in the Articles of Agreement or approval of new quota increases, for example) require an 85% vote. Because the U.S. vote exceeds 1 5%,however, no quota increases, amendments or other major actions can go into effect without its affirmative vote. The same can be said for other major blocks of IMF member countries.

As stated in its Articles of Agreement, the purposes of the IMF are (1) to promote international cooperation on international monetary problems, (2) to facilitate the expansion and balanced growth of international trade, promoting high levels of employment and real income and the development of productive resources in all member countries, (3) to promote exchange rate stability and to avoid competitive exchange rate depreciation, (4) to help establish a multilateral system of payments among countries for current transactions and to help eliminate foreign exchange restrictions which hamper world trade, (5) to make loans to countries on a temporary basis with adequate safeguards for repayment, "thus providing them with opportunity to correct maladjustments in their balance of payments without resorting to measures destructive of national or international prosperity," and (6) to shorten with such loans the duration and to lessen the degree of disequilibrium in countries' balances of payments.

The IMF is an international financial institution (IFI) which deals mainly with balance of payments (BOP), exchange rate, and international monetary concerns. It originally focused mainly on macroeconomic issues. It monitored the macroeconomic and exchange rate policies of member countries and it helped countries overcome BOP crises with short-term loans conditioned on their making improvements in macroeconomic performance. It left microeconimic issues and domestic institutional issues to the World Bank and the other multilateral development banks (MDBs). In recent years, however, the Fund has found that these issues have a much larger impact on countries' abilities to pursue effective macroeconomic and exchange rate policies. Increasingly, it has included them among the subjects which need to be addressed in the context of its loan programs.

Box 1. (Continued)

It has also given these issues more attention in its consultations with member country governments, its surveillance activities, and its technical assistance activity.

The IMF is a monetary institution, not a development agency. Its sister agency, the World Bank, was created at the same time as the IMF in order to provide long-term loans and to stimulate growth and economic development in war-damaged and developing countries. Even so, economic development and growth are core objectives of the IMF, as specified in purposes 2 and 4 above. The founders believed that international monetary stability would facilitate the growth of world trade and that this in turn would generate higher levels of employment, increased income, and expanded growth and development in the countries participating in the post-World War II international economy.

The founders expected (purposes 5 and 6) that the IMF would be a means through which countries could remedy their domestic economic problems without resorting to the kinds of "beggar-thy-neighbor" practices which sought to shift the burden of adjustment onto other countries. Countries with chronic BOP deficits could get short-term IMF loans to help them weather a balance of payments crisis. It was generally presumed that BOP deficits, inflation, unemployment and low levels of economic activity were the result of inappropriate domestic economic policies. Better policies and adjustments in the exchange rate for the country's currency were deemed to be the appropriate response to this situation. It was expected that IMF assistance would help countries shorten the depth and duration of their economic problems and help contain or prevent the spread of monetary instability to other countries.

Economic Growth Rates

On April 22, 2009, the International Monetary Fund (IMF) revised its forecast for world economic growth down to -1.3% for 2009. This would be the lowest level of growth since World War II and would be down from the IMF’s forecast in January 2009 that global economic output would grow by 0.5% this year and its projection in November 2008 that growth in 2009 would be around 1.7%. The World Bank, in March 2009, issued an equally pessimistic outlook, projecting (without providing a specific figure) that the world economy will contract (negative growth) in 2009 [4]

As shown in Figure 1, countries world-wide are experiencing a simultaneous downturn in economic activity. The advanced industrialized countries of North America, Europe, and Japan are declining into recession, and economic growth rates in most developing and emerging market countries are also in marked decline. Even China, though its economy continues to expand, has experience a substantial reduction in its rate of economic growth. These declines in economic activity have been accompanied by losses of trillions of dollars in equity markets and a credit squeeze that not only are affecting households and businesses worldwide but are putting a damper on the financing of activities such as world trade and oil exploration. The International Labor Organization expects global unemployment in 2009 to increase over 2007 by a range of 18 million to 30 million workers, and more than 50 million if the situation continues to deteriorate [5]. In the latter case, some 200 million workers, mostly in developing economies, could find themselves in extreme poverty.

Developing and emerging market countries are seeing the collapse in growth through several channels. First, economic slowdown in the advanced economies is leading to decreased demand for exports (Figure 2) and a contraction of capital flows (Figure 3).

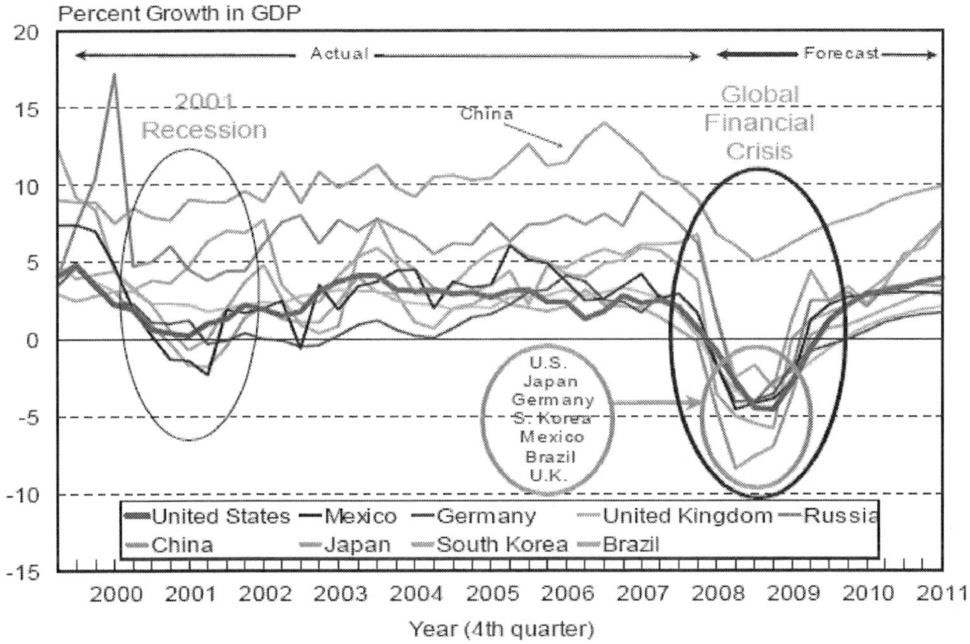

Source: Congressional Research Service with data from Global Insight, March 15, monthly forecast, using annualized quarterly changes in growth rates.

Figure 1. Selected Economic Growth Rates, 2000-2001.

Developing countries also suffer from the collapse of commodity prices (Figure 4). Rapid economic growth in China and India over the past decade led to record prices for petroleum, minerals, and other commodities. Between 2003 and 2008, oil prices rose by 320% and food prices by 138%. Since mid-2008, however, weakening demand for these exports has led to a rapid decline in the price of many of these commodities. Because many of the poorest countries are heavily dependent on a few primary export commodities, rapid swings in commodity prices can wreak havoc on their domestic economies. Yemen, for example, announced in January that it would have to decrease public expenditures by 50% because of the financial crisis and the lower government revenues from its oil exports.

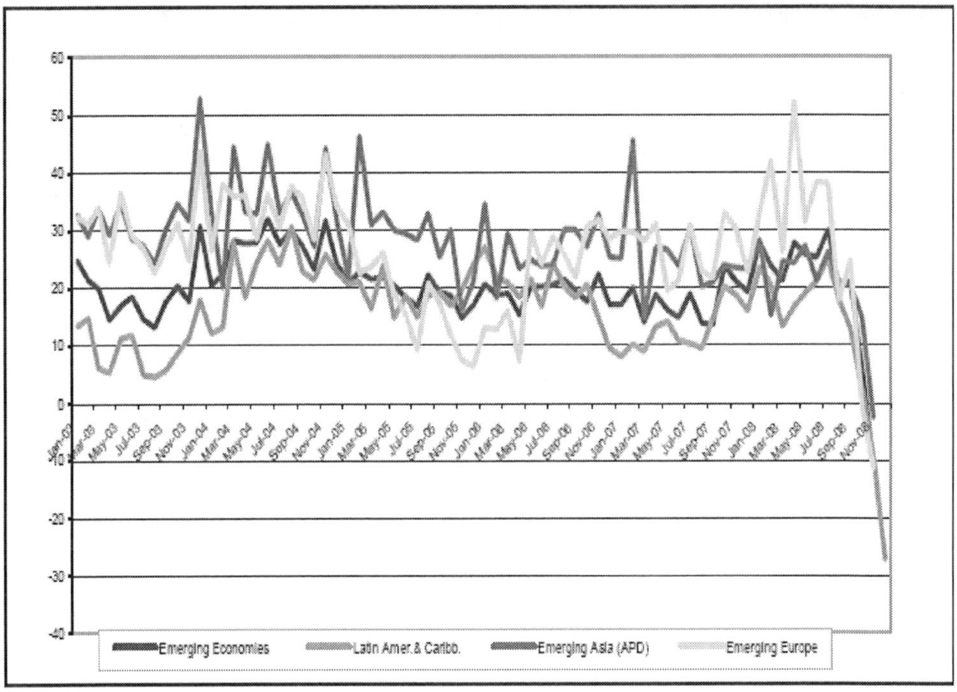

Source: International Monetary Fund.

Figure 2. Merchandise Exports from Emerging Markets, 2003 – 2008 (in percentage change from year earlier).

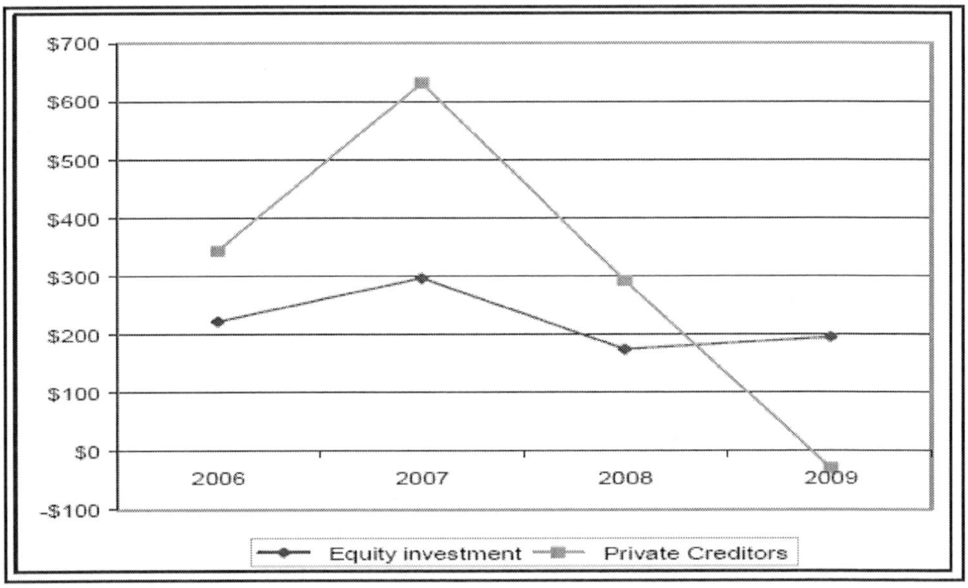

Source: Institute for International Finance: "Capital Flows To Emerging Market Economies." January 27, 2009.

Figure 3. Net Private Capital Flows to Emerging Markets ($ in billions).

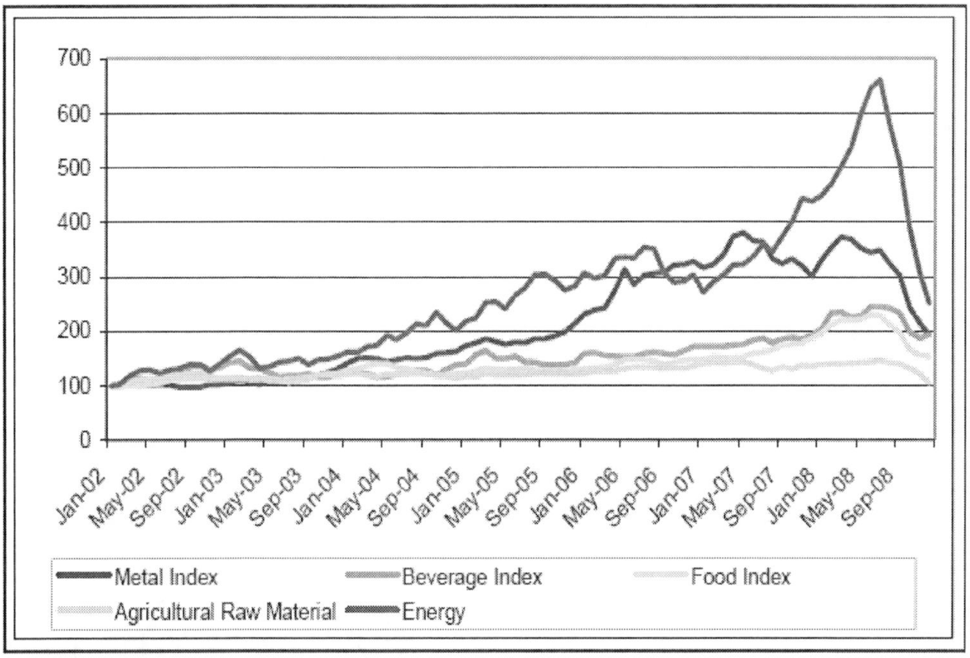

Source: International Monetary Fund.

Figure 4. Commodity Price Indices (index: Jan. 2002=100).

Impact of the Financial Crisis on World Poverty

While the poorest countries, many in sub-Saharan Africa, are less integrated into global capital markets than the advanced industrial nations or emerging economies in Eastern Europe, the global economic slowdown is affecting their standards of living and is expected to lead to higher levels of global poverty – and not just in the least developed countries. Many argue that the impact on poverty may be felt most strongly in the large, middle-income countries such as China and India, the world's two most populous nations. Over the past two decades, the largest gains in raising people out of poverty have been made in these two countries. For several years China has averaged 10% annual economic growth, while India has grown upwards of 8% annually between 2002 and 2007. The World Bank estimates each one percentage point drop in world economic growth could trap another 20 million people in poverty. Slow economic growth in both of these countries could push millions into poverty as well as have other adverse effects in less-developed economies. The International Labor Organization predicts that some 50 million more peoplearound the world will be unemployed in 2009 compared to 2007. The majority of these newly unemployed will likely be in developing countries [6]

According to recent World Bank research, almost 40% of developing countries are highly exposed to the poverty effects of the crisis due to both declining growth rates and high initial poverty levels. An additional 56% of countries are moderately exposed due to either decelerating growth or high poverty levels, but not both. Over 90% of developing countries face a greater risk of increased poverty because of the financial crisis. While advanced economies are expanding their fiscal deficits with robust stimulus packages, the World Bank finds that only one quarter of the exposed countries have the ability to expand their fiscal deficits. One third of developing countries with reasonable fiscal capacity are aid-dependent and will require extensive bilateral and multilateral support if they are to increase fiscal spending [7]

Lower levels of world remittances will also impact poverty levels. The combination of slow growth rates, job losses, and the rising cost of living in advanced countries has led to fewer economic migrants from developing countries and lower levels of remittances. This could have major effects in countries which provide large numbers of migrant workers, including Mexico, India, Bangladesh, and the Philippines. The volume of remittances soared over the past decade, but recent data show significant deceleration since the beginning of the current crisis with Latin America and Caribbean the hardest hit. The Inter-American Development Bank calculates that remittances to the region declined by 1.7% between 2007 and 2008.

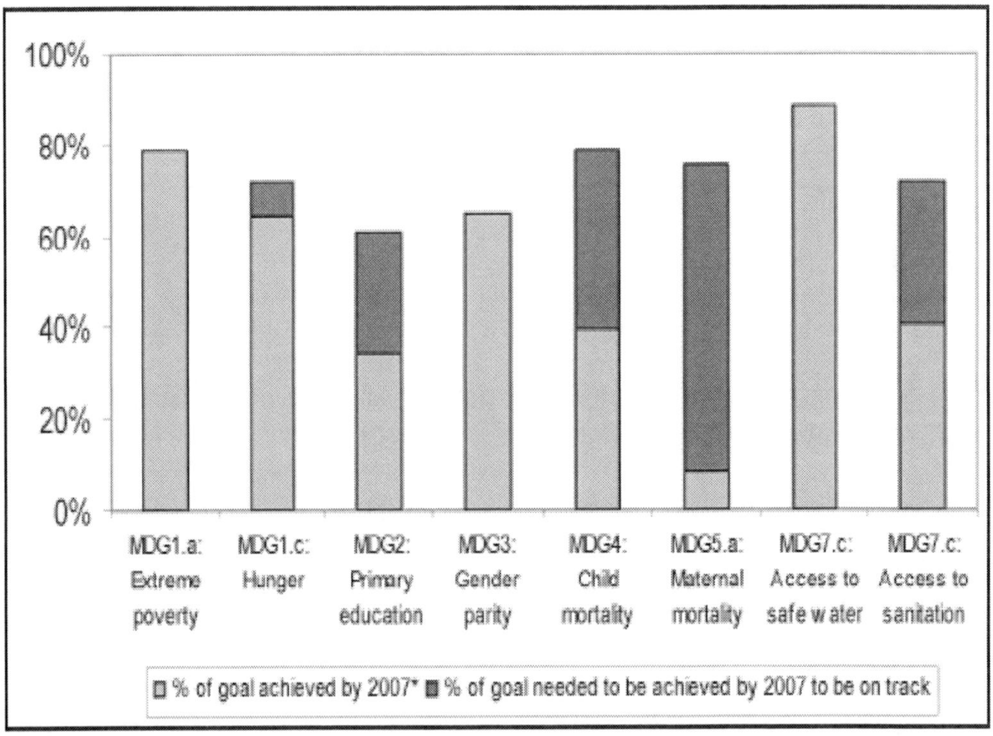

Source: World Bank.

Figure 5. Progress towards MDGs – All Developing Countries.

While many countries were already having difficulties making progress in meeting the Millennium Development Goals (MDGs), [8] the financial crisis will likely further hinder their efforts. According to the World Bank, by 2007, countries had only made sufficient progress toward achieving two MDGs, those for poverty reduction and access to safe water to be on track of reaching the 2015 targets (Figure 5). The decline in world employment; the shift away from export-oriented industries; and the decline of remittances are expected to jeopardize many of the recent gains in poverty reduction throughout the developing world.

The World Bank notes that it is difficult to assess the exact impact the financial crisis is likely to have. However, research on prior crises suggests that:

> countries that suffered economic contractions of 10 percent or more between 1980 and 2004 experienced, for example, more than one million excess infant deaths. Evidence suggests that growth collapses are costly for human development outcomes, as they deteriorate more quickly during growth decelerations than they improve during growth accelerations. The average GDP growth rate of developing countries is now projected to fall in 2009 to less than half the pre-crisis rate. The projected lower growth path will sharply slow the reduction in infant mortality. Preliminary analysis shows that, as a result, infant deaths in developing countries may be 200,000 to 400,000 per year higher on average between 2009 and the MDG target year of 2015 than they would have been in the absence of the crisis [9]

Despite the current global economic slowdown, estimates suggest that poverty rates are still likely to decline in the long-term. Over the medium-term (3-to-5), economic growth rates may still be higher than they were in the 1990s due to macroeconomic policy improvements and structural reforms such as privatization and regulatory initiatives within developing countries. This depends, however, on how quickly and fully the world can recover from current recessionary economic conditions.

Impact of the Crisis on the IMF

The severity of the current financial crisis is a challenge for the IMF, whose financial resources have not kept pace with the global economy over the past decade. The IMF reports that its resources would need to grow by 55% to match the levels relative to global output that prevailed during the Asian financial crisis of 1997-1998. The leaders of the G-20 countries agreed in April 2009 that resources available to the IMF needed to be increased three-fold in order to deal with current world financial crisis and the risk that it might become even more serious in the future.

Demand for IMF resources in 2009 has been strong, though, as Figure 6 indicates, the recent rise in IMF lending was preceded by historic lows in loan demand.

On August 31, 2008, total IMF lending was SDR1 1.65 billion (about $16.65 billion), down from a peak of SDR76.84 billion (then around $116 billion) in September 2003 [10]. Since the IMF 's main source of income is the interest paid for its loans, the decrease in demand for IMF loans resulted in shortfalls in the IMF 's administrative budget and a roughly 20% reduction in IMF staff during 2007-2008. The latest annual review of the IMF 's income position was prepared in April 2008 and publicly released in July. Fund officials suggest that the projected shortfall for FY2009 is about SDR150 million or $242 million. According to IMF officials, the Fund's income in FY2009 is likely to be somewhat higher, given the recent surge in lending in response to the global financial crisis. Between October and December 2008, lending almost doubled, from SDR1 1.3 billion ($17.1 billion) to SDR2 1.48 billion ($32.54 billion).

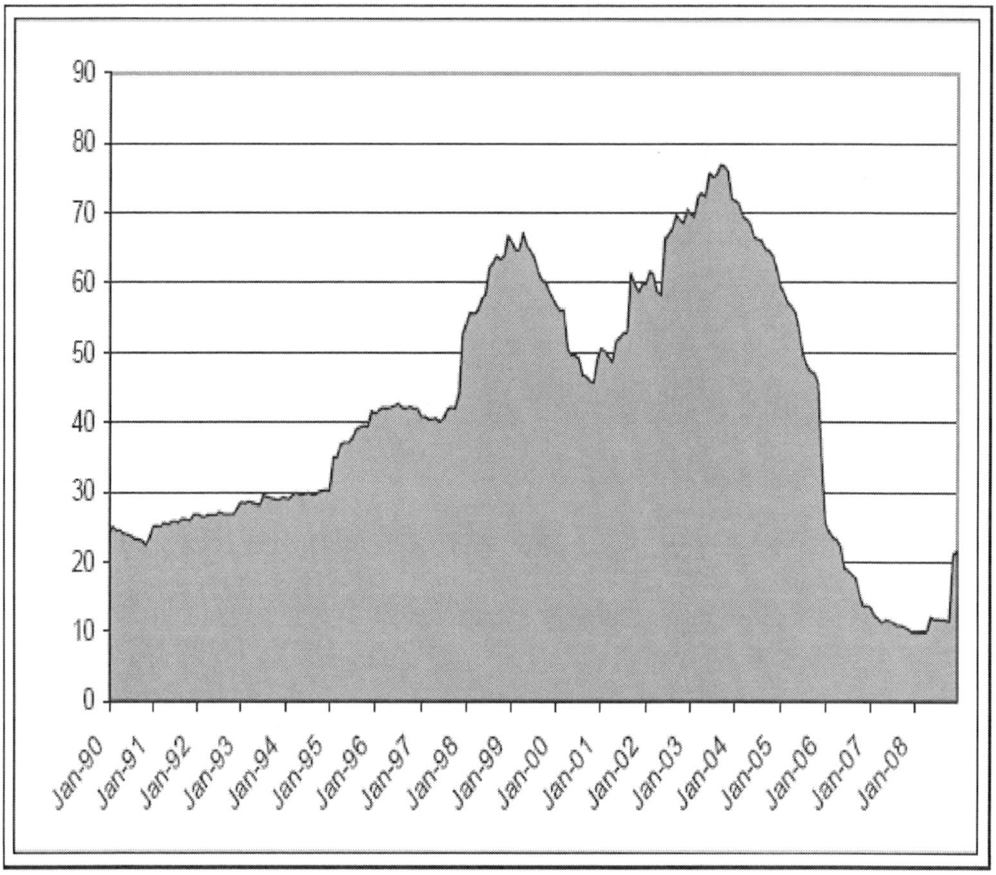

Source: International Monetary Fund.

Figure 6. Outstanding IMF Lending (1990-2008, billion SDR).

The current financial crisis represents a major challenge for the IMF. The United States and other advanced industrial economies are at the center of the crisis, but the IMF would not have enough resources to provide them with significant financial assistance if they sought IMF aid. The IMF 's total financial resources as of April 2009 were $335.4 billion, of which $228.2 billion were usable resources [11]. This is small compared to amount owed to other creditors by the emerging market countries. At the end of the third quarter of 2008, the latter had borrowed about $2.75 trillion from the world's banks. Developing countries also had around $4.5 trillion in foreign exchange reserves. If the G-20 pledges of $500 billion in new resources are realized, the IMF would once again have the financial resources to credibly lend to developing countries impacted by the crisis.

Increasing Fund Resources

At the 2009 Davos World Economic Forum, John Lipsky, the IMF's First Deputy Managing Director, said that to be able to effectively lend to all the potential countries affected by the crisis, the IMF should double its lending resources to around $500 billion [12]

Momentum to boost IMF resources increased during the spring as the global economy worsened and many countries sought IMF financial assistance through a variety of the IMF's lending facilities (Table 1).

Box 2. IMF Lending Facilities

The Flexible Credit Line. In April 2009, the IMF announced the creation of its new Flexible Credit Line (FCL). Countries with good economic track records may borrow – in amounts not subject to the Fund's normal access limits – for periods of 6 to 12 months. Unlike other IMF loan programs, FCL loans can be disbursed up front rather than over a period of time.. The FCL replaced earlier facilities -- the Short-Term Liquidity Facility (SLF), created in 2008, the Contingent Credit Line (CCL), created in 1999 and closed in 2003, and the Supplemental Reserve Facility (SRF). No countries ever borrowed from the SLF or CCL. Colombia, Mexico, and Poland have borrowed from the new facility. FCL borrowers can borrow on a precautionary basis based on potential balance of payments needs. That is, they can use the loan as a line of credit, to bolster their foreign exchange reserves and improve their financial situation, without any requirement that funds need actually be disbursed. This aims to provide stability and to lessen the chance that incidental events might trigger capital flight or a run on the nation's economy. Access is normally not to exceed 1000% of quota.

Stand-By Arrangements (SBA) are the IMF's standard loan program and its most commonly used facility. Designed to address short-term BOP problems, these are lines of credit which may be used as needed during a specific period of time (generally 12 to 18 months). Repayment is expected within 31/4 to 5 years after each disbursement is made.

SBA loans carry performance conditionality and are disbursed in stages as countries meet specified policy and performance goals. These generally address fiscal, and monetary criteria, though in recent years the IMF has also monitored institutional goals and sought steps to preserve borrower countries' social safety nets. SBA loans can be approved on a precautionary basis, with funds being drawn only if the country needs them to address deteriorating conditions. In April 2009, the executive board decided that high-access precautionary SBAs (HAPAs) should be available on a more regular basis. It also said the design of SBAs should be more flexible, with respect to phasing, frontloading of access and the frequency of performance reviews, to take into account the borrowers' varying circumstances.

The Extended Fund Facility (EFF) was created in 1975 to help countries address long-term BOP problems which required major restructuring of their economies. These loans are similar to SBAs, but credit is generally kept available for a longer period (3 years) and repayment is expected within 4 1/2 to 7 years of disbursement. Surcharges also apply. The executive board decided in April 2009 to retain the EFF because of its importance for low-income countries.

The Supplemental Reserve Facility (SRF) was created in 1997 to provide short-term financing (2 to 21/2 years) on a large scale.

The IMF used this facility to fund the large loans it made to emerging market economies during the international financial crises of the 1 990s. SRF loans carried a substantial surcharge of 3- to-5% and were intended to supplement SBA or EFF arrangements. The SRF was abolished in April 2009 when the FCL was established

The Compensatory Financing Facility (CFF) was created in the 1 960s to help countries experiencing a sudden loss of export income or a sudden rise in imported cereal prices due to fluctuating world prices. SBA repayment terms apply. The CFF was abolished in April 2009 when the FCL was established.

Concessional Rate Facilities. Low income countries may borrow on concessional repayment terms from the Poverty Reduction and Growth Facility (PRGF) and the Exogenous Shocks Facility (ESF). To qualify for such loans, countries must be eligible to borrow from the World Bank only through its concessional aid facility, the International Development Association (IDA). Most borrowers have per capita income levels of about $865 a year. PRGF loans are intended to help low-income countries surmount BOP or financial crises. Unlike SBA and other loans, however, conditionality for PRGF loans is based more on the economic strategies outlined in Poverty Reduction Strategy Papers (PRGF), which are prepared jointly by the borrower country, the IMF and World Bank staff, and civil society groups. The ESF is intended to provide countries with quicker and easier access to assistance to help them cope with economic shocks that have a negative impact on their economy but are beyond their governments' control. Conditionality is focused on steps needed to adjust to the economic shock, with less attention to the structural adjustment measures more commonly associated with SBA, EFF and PRGF assistance. In 2008, access was made more flexible and the earlier requirement that countries must have PRGF in place was dropped.

Loan Terms. The IMF funds its loans from its General Resources Account (GRA), using money paid in quotas or money borrowed through the NAB or other procedures. The amount a country may borrow will depend on the type of loan but is generally a multiple of its quota. Surcharges are applied to loans which represent high multiples of the borrower country's quota. IMF non-concessional loans carry an interest rate ("rate of charge") which is based on the IMF's SDR interest rate. The SDR rate is calculated weekly, for a basket of major currencies, based on a weighted average for short-term government debt in major international money markets. There is a margin (currently 100 basis points) over the SDR interest rate to cover intermediation costs and build reserves. There is also an interest rate premium ("surcharge.") In April 2009, the rate was 2.1%, Loans from the PRGF and ESF carry an interest charge of 0.5% and are repayable over a period of between 5 1/2 and 10 years, depending on the borrower's situation. A subsidy account funded by donor countries enables the IMF to charge this reduced rate to PRGF and EFF borrowers.

Expanding the NAB

At the G-20 meeting in April 2009, the major countries agreed that the resources of the New Arrangements to Borrow (NAB) should be expanded by about $500 billion. This would not expand the IMF 's core resources, but it would triple the funds available to the IMF for use in fighting the current crisis. The G-20 leaders said the expanded NAB would be more flexible than the existing program, but the details are still being worked out and have not yet been released.

Table 1. IMF Financial Arrangements as of May 4, 2009 (in millions of SDR)

Member	Effective Date	Expiration Date	Amount Agreed	Undrawn Balance	Total Credit Outstanding
Stand By Arrangements					
Armenia	03/06/09	07/05/11	368	206	162
Belarus	01/12/09	04/11/10	1,618	1,100	518
Costa Rica	04/11/09	07/10/10	492	492	--
El Salvador	01/16/09	03/31/10	514	514	--
Gabon	05/07/07	05/06/10	77	77	--
Georgia	09/15/08	03/14/10	477	189	288
Guatemala	04/22/09	10/21/10	631	631	--
Hungary	11/06/08	04/05/10	10,538	4,215	6,323
Iceland	11/19/08	11/18/10	1,400	840	560
Latvia	12/23/08	03/22/11	1,522	986	535
Mongolia	04/01/09	10/01/10	153	102	51
Pakistan	11/24/08	10/23/10	5,169	2,533	2,639
Romania	05/04/09	05/03/11	11,400	11,400	--
Serbia	01/16/09	04/14/10	351	351	--
Seychelles	11/14/08	11/13/10	18	11	07
Ukraine	11/15/08	11/04/10	11,000	8,000	3,030
Flexible Credit Line					
Colombia	05/11/09	05/10/10	6,966	6,966	--
Mexico	04/17/09	04/16/10	31,528	31,528	--
Poland	05/06/09	05/05/09	13,690	13690	--
Exogenous Shocks Facility					
Kyrgyz Rep	12/10/08	06/09/10	67	50	100
Malawi	12/03/08	12/02/09	52	17	81
Senegal	12/19/08	12/18/09	49	24	223

Source: IMF Financial Activities – Update April 30, 2009.
Note: 1 U.S. dollar equals approximately 0.67 SDR.

The NAB is a facility from which the IMF may borrow supplemental funds to help it respond to financial crises in countries of key significance to the world economy. An 85% majority of the NAB creditor countries must agree before NAB resources can be used for assistance to a specific country, and the IMF must repay the NAB creditors within five years. The NAB was proposed in 1994 and created in 1998 after the Mexican debt crisis raised concerns about the adequacy of IMF resources in the face of a worldwide crisis. An earlier facility, the General Arrangement to Borrow (GAB), was created in 1962 to augment the

IMF's resources in case it were needed to backstop the major European currencies after they became freely convertible after the Second World War. The NAB/GAB currently has commitments totaling $50 billion from 26 countries [13].

The G-20 agreed that $250 billion should be made available immediately through bilateral arrangements between the IMF and individual countries (Japan had just signed an agreement loaning $100 billion to the IMF and the European Union had pledged to do the same). The also agreed that the NAB would be increased in size by an additional $250 billion as more countries pledged their participation. At the time of the G-20 meeting, Japan had already lent $100 billion to the IMF, and members of the European Union had agreed to provide an additional $100 billion. Subsequently, Canada ($10 billion), South Korea ($10 billion), Norway ($4.5 billion), and Switzerland ($10 billion) agreed to subscribe additional funds. The Obama Administration has asked Congress to approve a U.S. subscription of $100 billion to the NAB and expects that major emerging market countries will also agree to lend supplemental funds to the IMF. The sources for the remaining funds have not been announced.

China has agreed, in principle, to contribute another $40 billion to the IMF to be invested in IMF SDR-denominated bonds [14]. The IMF, however, has not publicly announced a plan to issue SDRdenominated bonds, although it has the legal authority to do so. If these bonds are issued, an additional $125.5 billion will still need to be pledged by other countries if the $500 billion goal announced by the G-20 is to be achieved (Table 2).

Table 2. G-20 Commitments to the NAB (in billions of U.S. Dollars)

Country	Amount
Japan	$100.0
European Union	$100.0
Switzerland	$10.0
Norway	$4.5
South Korea	$10.0
Canada	$10.0
China	$40.0*
U.S.	$100.0
Needed from others to reach $500 billion target	$125.5

* Possibly through SDR bond purchases.

SDR Allocation

In addition to the planned expansion of the NAB, the G-20 leaders agreed that the IMF should create $250 billion worth of new SDRs and allocate them to its member countries. The First Amendment to the IMF Articles, which went into effect in 1969, authorized the IMF to create a new international reserve asset that could be used to supplement its member countries' foreign exchange reserves. SDRs are distributed to member countries in proportion to their IMF quotas. They are held in the SDR Department of the IMF and are separate from quota resources. The SDR serves as the unit of account of the IMF and some other international organizations. Its value is based on a basket of key international currencies.

The new $250 billion allocation of SDRs is not an expansion of the IMF 's resources but rather is an expansion of the international reserves of all its member countries. Each country will get a portion of the new SDRs based on its ownership share (its quota) in the IMF. This will increase the size of each country's foreign exchange reserves without any requirement that some country must run a deficit in order for another to accrue a surplus.

If a country wishes to exchange some of its allocated SDRs for money, it applies to the IMF and the IMF sells those SDRs to another participating country in order to generate the needed funds. The IMF does not use its own resources to fund these operations. In effect, the IMF's SDR Department is a medium through which countries trade resources among themselves. Technically speaking, there is no borrowing or lending, since the value of each country's assets stays the same even though the composition of their assets (SDRs or cash) may change. However, countries pay interest to the IMF whenever the number of SDRs they hold is less than the amount originally allocated to them and the IMF pays interest to countries that hold more SDRs than the amount they originally received. Because these are not "loans," countries are not required to repurchase their SDRs within any specific period of time, but they pay interest on the outstanding balance.

Articles XVII, XVIII, and XIX of the IMF Articles of Agreement set down the rules by which SDRs may be created and exchanged among members for usable currency. If a country wants to encash some of its SDRs, the IMF facilitates the exchange among member countries. In recent years, all transactions in SDRs have been conducted on a voluntary basis. Countries must pay interest if the number of SDRs they possess is less than the amount originally issued to them, and these payments are received by those members that own more SDRs than they were originally allocated. The rate of interest paid and received in connection with use of SDRs is fixed by the IMF – currently a weighted average of short-term dollar, euro, yen, and sterling interest rates.

The $250 billion allocation of SDRs would greatly expand the volume of SDRs allocated to date (currently worth about $32 billion). A proposal has been pending since 1997 (commonly referred to as the "Fourth Amendment" to the IMF Articles) that would roughly double the number of SDRs allocated to date. The Obama Administration has asked Congress approve U.S. consent to this amendment. With U.S. approval, the amendment will have received sufficient votes to go into effect. An amendment is required for this allocation of SDRs because it is not a straight pro rata distribution. Rather, countries that did not receive previous allocations because they were not members of the IMF (or participants in the SDR Department) would get a catch-up allocation to remedy that situation.

IMF Bond Sales

Several developing countries with considerable foreign exchange reserve holdings have been approached about contributing to the G-20 pledge to increase IMF resources. Many have expressed their unwillingness to lend money to the institution until broader governance reform at the institution is achieved. While some changes were agreed on at the April 2008

IMF spring meetings (these are discussed in more detail below) that will increase developing country representation, they have been widely characterized as modest. Many developing countries have thus sought a temporary means to provide assistance to the IMF, while delaying a more permanent contribution until more substantial governance reforms give them a larger representation in the institution [15]. At the IMF 's spring 2009 annual meetings, Brazil, China, India, and Russia signaled their interest in purchasing bonds issued by the IMF in SDRs [16]. For countries with large reserves, these bonds could prove an attractive way to diversifying the currency composition of their foreign exchange reserves. (Most foreign exchange reserves are currently held in only a few currencies including U.S. dollars, euros, and Japanese yen.)

Article 7 of the IMF 's Articles of Agreement provides the Fund the authority to borrow from the capital markets. No additional congressional authorization is needed. While the IMF has never issued bonds in its 60-year history, a framework for issuing bonds in the official sector was developed in the early 1980s. While details about the current proposal are still being negotiated, some details have emerged. It is expected that the bonds would be traded only amongst official agencies, and countries would not be allowed to sell the bonds to private firms or individuals on the secondary market [17]. The implication for the United States of the proposal would be mixed. If successful, the proposal could lead to greater international macroeconomic security from which the United States could benefit.

A concern about the bond sales is that if increasing amounts of foreign exchange reserves are transferred out of dollars into IMF bonds, the future demand for U.S. Treasury bills and agency instruments, which are used to finance the country's deficits, might decrease, thus increasing the yield on low-risk assets. This would raise the cost to the United States of future debt placements and possibly accentuate a trend of countries slowly diversifying their reserves out of the dollar. Many analysts have argued that since the Asian financial crisis (and during the current crisis), foreign demand for U.S. Treasury assets (largely from central banks) has played a crucial role in depressing U.S. interest rates. Should demand for U.S. Treasury assets decrease because of asset allocation decisions by foreign central banks, or because foreign governments need to spend more of the reserves domestically and have less to invest, there could be upward pressure on U.S. interest rates. However, the overall demand for U.S. Treasury bonds may also be little affected, if they are held instead by an emerging market country that receives IMF loans rather than by an emerging market country purchasing IMF bonds.

Other Pending IMF Reforms

Several proposals affecting the IMF were already pending at the time of the G-20 meeting on April 2, 2009. These proposals are part of an IMF governance reform package negotiated between 2006 and 2008. The George W. Bush Administration submitted proposed legislation regarding these reforms in November 2008, but it was not taken up by the 110th Congress. The reforms included plans for a an increase in IMF quotas for selected members and several procedural, policy and financial reforms. Also pending was an amendment to the IMF Articles of Agreement, originally proposed in 1997, that would permit a special allocation of SDRs to IMF member countries as discussed above.

The quota increase involves a targeted realignment in the voting shares of member countries in order to give poor countries and dynamic emerging market countries more say in the organization. The U.S. voting share in the IMF would remain at its present 16.77% and the United States would retain the capacity to block the 85% vote that is required to approve most major initiatives in the Fund. Under this reform of IMF quotas, 54 under-represented countries would see their combined quota share in the Fund increase by about 5% of the total.

Other reforms included in the governance reform package include:

1. a new formula for determining country quotas, giving much more weight to GDP and thus better reflecting countries' weight in the world economy;
2. a tripling of "basic votes" – equally allocated votes – thus giving the poor countries an increased voice in the organization;
3. an additional Alternate Executive Director for the two constituencies of the executive board representing countries in sub-Saharan Africa; and
4. changes in the IMF 's investment and financial procedures, including the sale of gold to finance the establishment of an income-generating endowment fund to help pay for the IMF's activities (research, policy and technical assistance, etc.) that are not related to its loan operations.

The proposed Fourth Amendment to the IMF Articles would permit a one-time allocation of about SDR 21.4 billion disproportionately to all IMF member countries in order to make total SDR allocations more equitable. In dollar terms, the allocation would be worth about $32 billion and would include about $5 billion in new resources for Eastern Europe. Under the IMF's Articles of Agreement, specifically Article XVIII, each allocation of SDRs is made to members on a pro rata basis according to quota. However, the proposed allocation of resources under the proposed Fourth Amendment is not a straight pro rata distribution. Rather, in this allocation, in which all countries would receive some additional SDRs, countries that joined the Fund after 1981, or between 1972 and 1978, and therefore did not participate in the SDR allocations that took place before those dates (about one-fifth of the total membership), would receive additional SDRs equivalent to the amounts they would have received had they been members before that date. An amendment to the IMF Articles is required to allow this "catch-up" allocation of SDR resources.

THE ROLE OF CONGRESS

Some Initiatives Would Require Congressional Approval

Some of the provisions discussed above would require congressional assent and some do not. In general, action by Congress is not required before the United States can vote for increases in IMF resources that do not require contributions from the United States, changes in IMF policy, or procedures that implement existing provisions of the IMF Articles. On the other hand, congressional action is required before the United States can vote for amendments to the IMF Articles, for gold sales, or for quota increases that involve contributions by the United States.

Table 3. Congressional Action Needed on Various IMF Options

Option	Congressional Action
Ad Hoc Quota Increase for selected countries	None required (even though this may lower the U.S. voting share.)
Quota increase for the United States	Requires congressional authorization (because it changes the amount of quota resources held by the United States) .
Loan to IMF Through NAB	Requires congressional authorization.
Sale of IMF Gold	Requires congressional authorization under most circumstances.
Revise quota formula	No congressional authorization or appropriation required.
Reorganize Executive Board	No authorization or appropriation required under most circumstances. However, if Board reform is done through an amendment of the Articles, congressional authorization is required. This is the case for the current proposed amendment to allow the largest Board constituencies to be represented by two Alternate Executive Directors.
Increase Basic Votes	The proposal requires amending the IMF's Articles of Agreement and thus requires congressional authorization.
4th Amendment Allocating SDRs	Requires congressional authorization, as it is an amendment to the IMF Articles,. It would allocate SDR 21.4 billion, some countries getting more because they did not participate in the earlier allocations.
New Allocation of SDRs	Not required if the total amount of SDRs allocated to the United States is smaller than the current U.S. quota in the fund. U.S. receipts in the new allocation would be smaller than that amount.

Congress and the New Allocations of SDRs

Two new allocations of SDRs are currently under discussion. Under U.S. law, the smaller allocation requires the assent of Congress before it can go into effect, but no action by Congress is needed before the larger allocation may occur. The Bretton Woods Agreements Act (BWAA) says that Congress must give its assent before the United States may vote for any amendment to the IMF or World Bank Articles of Agreement [18]. The smaller (SDR 21.4 billion) allocation would be accomplished through adoption of the Fourth Amendment to the IMF Articles. As noted before, this allocation provides countries that did not participate in the earlier allocations of SDRs with a catch-up distribution equivalent to the amount they would have received if they had been members when the previous allocations were made. Because of this catch-up provision, the allocation must be done through an amendment rather than through the regular SDR allocation process. Because it is an amendment to the IMF Articles of Agreement, Congress would be required to give its assent before the United States may vote for the plan.

Box 3. U.S. Participation in the IMF

As the largest single contributor ($50.4 billion cumulatively) to the IMF, the United States has a leading role in shaping the IMF's lending, surveillance, and advisory operations. Both House and Senate committees frequently hold hearings on IMF activities in developing countries and on IMF reform. Other countries are also concerned that steps should be taken to make the IMF more effective.

The President has the ultimate authority under U.S. law to direct U.S. policy and instruct the U.S. representatives at the IMF, and the multilateral development banks (MDBs). The President, in turn, has generally delegated authority to the Secretary of the Treasury. The Treasury's Under Secretary for International Affairs and his staff manage day-to- day U.S. participation. With the advice and consent of the Senate, the President names individuals to represent the United States on the executive boards of the IMF and MDBs. The Executive Boards have authority over operations and policy and must approve any loan or policy decision. The Secretary of the Treasury serves as the U.S. representative on the World Bank Board of Governors, where each country has its own representative. The Board of Governors is the highest level decision making body of the World Bank. In both the World Bank Executive Board and Board of Governors countries have voting shares comparable to their financial contributions. At the World Bank, the United States has a 16.84% vote in the principal loan window.

Congress must give its consent by law before the United States may agree to participate in any new funding agreements. The Senate has advise and consent authority over all persons nominated to represent the United States at the IMF and the multilateral development banks. On many occasions, Congress has enacted legislation specifying what U.S. policy shall be in the international financial institutions (IFIs) and how the U.S. executive directors at these institutions shall vote and the objectives they shall pursue. Congress has also frequently made specific suggestions to the Administration through Sense of Congress resolutions or language in committee reports accompanying legislation suggesting specific goals and priorities the United States ought to emphasize in the IFIs. Since the World Bank and the other multilateral institutions are not agencies of the U.S. government, but rather international institutions, their activities and policies are not subject to U.S. law.

By contrast, the proposed $250 billion allocation of new SDRs would be accomplished through the procedure set forth in Article XVIII of the IMF Articles of Agreement. This says that, upon an 85% majority of the IMF membership, the SDR Department of the Fund may create new SDRs and allocate them to member countries in proportion to their IMF quotas in the institution. The SDR mechanism at the IMF was created in 1969, following adoption of the First Amendment to the Articles. In the Special Drawing Rights Act of 1968, Congress gave the Administration authority to vote for the First Amendment, and it set forth the guidelines for U.S. participation in the SDR Department.19 Section 6 of the Act says that, before the United States can vote for any allocation of SDRs that would be equal to or greater than the existing U.S. quota in the Fund, Congress must give its consent. However, the Act also says that, if the U.S. share of a new allocation of SDRs is less than the size of the U.S. quota, the United States can support it as long as the Treasury Department consults with leaders of the House and Senate authorizing committees at least 90 days in prior to the vote. The 90-day period began on April 13, 2009, when a Treasury official notified Congress that the United States planned to vote in favor of the proposed new allocation of SDRs.

The IMF's total quota resources amount to about SDR 217 billion and the U.S. quota is equal to about SDR 37.15 billion. The $250 billion allocation is equivalent to about SDR 168 billion and the U.S. share would be worth about SDR 28 billion. On May 1, 2009, the U.S. dollar was worth about SDR 0.67. If the dollar goes up in value compared to the euro, UK pound or Japanese yen, the dollar's value vis-à-vis the SDR would increase. Therefore, a $250 billion allocation of SDRs allows some scope for the dollar to appreciate relative to the other currencies in the SDR basket without triggering the requirement for congressional action.

Gold Sales

It also expected that President Obama will request congressional authorization for the Administration to vote in favor of selling 403 metric tons of IMF gold for the purpose of increasing the Fund's liquid reserves. Income earned on these reserves, in turn, would finance a portion of the IMF budget related to its provision of global public goods, such as economic and financial surveillance. The gold sales to benefit poor countries, announced by the G-20 leaders, would be included in this agreed total, as it is expected that the currently high price of gold may provide some additional income beyond what is expected for budget financing. However, any additional income would likely be modest since the current price of gold (around $925 an ounce on May 14, 2008) is not significantly difference from the assumption on which the new income model was based ($850 per ounce). The IMF Articles of Agreement specify that any sale of IMF gold must receive an 85% affirmative vote by the member countries.

In the late 1 990s, limited gold-sales were proposed to finance the IMF 's initial contribution to the Heavily Indebted Poor Countries (HIPC) initiative. Due to the concerns raised above, 13 million ounces of gold were sold in off-market transactions with two members, Brazil and Mexico, that had financial obligations to the IMF. Gold was sold at the market price, and profits were placed in a special IMF HIPC account. At the same time, the IMF accepted back the gold sold to Brazil and Mexico in settlement of their financial obligations to the Fund. The result was that the balance of the IMF 's holdings of physical gold remained unchanged, although its usable resources shrank relative to what they otherwise would have been if the Fund had received currencies in settlement of these financial obligations [20]. The transaction was structured in this way because, in the past, proposals to sell IMF gold reserves have been unpopular among some Members of Congress. Some have argued that there is a potential lack of IMF transparency. Some claim that the gold held by the IMF belongs to the member nations and that it is not the IMF 's place to propose gold sales to fund current operating expenses. Some also argue that gold sales have the potential to weaken the global price of gold, and the effect on the IMF balance sheet is unclear. The sale contemplated now, however, would only include gold acquired by the Fund after the Second Amendment to the IMF Articles of Agreement, which occurred in 1978, after which members no longer paid quota contributions in gold. Therefore, the gold sold is in no way attributable to member countries.

Under Article V, Sec. 12 of the IMF 's Articles of Agreement, approval of gold sales by the IMF requires an 85% IMF voting majority. The United States has almost a 1 6.77%vote and could thus block any sale of IMF gold. Understanding this "virtual" veto, Congress, in

1999, enacted legislation in the FY 2000 Consolidated Appropriations Act that authorized the United States to vote at the IMF in favor of a limited sale of IMF gold to fund the IMF 's participation in HIPC debt cancellation. However, the act, amending section 5 of the Bretton Woods Agreements Act (22 U.S.C. 286c), requires the explicit consent of Congress before the executive branch can support future gold sales. However, the law provides that the United States may support the sale of IMF gold without congressional action if the Secretary of the Treasury certifies to Congress that the sale of gold is necessary for the Fund to restitute gold to its members, or to provide liquidity that will enable the Fund to meet member countries' claims on it or to meet threats to the systemic stability of the international financial system [21]

Budgetary Treatment of IMF Contributions

On May 12, the White House and Congress reached an agreement to treat the U.S. subscription to the IMF as a line of credit for budgetary purposes. Reminiscent of the method used for the 1966 quota increase, Congress has been asked by the Administration to authorize the United States to extend a line of credit to the IMF for the NAB and quota subscriptions that total $108 billion. Unlike IMF quota increases since 1967, that were treated as an exchange of assets with no budgetary impact, under the new agreed framework, the U.S. contribution would be scored for budgetary purposes under the existing credit reform legislation. This legislation says that Congress need not appropriate the full face value but only the expected amount of loss for any loans made by the United States Government. When U.S. contributions to the IMF were treated as an exchange, there was considered to be no risk of default by the IMF in its obligations to the United States. Under credit reform, a small fraction of the total would be appropriated to cover possible losses. Reportedly, CBO has determined that the U.S. contributions to the IMF would require $5 billion to be appropriated [22]. This re-calculation of the cost is expected by many to ease the prospects for enacting this legislation.

Prior to the May 12th agreement, Congress had appropriated budget authority to facilitate U.S. subscriptions to the IMF, but the actual payments were treated as an exchange of assets with the IMF. Thus, from a U.S. budgetary perspective, there were no net outlays and no net impact on the U.S. budget. In the past 60 years, Congress has handled the bookkeeping aspects for U.S. participation in the IMF in a variety of ways. This system was the result of a compromise among the leading figures on the relevant congressional committees in 1980.

Payments to the IMF were considered to be an exchange of assets because the United States receives back from the IMF a monetary instrument of equal value which it adds to its foreign exchange reserves. The United States receives an increased holding of SDRs in the Fund's SDR Department whenever it purchases SDRs from another country, and an increased reserve tranch position whenever the IMF draws on the U.S. quota to finance loans to borrower countries. Both the SDR and reserve tranche positions are liquid interest bearing assets. SDRs cannot be used to make purchases in the marketplace, but they can be exchanged with other IMF members for currencies or used to satisfy international obligations which in most cases involve the Fund. In the case of loans through the NAB, the United States receives a promissory note from the IMF pledging to repay the loan with interest at a certain time. Credits provided to the IMF through the NAB are considered to be monetary assets and are included in countries' foreign exchange reserves. The proceeds are considered to be readily available because NAB participants can obtain immediate early repayment from the IMF if they have a balance of payments need.

In 2009, there was concern that the procedural aspects of the budget process may have an impact on congressional consideration of the proposed new U.S. subscriptions to the IMF. Some are concerned that Members of Congress may vote against providing budget authority for the proposed $100 billion line of credit to the IMF through the NAB on account of "bailout fatigue," even though the payment would have no outlay effect under then-existing congressional budget scorekeeping procedures.

Peter Orszag, director of the Office of Management and Budget (OMB), was quoted in April 2009 as saying that he cannot see "any analytical rationale for why something would score zero as an outlay but then score as something in budget authority." He reportedly urged the Congressional Budget Office (CBO) and the House and Senate Budget Committees to use an alternative "exchange of assets" procedure (like that use for IMF payments in 1976 and 1977) in which no appropriations would be required to put the $100 billion line of credit through the NAB and U.S. participation in the IMF quota increase into effect [23]. Others have been concerned, though, that changing the existing budgetary procedure for IMF subscriptions at the present moment might weaken their support because it might be seen as an effort to change the rules in the face of controversy or a signal that the Administration fears that it may not have the votes to approve the measure through the established process. By contrast, critics of the current scorekeeping system say that it would be unfortunate if bookkeeping procedures hindered Congress from considering the IMF proposals on their merits.

The Treasury Department is required by law to report to Congress quarterly the financial cost of U.S. participation in the IMF. The most recent report, current through 2007, was submitted in April 2009 [24]. The Department reports that, in 2007, the United States earned a net $68 million from its participation in the SDR Department, and it earned a net $362 million from its transactions with the IMF General Department (which deals with quota accounts)

The United States has used various methods over the years to account for the cost of its participation in the IMF. Before 1967, the United States funded its participation in the IMF through a variety of procedures, including public debt transactions and payments from the Exchange Stabilization Fund. In the 1966 quota increase, the U.S. payment took the form of a letter of credit to the IMF which, for technical reasons, the United States mostly borrowed back during the following years.

In 1967, the U.S. Government adopted a unified Federal budget that consolidated the operating budget of the government with other previously off-budget accounts. This was intended to improve clarity and to enhance the government's management of fiscal policy. In the process, the President's Commission on Budget Concepts (PCBC) also examined the procedures by which the United States managed its payments to the IMF. It recommended that payments to the IMF should be treated as monetary exchanges akin to bank withdrawals and deposits rather than as international lending operations. As such, these payments would be handled as an exchange of assets and would be excluded from budget receipts and expenditures. Congress would be asked to authorize new U.S. payments to the IMF, but the cost of those payments would not be included in the Federal budget.

The new budget concept was not fully implemented when the next quota increase was considered by Congress. In addition to legislation authorizing U.S. participation, the Nixon Administration sought and Congress approved appropriations to effect U.S. participation in the plan. They agreed, however, that the exchange of assets concept was sufficient to cover the resulting payments, and they would have no net outlay impact on the U.S. budget [25].

In 1976, when the following quota increase was considered, the Ford Administration proposed and Congress agreed that the transaction would be treated solely as an exchange of assets. Legislation was enacted authorizing U.S. participation in the plan, but no appropriations were required. The same procedure was used the following year to approve a loan by the United States to the IMF 's Supplemental Financing Facility ("Witteveen Facility") [26] CBO found, in a study of the budgetary scorekeeping issue in 1978, that any procedure – appropriated, exchanged, on-budget, off-budget – is intrinsically arbitrary and not consistent with similar or comparable programs that are treated differently from a scorekeeping perspective elsewhere in the U.S. budget process [27].

Many Members of Congress, reportedly, were not happy with this arrangement. Some argued, citing the provision of the U.S. Constitution which says that no money shall be drawn from the Treasury except through an appropriation by law, that the funding for U.S. participation in the IMF must be appropriated. Some also said that treating the U.S. payments to the IMF as an off- budget transaction was inconsistent with the principle of budgetary unity which underlay the work of the Presidential budget commission in 1967 and a violation of the prohibition against "backdoor spending" in the Congressional Budget Act of 1974.

The issue came to a head in 1980 during congressional consideration of legislation to approve U.S. participation in a new quota increase for the IMF. A compromise was ultimately agreed to. Under this arrangement, the full amount of the U.S. subscription to the IMF would be appropriated as budget authority [28]. This gave Congress control over the size of the U.S. payments and the amount of contingent liability the United States undertook through its participation in the IMF. However, consistent with the exchange of assets concept, no outlays would be counted and the payments to the IMF would be deemed to have no net impact on the U.S. budget. This procedure remains in effect to this day.

Congress has taken a different approach in its budgetary treatment of the contingent liability associated with U.S. participation in the multilateral development banks (MDBs). The MDBs fund their market-rate loan programs with money borrowed in commercial markets. Because they are backed by substantial reserves and by the callable capital subscriptions of their member countries, the banks can sell their bonds and notes at favorable interest rates, and they pass these relatively low rates on to their borrower countries. MDB member countries subscribe some of their purchases of capital stock in callable capital and some (a fixed ratio, now a very small percent of the cost for each share) in paid-in capital. Callable capital is a type of full faith and credit guarantee to the banks' bondholders from their member countries. Most analysts believe that it is very unlikely that one of the MDBs would go bankrupt, exhausting all its resources, and needing to call on the callable capital of its members in order to satisfy its creditors.

Before 1982, Congress appropriated the full amount necessary for the callable portion of U.S. subscriptions to capital stock in the multilateral development banks (MDB). About $12 billion for callable capital had been appropriated by that time, roughly $8 billion for the World Bank and $4 billion for the regional development banks. No outlays were associated with this budget authority and it had no impact on the budget or the budget deficit. During the

1970s, however, cuts were adopted reducing the appropriations for MDB callable capital. The proponents of these cuts often claimed that they were saving the taxpayers and reducing the budget deficit by hundreds of millions of dollars. The cuts in callable capital were not program oriented, since the full paid-in portion of the subscriptions for MDB capital stock was generally appropriated. The resulting mismatch in appropriations had a negative effect on U.S. participation in the banks.

Consequently, in 1981, Congress decided that funds would no longer need to be appropriated for new U.S. subscriptions to callable capital. Instead, as is now the current arrangement, the size of the annual U.S. subscription is regulated through program limitations in appropriations acts [29]. No formal appropriations are required, though appropriations would be required if there ever were to be a call on callable capital. In the case of the IMF, neither the Balanced Budget Act of 1977 nor Sec. 17 of the BWAA require that budget authority must be appropriated to facilitate future increases in the U.S. quota in the IMF or future loans to the IMF through the NAB. The law is silent as to the budgetary procedures that Congress should use on such occasions.

The procedures are different for the IMF and the multilateral banks, but the budgeting issue in both situations is essentially the same. Should the outlay effect of the U.S. commitment to these institutions be counted as zero or is there a likelihood that the IMF will not pay the United States back or a possibility that a call might be made on callable capital? Congress has used a variety of mechanisms to effect the U.S. payments to international financial institutions – in some cases appropriating the full amount in budget authority, in other cases setting a program limitation on new liability, and in other cases treating the entire transaction as an off-budget exchange of assets. None of these arrangements seems to be superior to the others, either in terms of maintaining congressional control or in reflecting or controlling the liabilities that the United States faces through its participation in international financial programs.

In 2004, CBO Director Douglas Holtz-Eakin told the Senate Banking Committee that, "The current budgetary treatment does not fully reflect the U.S. share of the credit risk associated withthe lending and other transactions of the international financial institutions." He had no recommendations for change, however. He said that CBO hoped to discuss these issues further in a future paper [30]. For various reasons, that study was never completed and no paper was released. It may be difficult, in the present moment, for Congress to determine what the "right" budgeting procedure might be in this situation. Over the longer term, however, Congress may want to consider whether an analysis of these budgetary issues might be desirable and whether some changes in the scorekeeping system for international financial institutions might be appropriate.

REFERENCES

[1] Members of the G-20 are: Argentina, Australia, Brazil, Canada, China, France, Germany, India, Indonesia, Italy, Japan, Mexico, Russia, Saudi Arabia, South Africa, South Korea, Turkey, the United Kingdom, the United States, and the European Union.

[2] Global plan for recovery and reform: the Communiqué from the London Summit, available at: http://www.londonsummit.gov.uk/en/summit-aims/summit-communique/

[3] The IMFC has the responsibility of advising, and reporting to, the Board of Governors on matters relating to the Board of Governors' functions in supervising the management and adaptation of the international monetary and financial system, reviewing developments in global liquidity and the transfer of resources to developing countries; considering proposals by the Executive Board to amend the Articles of Agreement; and dealing with disturbances that might threaten the system. The IMFC has 24 members who are governors of the Fund, ministers, or others of comparable rank. The membership reflects the composition of the IMF's Executive Board: each member country that appoints, and each group of member countries that elects, an Executive Director appoints a member of the IMFC.

[4] *Swimming Against the Tide: How Developing Countries are Coping with the Global Crisis*, Background Paper prepared by World Bank Staff for the G20 Finance Ministers and Central Bank Governors Meeting, Horsham, United Kingdom on March 13-14, 2009.

[5] *Global Employment Trends Report 2009*, International Labour Organization, January 2009.

[6] "Unemployment, working poor and vulnerable employment to increase dramatically due to global economic crisis," *International Labor Organization*, January 28, 2009.

[7] "The Global Economic Crisis: Assessing Vulnerability with a Poverty Lens," *The World Bank*, February 2009.

[8] In September 2000, at the United Nations General Assembly's Millennium Summit, world leaders issued the United Nations Millennium Declaration (A/RES/55/2) agreeing to a set of time-bound, measurable goals to fight poverty, hunger, and disease, combat illiteracy, protect the environment and promote gender equality. One hundred eighty-seven nations unanimously agreed to these objectives which became the eight Millennium Development Goals. These goals, which are to be achieved by 2015, are to serve as a framework as nations plan their development assistance programs.

[9] *Swimming Against the Tide: How Developing Countries are Coping with the Global Crisis*, Background Paper prepared by World Bank Staff for the G20 Finance Ministers and Central Bank Governors Meeting, Horsham, United Kingdom on March 13-14, 2009. pg. 11.

[10] Total IMF Credit Outstanding for all members from 1984-2008, available at http://www.imf.org/external/np/fin/tad/ extcred1.aspx.

[11] The IMF resources considered non-usable to fund its operations are (1) its gold holdings, (2) currencies of members that are using IMF resources and are therefore, by definition, in a weak balance of payments or reserve position, (3) the currencies of other members with relatively weak external positions, and (4) other non-liquid IMF assets.

[12] "As Contingency, IMF Aims to Double its Lendable Resources," *IMF Survey Magazine: Policy,* February 2, 2009.

[13] The NAB are a set of credit arrangements between the IMF and 26 developed country members and institutions. These arrangements have been renewed twice, most recently in November 2007 for a further period of five years from November 2008. The NAB are a supplemental, emergency mechanism. They provide temporary financing for the IMF only when necessary. Thus, they are a non-quota based source of financing for the IMF. The NAB are not, therefore, intended to substitute for a quota or capital increase. The NAB has been activated once to finance a Stand-by Arrangement for Brazil in

December 1998, when the IMF called on funding of SDR 9.1 billion, of which SDR 2.9 billion was used.

[14] Daisy Ku, "China to contribute to IMF through SDR bond-sources," *Reuters*, April 8, 2009.

[15] For background, see: CRS Report RL33626, *International Monetary Fund: Reforming Country Representation*, by Martin A. Weiss.

[16] Cai Hong, "Use IMF Bonds to Fight Crisis," *China Daily*, April 24, 2009.

[17] Eswar Prasad, "*Details and Implications of IMF Bonds*," May 4, 2009.

[18] The Bretton Woods Agreements Act, P.L. 79-171 (22. U.S.C. 286, et seq.), is the key act governing procedures for U.S. participation in the IMF and World Bank. Sec.5 says that that no one may vote on behalf of the United States for an increase in the U.S. quota in the IMF or an amendment to the IMF Articles unless Congress authorizes that action.

[19] P.L. 90-349, 22 U.S.C. § 286o. Any SDRs allocated by the IMF or otherwise acquired by the United States are resources of the Exchange Stabilization Fund. For background on the ESF, see: CRS Report RL30125, *The Exchange Stabilization Fund of the U.S. Treasury Department: Purpose, History, and Legislative Activity*, by Arlene E. Wilson, T*he Exchange Stabilization Fund of the U.S. Treasury Department*, by Arlene Wilson.

[20] The IMF may hold gold as an asset, but it cannot lend gold nor can it use gold as security for borrowing funds. The transactions in 1999 shifted money out of the IMF's general resources account into a special fund for HIPC debt cancellation. To offset this deduction, the IMF revalued some of its gold by an equal amount. See Jonathan E. Sanford, "IMF Gold and the World Bank's Unfunded HIPC Mandate," *Development Policy Review*, January 2004.

[21] P.L. 106-113, Consolidated Appropriations Act, 2000, Sec. 504(d).

[22] "Obama IMF Aid Request goes into Senate Bill," *Reuters*, May 13, 2009.

[23] David Rogers. "How to spend without 'spending.'" *Politico*, April 22, 2009, p. 1.

[24] [Department of the Treasury.] Report to Congress on Financial Implications of U.S. Participation in the International Monetary Fund. Available at http://www.ustreas.b gov/press/releases/reports/imfreportq1q42007.pdf

[25] P.L. 9 1-599 and P.L. 91-619, enacted in December 1970, added Sec. 22 to the BWAA and appropriated necessary funds. The Administration had requested that funds for the quota increase be both authorized and appropriated. U.S. Bureau of the Budget. *The Budget of the United States Government, Fiscal Year 1971*, Appendix, p. 105.

[26] P.L. 94-564, enacted in October 1976, added Sec. 25 to the BWAA, saying that "the U.S. Governor of the Bank (sic) is authorized to consent to an increase in the quota of the United States in the Fund equivalent to 1,705 million Special Drawing Rights." The next year, P.L. 95-435, enacted in October 1977, added Sec. 28 to the BWAA, saying that "The Secretary of the Treasury is authorized to make resources available as provided in decision 5509-(77/127) of the Fund, in amounts not to exceed the equivalent of 1,450 million Special Drawing Rights." In neither case were appropriations required. See also Treasury Secretary William E. Simon's paper, "The Exchange of Assets Concept," reprinted in U.S. Congress. Committee on Banking, Currency and Housing. Subcommittee on International Trade, Investment and Monetary Policy. *Hearings on H.R. 13955, June 1 and 3, 1976*. USGPO, 1976, p. 31.

[27] Congressional Budget Office. *U.S. Participation in the Witteveen Facility: The Need for a New Source of International Finance*. March 1978. This paper is available at http://www.cbo.gov/ftpdocs/67xx/doc6727/78-CBO027.pdf.

[28] P.L. 96-3 89, enacted in October 1980, added Sec. 32 to the BWAA. This says the ecretary of the Treasury "is authorized to consent to an increase in the quota of the SUnited States in the Fund equivalent to 4,202.5 million Special Drawing Rights, limited to such amounts as are appropriated in advance in appropriation Acts." Congress substituted the latter language for the original text, which approved participation in the quota increase "to such extent or in such amounts [as] are provided in appropriation Acts." The latter language would have required action by the appropriations committees but would not have required formal appropriations to effect the U.S. increase in the IMF.

[29] P.L. 97-35, enacted August 1981, adding Sec. 39 to the Bretton Woods Agreement Act. This authorized U.S. participation in a new capital increase for the World Bank, providing that 'any subscription to such additional shares shall be effective only to such extent or in such amounts as are provided in advance in appropriations acts." This is the same language Congress had chosen not to enact the previous year in connection with U.S. payments to the IMF.

[30] Statement of Douglas Holtz-Eakin, Director. Congressional Budget Office. *The Costs and Budgetary Treatment of Multilateral Financial Institutions' Activity*. Testimony before the Senate Committee on Banking, Housing and Urban Affairs, May 19, 2004. A copy of this testimony is available at http://www.cbo.gov/ftpdocs/54xx/doc5458/05-19-MFIs.pdf. CBO's last scored IMF legislation in 1998 when it considered H.R. 3114, the International Monetary Fund Reform and Authorization Act of 1998, a bill that was reported by committee but not considered by the House. A copy of the CBO cost estimate is available http://www.cbo.gov/ftpdocs/3xx/doc385/H.R.3114.pdf.

In: The Global Financial Crisis: Policies and Implications ISBN 978-1-61470-317-4
Editor: J. P. Gallagher and E. C. Wilkins © 2012 Nova Science Publishers, Inc.

Chapter 3

THE GLOBAL FINANCIAL CRISIS: ANALYSIS AND POLICY IMPLICATIONS[*]

Dick K. Nanto

ABSTRACT

What began as a bursting of the U.S. housing market bubble and a rise in foreclosures has ballooned into a global financial and economic crisis. The world now appears to have entered a global recession that is causing widespread business contraction, increases in unemployment, and shrinking government revenues. Some of the largest and most venerable banks, investment houses, and insurance companies have either declared bankruptcy or have had to be rescued financially. The world is facing the worst economic conditions since the great depression. Nearly all industrialized countries and many emerging and developing nations have announced economic stimulus and/or financial sector rescue packages, such as the American Recovery and Reinvestment Act of 2009 (H.R. 1, P.L. 111-5). Several countries have resorted to borrowing from the International Monetary Fund as a last resort. The crisis has exposed fundamental weaknesses in financial systems worldwide, demonstrated how interconnected and interdependent economies are today, and has posed vexing policy dilemmas for governments.

The process for coping with the crisis by countries across the globe has been manifest in four basic phases. The first has been intervention to contain the contagion and restore confidence in the system. This has required extraordinary measures both in scope, cost, and extent of government reach. The second has been coping with the secondary effects of the crisis, particularly the slowdown in economic activity and flight of capital from countries in emerging markets and elsewhere that have been affected by the crisis. The third phase of this process is to make changes in the financial system to reduce risk and prevent future crises. In order to give these proposals political backing, world leaders have called for international meetings to address changes in policy, regulations, oversight, and enforcement. Some are characterizing these meetings as Bretton Woods II. On April 2, heads of the G-20 nations met in the Leaders' London Summit and announced measures to bolster the international financial institutions, stabilize the world economy, and reform and improve the financial regulatory system. The fourth phase of

[*] This is an edited, reformatted and augmented version of CRS Report RL34742, dated May 12, 2009.

the process is dealing with political, social, and security effects of the financial turmoil. Significant foreign policy implications of the crisis are now emerging.

The role for Congress in this financial crisis is multifaceted. While the recent focus has been on combating the recession, the ultimate issue perhaps is how to ensure the smooth and efficient functioning of financial markets to promote the general well-being of the country while protecting taxpayer interests and facilitating business operations without creating a moral hazard. In addition to preventing future crises through legislative, oversight, and domestic regulatory functions, Congress plays a key role in generating policy options and informing the public. On the regulatory side, the largest questions seem to be how U.S. regulations should be changed and, if changed, how closely those changes are to be harmonized with international recommendations. Other questions include: should the United States promote global regulatory standards to be voluntarily adopted by countries or should a supranational regulatory institution be created? Where would enforcement authority reside; at the state, national, or international level? Congress also plays a role in measures to reform and recapitalize the International Monetary Fund, the World Bank, and regional development banks.

Recent Developments and Analysis [1]

May 7. The government's "stress tests" indicated that ten of the largest U.S. banks would have to raise a combined $74.6 billion in capital to cushion themselves against economic under- performance.

May 5. The European Commission lowered its growth forecast for the European Union to -4% in 2009 and -0.1% in 2010.

May 4. The International Monetary Fund approved a 24-month $17.1 billion Stand-By Arrangement for Romania. The total international financial support package will amount to $26.4 billion, with the European Union providing $6.6 billion, the World Bank $1.3 billion, and the European Bank for Reconstruction and Development, the European Investment Bank, and the International Finance Corporation a combined $1.3 billion.

April 30. Chrysler announced merger with Fiat and filed for bankruptcy. Separately, the Financial Accounting Standards Board changed the mark-to-market accounting rule to give banks more discretion in reporting value of assets.

April 29. The World Health Organization raised the Swine flu pandemic alert to phase 5 (humanto-human spread of the virus into at least two countries indicating that a pandemic is imminent).

April 22. The International Monetary Fund projected global economic activity to contract by 1.3% in 2009 with a slow recovery (1.9% growth) in 2010. Overall, the advanced economies are forecast to contract by 3.8% in 2009, with the U.S. economy shrinking by 2.8%.

April 21 .The IMF estimated that banks and other financial institutions faced aggregate losses of $4.05 trillion in the value of their holdings as a result of the crisis. Of that amount, $2.7 trillion is from loans and assets originating in the United States, the fund said. That estimate is up from $2.2 trillion in the fund's interim report in January, and $1.4 trillion last October.

April 14. The IMF granted Poland a $20.5 billion credit line using a facility intended to backstop countries with sound economic policies that have been caught short by the global financial crisis. On April 1, Mexico said that it was tapping the new credit line for $47 billion.

As for the impact of a swine flu pandemic in the United States, according to Global Insight, an economic consulting firm, in a mild epidemic of roughly 75 million infected with 100,000 fatalities the impact on U.S. economic growth would be less than -0.5% per year, but in a more severe epidemic the consequences could be quite dire.

THE GLOBAL FINANCIAL CRISIS AND U.S. INTERESTS [2]

What began as a bursting of the U.S. housing market bubble and a rise in foreclosures has ballooned into a global financial and economic crisis. Some of the largest and most venerable banks, investment houses, and insurance companies have either declared bankruptcy or have had to be rescued financially. In October 2008, credit flows froze, lender confidence dropped, and one after another the economies of countries around the world dipped toward recession. The crisis exposed fundamental weaknesses in financial systems worldwide, and despite coordinated easing of monetary policy by governments and, trillions of dollars in intervention by central banks and governments, and large fiscal stimulus packages, the crisis seems far from over.

This financial crisis which began in industrialized countries quickly spread to emerging market and developing economies. Investors have pulled capital from countries, even those with small levels of perceived risk, and caused values of stocks and domestic currencies to plunge. Also, slumping exports and commodity prices have added to the woes, pushing economies world wide either into recession or into a period of slow economic growth. The global crisis now seems to be played out on two levels. The first is among the industrialized nations of the world where most of the losses from subprime mortgage debt, excessive leveraging of investments, and inadequate capital backing credit default swaps (insurance against defaults and bankruptcy) have occurred. The second level of the crisis is among emerging market and other economies who may be "innocent bystanders" to the crisis but who also may have less resilient economic systems that can often be whipsawed by actions in global markets. Most industrialized countries (except for Iceland) seem to able to finance their own rescue packages by borrowing domestically and in international capital markets, but many emerging market and developing economies have insufficient sources of capital and have turned to help from the International Monetary Fund (IMF), World Bank, or from capital surplus nations, such as Japan, and the European Union.

For the United States, the financial turmoil touches on the fundamental national interest of protecting the economic security of Americans. It also is affecting the United States in achieving national foreign policy goals, such as maintaining political stability and cooperative relations with other nations and supporting a financial infrastructure that allows for the smooth functioning of the international economy. Reverberations from the financial crisis, moreover, are not only being felt on Wall Street and Main Street but are being manifest in world flows of exports and imports, rates of growth and unemployment, government revenues and expenditures, and in political risk in some countries. The simultaneous slowdown in economic activity around the globe indicates that emerging market and developing economies have not decoupled from industrialized countries and governments cannot depend on exports to pull them out of these recessionary conditions.

This global financial and economic crisis has brought to the public consciousness several arcane financial terms usually confined to the domain of regulators and Wall Street investors. These terms lie at the heart of both understanding and resolving this financial crisis and include:

- Systemic risk: The risk that the failure of one or a set of market participants, such as core banks, will reverberate through a financial system and cause severe problems for participants in other sectors. Because of systemic risk, the scope of regulatory agencies may have to be expanded to cover a wider range of institutions and markets [3]
- Deleveraging: The unwinding of debt. Companies borrow to buy assets that increase their growth potential or increase returns on investments. Deleveraging lowers the risk of default on debt and mitigates losses, but if it is done by selling assets at a discount, it may depress security and asset prices and lead to large losses. Hedge funds tend to be highly leveraged.
- Procyclicality: The tendency for market players to take actions over a business cycle that increase the boom-and-bust effects, e.g. borrowing extensively during upturns and deleveraging during downturns. Changing regulations to dampen procyclical effects would be extremely challenging [4]
- Preferred equity: A cross between common stock and debt. It gives the holder a claim, prior to that of common stockholders, on earnings and on assets in the event of liquidation. Most preferred stock pays a fixed dividend. As a result of the stress tests in early 2009, some banks may increase their capital base by converting preferred equity to common stock.
- Collateralized debt obligations (CDOs): a type of structured asset-backed security whose value and payments are derived from a portfolio of fixed-income underlying assets. CDOs based on sub-prime mortgages have been at the heart of the global financial crisis. CDOs are assigned different risk classes or tranches, with "senior" tranches considered to be the safest. Since interest and principal payments are made in order of seniority, junior tranches offer higher coupon payments (and interest rates) or lower prices to compensate for additional default risk. Investors, pension funds, and insurance companies buy CDOs.
- Credit default swap (CDS): a credit derivative contract between two counterparties in which the buyer makes periodic payments to the seller and in return receives a sum of money if a certain credit event occurs (such as a default in an underlying financial instrument). Payoffs and collateral calls on CDSs issued on sub-prime mortgage CDOs have been a primary cause of the problems of AIG and other companies.

The role for Congress in this financial crisis is multifaceted. The overall issue seems to be how to ensure the smooth and efficient functioning of financial markets to promote the general wellbeing of the country while protecting taxpayer interests and facilitating business operations without creating a moral hazard [5] In addition to preventing future crises through legislative, oversight, and domestic regulatory functions, Congress has been providing funds and ground rules for economic stabilization and rescue packages and informing the public through hearings and other means. Congress also plays a role in measures to reform the international financial system and in recapitalizing international financial institutions, such as the International Monetary Fund, and replenishing funds for poverty reduction arms of the World Bank (International Development Association) and regional development banks. As the force of the effects of the global financial meltdown are felt, popular and congressional concern has been intensifying. Are the financial sector executives mainly responsible for the crisis benefitting financially from it (in the form of large bonus payments)? Is the system too complex to be controlled, or is it an insider's game at the expense of Main Street? Should the U.S. domestic economy be given first priority in spending (Buy America), and should financial institutions receiving government funds direct their lending or repayment of debts to domestic, rather than foreign, firms? Opposition to globalization from various quarters and rising protectionist sentiment also may trigger new international trade disputes and work to shape the debate over rewriting U.S. and international financial rules.

The global financial crisis has brought home an important point: the United States is still a major center of the financial world. Regional financial crises (such as the Asian financial crisis, Japan's banking crisis, or the Latin American debt crisis) can occur without seriously infecting the rest of the global financial system. But when the U.S. financial system stumbles, it may bring major parts of the rest of the world down with it [6]. The reason is that the United States is the main guarantor of the international financial system, the provider of dollars widely used as currency reserves and as an international medium of exchange, and a contributor to much of the financial capital that sloshes around the world seeking higher yields. The rest of the world may not appreciate it, but a financial crisis in the United States often takes on a global hue.

Four Phases of the Global Financial Crisis

The process as it has played out in countries across the globe has been manifest in four overlapping phases. Although each phase has a policy focus, each phase of the crisis affects the others, and, until the crisis has passed, no phase seems to have a clear end point.

Contain the Contagion and Strengthen Financial Sectors

The first phase has been intervention to contain the contagion and strengthen financial sectors in countries [7]. On a macroeconomic level, this has included policy actions such as lowering interest rates, expanding the money supply, quantitative (monetary) easing, and actions to restart and restore confidence in credit markets. On a microeconomic level, this has entailed actions to resolve immediate problems and effects of the crisis including financial rescue packages for ailing firms, guaranteeing deposits at banks, injections of capital, disposing of toxic assets, and restructuring debt. This has involved decisive (and, in cases, unprecedented) measures both in scope, cost, and extent of government reach. Actions taken include the rescue of financial institutions considered to be "too big to fail" and government takeovers of certain financial institutions, government facilitation of mergers and acquisitions, and government purchases of problem financial assets. Nearly every industrialized country and many developing and emerging market countries have pursued some or all of these actions. Although the "panic" phase of containing the contagion may have passed, operations still are continuing, and the ultimate cost of the actions are yet to be determined. (See Appendix E for early containment actions)

In the United States, traditional monetary policy almost has reached its limit as the Federal Reserve has lowered its discount rate to 0.5% and has a target rate for the federal funds rate of 0.0 to 0.25%. The Federal Reserve and Treasury, therefore, have turned toward quantitative monetary easing (buying government securities and injecting more money into the economy) and dealing directly with the toxic assets being held by banks [8]

What has been learned from previous financial crises is that without a resolution of underlying problems with toxic assets and restoring health to the balance sheet of banks and other financial institutions, financial crises continue to drag on. This was particularly the case with Japan [9]. Even Sweden, often viewed as a successful model of how to cope with a financial crisis, had to take decisive action to deal with the nonperforming assets of its banking system [10]

In the United States, the Treasury, Federal Reserve, Federal Deposit Insurance Corporation, Office of Thrift Supervision, and Comptroller of the Currency have worked together to contain the contagion. Under the $700 billion Troubled Asset Relief Program [11] (TARP, H.R. 1424/P.L. 110-343), the Treasury has invested in dozens of banks, General Motors, Chrysler and the insurer A.I.G. The investments are in the form of preferred stock that pays quarterly dividends, which to date total $2.5 billion.

On March 23, 2009, The U.S. Treasury released the details of its $900 billion Public Private Partnership Investment Program to address the challenge of toxic (legacy) assets being carried by the financial system [12]

The U.S. Federal Reserve also has conducted about $1.2 trillion in emergency commitments to stabilize the financial sector. Its interventions have included a safety net for commercial banks, the rescue of Bear Stearns, a lending facility for investment banks and brokerages, loans for money-market assets and commercial paper, and purchases of securitized loans and lending to businesses and consumers for purchases of asset-backed securities [13]

Coping with Macroeconomic Effects

The second phase of this financial crisis is less uncommon except that the severity of the macroeconomic downturn confronting countries around the world is the worst since the Great Depression of the 193 0s. The financial crisis soon spread to real sectors to negatively affect whole economies, production, firms, investors, and households. Many of these countries, particularly those with emerging and developing markets, have been pulled down by the ever widening flight of capital from their economies and by falling exports and commodity prices. In these cases, governments have turned to traditional monetary and fiscal policies to deal with recessionary economic conditions, declining tax revenues, and rising unemployment.

Figure 1 shows the effect of the financial crisis on economic growth rates (annualized changes in real GDP by quarter) in selected nations of the world. The figure shows the difference between the 2001 recession that was confined primarily to countries such as the United States, Mexico, and Japan and the current financial crisis that is pulling down growth rates in a variety of countries. The slowdown—recession for many countries—is global. The implication of this synchronous drop in growth rates is that the United States and other nations may not be able to export their way out of recession. Even China is experiencing a "growth recession." There is no major economy that can play the role of an economic engine to pull other countries out of their economic doldrums.

In response to the recession or slowdown in economic growth, many countries have adopted fiscal stimulus packages designed to induce economic recovery or at least keep conditions from worsening. These are summarized in Table 2 and Appendix B and include packages by China ($586 billion), the European Union ($256 billion), Japan ($250 billion), Mexico ($54 billion), and South Korea ($52.5 billion).The global total for stimulus packages now exceeds $2 trillion, but some of the packages include measures that extend into subsequent years, so the total does not imply that the entire amount will translate into immediate government spending.

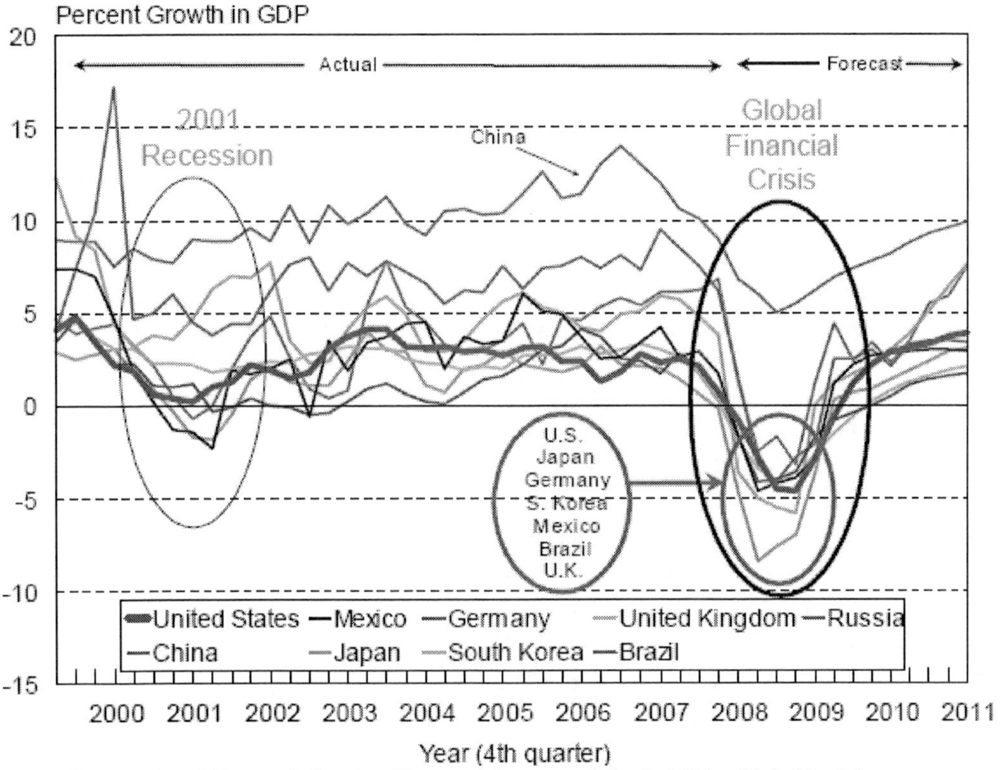

Source: Congressional Research Service. Data and forecasts (March 15) by Global Insight.

Figure 1. Quarterly (Annualized) Economic Growth Rates for Selected Countries.

The stimulus packages by definition are to be fiscal measures (government spending or tax cuts) but some packages include measures aimed at stabilizing banks and other financial institutions that usually are categorized as bank rescue or financial assistance packages. The $2 trillion total in stimulus packages amounts to approximately 3% of world gross domestic product, an amount that exceeds the call by the International Monetary Fund for fiscal stimulus totaling 2% of global GDP to counter worsening economic conditions worldwide [14]. If only new fiscal stimulus measures to be done in 2009 are counted, however, the total and the percent of global GDP figures would be considerably lower. An analysis of the stimulus measures by the European Community for 2009 found that such measures amount to an estimated 1.32% of European Community GDP [15] The IMF estimated that as of January 2009, the U.S. fiscal stimulus packages as a percent of GDP in 2009 would amount to 1.9%, for the euro area 0.9%, for Japan 1.4%, for Asia excluding Japan 1.5%, and for the rest of the G-20 countries 1.1%. [16]

At the G-20 London Summit, a schism arose between the United States and the U.K., who were arguing for large and coordinated stimulus packages, and Germany and France, who considered their automatic stabilizers (increases in government expenditures for items such as unemployment insurance that are triggered any time the economy slows) plus existing stimulus programs as sufficient. In their communiqué, the leaders noted that $5 billion will have been devoted to fiscal expansion by the end of 2010 and committed themselves to "deliver the scale of sustained fiscal effort necessary to restore growth." In the communiqué, the G-20 leaders decided to add $1.1 trillion in resources to the international financial institutions, including $750 billion more for the International Monetary Fund, $250 billion to boost global trade, and $100 billion for multilateral development banks. (See Appendix C for the London Summit communiqué)

The additional lending by the international financial institutions would be in addition to national fiscal stimulus efforts and could be targeted to those countries most in need. Several countries have borrowed heavily in international markets and carry debt denominated in euros or dollars. As their currencies have depreciated, the local currency cost of this debt has skyrocketed. Other countries have banks with debt exposure almost as large as national GDP. Some observers have raised the possibility of a sovereign debt crisis [17] (countries defaulting on government guaranteed debt) or as in the case of Iceland having to nationalize its banks and assume liabilities greater than the size of the national economy.

As of April 2009, the IMF, under its Stand-By Arrangement facility, has provided or is in the process of providing financial support packages for Iceland ($2.1 billion), Ukraine ($16.4 billion), Hungary ($25.1 billion), Pakistan ($7.6 billion), Belarus ($2.46 billion), Serbia ($530.3 million), Armenia ($540 million), El Salvador ($800 million), Latvia ($2.4 billion), and Seychelles ($26.6 million). The IMF also created a Flexible Credit Line for countries with strong fundamentals, policies, and track records of policy implementation. Once approved, these loans can be disbursed when the need arises rather than being conditioned on compliance with policy targets as in traditional IMF-supported programs. The IMF board has approved Mexico for $47 billion under this facility. Poland has requested a credit line of $20.5 billion.

Regulatory and Financial Market Reform

The third phase of the global financial crisis—to decide what changes may be needed in the financial system—also is underway. In order to coordinate reforms in national regulatory systems and give such proposals political backing, world leaders began a series of international meetings to address changes in policy, regulations, oversight, and enforcement. Some are characterizing these meetings as Bretton Woods II. [18] The G-20 leaders' Summit on Financial Markets and the World Economy that met on November 15, 2008, in Washington, DC, was the first of a series of summits to address these issues. The second was the G-20 Leader's Summit on April 2, 2009, in London, (See Appendix C) [19] and the third is to be held in November 2009.

In this third phase, the immediate issues to be addressed by the United States and other nations center on "fixing the system" and preventing future crises from occurring. Much of this involves the technicalities of regulation and oversight of financial markets, derivatives, and hedging activity, as well as standards for capital adequacy and a schema for funding and conducting future financial interventions, if necessary. In the November 2008 G-20 Summit, the leaders approved an Action Plan that sets forth a comprehensive work plan.

The leaders instructed finance ministers to make specific recommendations in the following areas:

- Avoiding regulatory policies that exacerbate the ups and downs of the business cycle;
- Reviewing and aligning global accounting standards, particularly for complex securities in times of stress;
- Strengthening transparency of credit derivatives markets and reducing their systemic risks;
- Reviewing incentives for risk-taking and innovation reflected in compensation practices; and
- Reviewing the mandates, governance, and resource requirements of the International Financial Institutions.

Most of the technical details of this work plan have been referred to existing international standards setting organizations or the National Finance Ministers and Central Bank Governors. These organizations include the International Accounting Standards Board, the Financial Accounting Standards Board, Basel Committee on Banking Supervision, the International Organization of Securities Commissions, and the Financial Stability Forum (Board).

At the London Summit, the leaders addressed the issue of coordination and oversight of the international financial system by establishing a new Financial Stability Board (F SB) with a strengthened mandate as a successor to the Financial Stability Forum with membership to include all G-20 countries, Financial Stability Forum members, Spain, and the European Commission. The FSB is to collaborate with the IMF to provide early warning of macroeconomic and financial risks and the actions needed to address them. The Summit left it to individual countries to reshape regulatory systems to identify and take account of macroprudential (systemic) risks, but agreed to regulate hedge funds and Credit Rating Agencies [20].

For the United States, the fundamental issues may be the degree to which U.S. laws and regulations are to be altered to conform to recommendations from the new Financial Stability Board and what authority the Board and IMF will have relative to member nations. Although the London Summit strengthened regulations and the IMF, it did not result in a "new international financial architecture." The question still is out as to whether the Bretton Woods system should be changed from one in which the United States is the buttress of the international financial architecture to one in which the United States remains the buttress but its financial markets are more "Europeanized" (more in accord with Europe's practices) and more constrained by the broader international financial order? Should the international financial architecture be merely strengthened or include more control, and if more control, then by whom? [21] What is the time frame for a new architecture that may take years to materialize?

For the United States, some of these issues are being addressed by the President's Working Group on Financial Markets (consisting of the U.S. Treasury Secretary, Chairs of the Federal Reserve Board, the Securities and Exchange Commission, and the Commodity

Futures Trading Commission) in cooperation with international financial organizations. Appendix D lists the major regulatory reform proposals and indicates whether they have been put forward by various U.S. and international organizations. Those that have been proposed by both the U.S. Treasury and the G-20 include the following:

- *System Risk:* All systemically important financial institutions should be subject to an appropriate degree of regulation. Use of stress testing by financial institutions should be more rigorous.
- *Capital Standards*: Large complex systemically-important financial institutions should be subject to more stringent capital regulation than other firms. Capital decisions by regulators and firms should make greater provision against liquidity risk.
- *Hedge Funds*: Hedge funds should be required to register with a national securities regulator. Systemically-important hedge funds should be subject to prudential regulation. Hedge funds should provide information on a confidential basis to regulators about their strategies and positions.
- *Over-the-Counter Derivatives*: Credit default swaps should be processed through a regulated centralized counterparty (CCP) or clearing house.
- *Tax Havens*: Minimum international standards—a regulatory floor—should apply in all countries, including tax havens and offshore banking centers.

Among the proposals put forward by the Treasury but not mentioned by the G-20 included creating a single regulator with responsibility over all systemically important financial institutions with power for prompt corrective action, strengthening regulation of critical payment systems, processing all standardized over-the-counter derivatives through a regulated clearing house and subjecting them to a strong regulatory regime, and providing authority for a government agency to take over a failing, systemically important non-bank institution and place it in conservatorship or receivership outside the bankruptcy system.

Dealing with Political, Social, and Security Effects

The fourth phase of the financial crisis is in dealing with political, social, and security effects of the financial turmoil. These are secondary impacts that relate to the role of the United States on the world stage, its leadership position relative to other countries, and the political and social impact within countries affected by the crisis. For example, on February 12, 2009, the U.S. Director of National Intelligence, Dennis Blair, told Congress that instability in countries around the world caused by the global economic crisis and its geopolitical implications, rather than terrorism, is the primary near-term security threat to the United States [22].

The political, social, and security effects of the global financial crisis can be divided roughly into the following categories:

- effects on political leadership and regimes inside countries;
- effects on ideologies, protectionism, and state capitalism;
- effects on international leadership and attitudes toward the United States;
- effects on supranational political and economic organizations; and
- effects on poverty and flows of aid resources.

Political Leadership and Regimes

The financial crisis works on political leadership and regimes within countries through two major mechanisms. The first is the discontent from citizens who are losing jobs, seeing businesses go bankrupt, losing wealth both in financial and real assets, and facing declining prices for their products. In democracies, this discontent often results in public opposition to the existing establishment or ruling regime. In some cases it can foment extremist movements, particularly in poorer countries where large numbers of unemployed young people may become susceptible to religious radicalism that demonizes Western industrialized society and encourages terrorist activity.

The precipitous drop in the price of oil holds important implications for countries, such as Russia, Mexico, Venezuela, Yemen, and other petroleum exporters, who were counting on oil revenues to continue to pour into their coffers to fund activities considered to be essential to their interests. While moderating oil prices may be a positive development for the U.S. consumer and for the U.S. balance of trade, it also may affect the political stability of certain petroleum exporting countries. The concomitant drop in prices of commodities such as rubber, copper ore, iron ore, beef, rice, coffee, and tea also carries dire consequences for exporter countries in Africa, Latin America, and Asia [23].

In Pakistan, a particular security problem exacerbated by the financial crisis could be developing. The IMF has approved a $7.6 billion loan package for Pakistan, but the country faces serious economic problems at a time when it is dealing with challenges from suspected al Qaeda and Taliban sympathizers, when citizen objections are rising to U.S. missile strikes on suspected terrorist targets in Pakistan, and the country faces a budget shortfall that may curtail the ability of the government to continue its counter terror operations [24].

The second way that the crisis works on ruling regimes is through the actions of existing governments both to stay in power and to deal with the adverse effects of the crisis. Any crisis generates centrifugal forces that tend to strengthen central government power. Most nations view the current financial crisis as having been created by the financial elite in New York and London in cooperation with their increasingly laissez faire governments. By blaming the industrialized West, particularly the United States, for their economic woes, governments can stoke the fires of nationalism and seek support for themselves. As nationalist sentiments rise and economic conditions worsen, citizens look to governments as a rescuer of last resort. Political authorities can take actions, ostensibly to counter the effects of the crisis, but often with the result that it consolidates their power and preserves their own positions. Authoritarian regimes, in particular, can take even more dictatorial actions to deal with financial and economic challenges.

Economic Philosophy, Protectionism, and State Capitalism

In the basic economic philosophies that guide policy, expediency seems to be trumping free- market ideologies in many countries. The crisis may hasten the already declining economic neoliberalism that began with President Ronald Reagan and British Prime Minister Margaret Thatcher. Although the market-based structure of most of the world economies is likely to continue, the basic philosophy of deregulation, non-governmental intervention in the private sector, and free and open markets for goods, services, and capital, seems to be subsumed by the need to increase regulation of new financial products, increased government intervention, and some pull-back from further reductions in trade barriers. Emerging market countries, particularly those in Eastern Europe, moreover, may be questioning their shift toward the capitalist model away from the socialist model of their past.

State capitalism in which governments either nationalize or own shares of companies and intervene to direct parts of their operations is rising not only in countries such as Russia, where a history of command economics predisposes governments toward state ownership of the means of production, but in the United States, Europe, and Asia. Nationalization of banks, insurance companies, and other financial institutions, as well as government capital injections and loans to private corporations have become parts of rescue and stimulus packages and have brought politicians and bureaucrats directly into economic decision-making at the company level.

While state ownership of enterprises may affect the efficiency and profitability of the operation, it also raises questions of equity (government favoring one company over another) and the use of scarce government resources in oversight and management of companies. When taxpayer funds have been used to invest in a company, the public then has an interest in its operations, but protecting that interest takes time and resources. This has already been illustrated in the United States by the attention devoted to executive compensation and bonuses of companies receiving government loans or capital injections and by the threatened bankruptcy of Chrysler and General Motors.

In the G-20 and other meetings, world representatives have been vocal in calling for countries to avoid resorting to protectionism as they try to stimulate their own economies. Still, whether it be provisions to buy domestic products instead of imports, financial assistance to domestic producers, or export incentives, countries have been attempting to protect national companies often at the expense of those foreign. Overt attempts to restrict imports, promote exports, or impose restrictions on trade are limited by the rules of the World Trade Organization (WTO), but there is ample scope for increases in trade barriers that are consistent with the rules and obligations of the WTO. These include raising applied tariffs to higher bound levels as well as actions to impose countervailing duties or to take antidumping measures. Certain sectors also are excluded from trade agreements for national security or other reasons. Moreover, there are opportunities to favor domestic producers at the expense of foreign producers through industry- specific relief or subsidy programs, broad fiscal stimulus programs, buy-domestic provisions, or currency depreciation.

Several countries have imposed trade related measures that tend to protect or assist domestic industries. Although the WTO reported in January 2009 that most WTO members had successfully kept domestic protectionist pressures under control "with only limited evidence of increases in trade restricting or trade distorting measures," the WTO also compiled a list of new trade and trade-related policy measures that had been taken since September 2008. These included increases in steel tariffs by India, increases in tariffs on 940 imported products by Ecuador, restrictions on ports of entry for imports of certain consumer goods by Indonesia, imposition of non-automatic licensing requirements on products considered as sensitive by Argentina, increase in tariffs on imports of crude oil by South Korea, re-introduction of export subsidies for certain dairy products by the European Commission, and a rise in import duties on cars and trucks by Russia [25]

China has announced a number of policy responses to deal with the crisis, including a pledge to spend $586 billion to boost domestic spending. However, China has also announced plans to provide subsidies to various industries (such as steel and motor vehicles) and to boost export tax rebates. Also, despite calls to allow its currency to appreciate, the Chinese government has depreciated its currency vis-à-vis the dollar in recent months arguably to help its export industries.

In the United States, the Buy America provision in the February 2009 stimulus package [26] has been widely criticized. Even though the provision applies only to steel, iron, and manufactured goods used in government funded construction projects and language was included that the provision "shall be applied in a manner consistent with United States obligations under international agreements," many nations have protested the Buy America language as "protectionist" [27] and as possibly starting down a slippery slope that could lead to WTOinconsistent protectionism by countries.

A concern also is rising among developing nations that a type of "financial protectionism" may arise. Governments may direct banks that have received capital injections to lend more domestically rather than overseas. Borrowing by the U.S. Treasury to finance the growing U.S. budget deficit also pulls in funds from around the world and could crowd out borrowers from countries also seeking to cover their deficits. Also of concern to countries such as Vietnam, China, and other exporters of foreign brand name exports is that private flows of investment capital may decline as producers face rising inventories and excess production capacity. Why build another factory when existing ones sit idle?

U.S. Leadership Position

Another issue raised by the global financial crisis has been the role of the United States on the world stage and the U.S. leadership position relative to other countries. How this will play out with the Obama Administration is yet to be seen, but the rest of the world seems to be expressing ambivalent feelings about the United States.

On one hand, many blame the United States for the crisis and see it as yet another of the excesses of a country that had emerged as the sole superpower in a unipolar world following the end of the Cold War. Although not always explicit, their willingness to follow the U.S. lead appears to have diminished. On the other hand, countries recognize that the United States is still one of a scant few that can bring other nations along and induce them to take actions outside of their political comfort zone. The combination of U.S. military power, extensive economic and financial clout, its diplomatic clout, and its veto power in the IMF put the United States at the center of any resolution to the global financial turmoil.

During the early phase of the crisis, European leaders (particularly British Prime Minister Gordon Brown, French President Nicolas Sarkozy, and German Chancellor Angela Merkel) played a major role and have been influential in crafting international mechanisms and policies to deal with adverse effects of the crisis as well as proposing long-term solutions. Also, dealing with the financial crisis has enabled countries with rich currency reserves, such as China, Russia, and Japan, to assume higher political profiles in world financial circles.

If China [28] helps to finance the various rescue measures in the United States, Washington may lose some leverage with Beijing in pursuing human and labor rights, product safety, and other pertinent issues. Also, the inclusion of China, India, and Brazil in the G-20 Summits rather than just the G-7 or G-8 countries as originally proposed, seems to indicate the growing influence of the non-industrialized nations in addressing global financial issues [29]

The recession in the United States and elsewhere also may hamper efforts to reach agreement on international issues such as climate change. In addition, U.S. trade and foreign investments are key components of American soft power. At a time when U.S. policymakers are turning more toward the use of soft power (or what is sometimes termed "smart power"), if the United States is blamed for what is becoming the worst global recession in decades and U.S. companies are perceived as reducing their overseas business activities because of the global financial crisis, the ability of the United States to induce other countries to coalesce around U.S. goals may be diminished.

International Financial Organizations

The financial crisis has brought international financial organizations and institutions into the spotlight. These include the International Monetary Fund, the Financial Stability Board (an enlarged Financial Stability Forum), the Group of Twenty (G-20), the Bank for International Settlements, the World Bank, the Group of 7 (G-7), and other organizations that play a role in coordinating policy among nations, provide early warning of impending crises, or assist countries as a lender of last resort. The precise architecture of any international financial structure and whether it is to have powers of oversight, regulatory, or supervisory authority is yet to be determined. However, the interconnectedness of global financial and economic markets has highlighted the need for stronger institutions to coordinate regulatory policy across nations, provide early warning of dangers caused by systemic, cyclical, or macroprudential risks [30] and induce corrective actions by national governments. A fundamental question in this process, however, rests on sovereignty: how much power and authority should an international organization wield relative to national authorities?

As a result of the global financial crisis, the IMF has expanded its activities along several dimensions. The first is its role as lender of last resort for countries less able to access international capital markets. It also is attempting to become a lender of "not-last" resort by offering flexible credit lines for countries with strong economic fundamentals and a sustained track record of implementing sound economic policies. The second area of expansion by the IMF has been in oversight of the international economy and in monitoring systemic risk across borders. The IMF also tracks world economic and financial developments more closely and provides countries with the forecasts and analysis of developments in financial markets. It additionally provides policy advice to countries and regions and is assisting the G-20 with recommendations to reshape the system of international regulation and governance. Although the London Summit provided for more funding for the IMF and international development banks, some larger issues, such as governance of and reform of the IMF are now being determined. (For further discussion of the IMF, see sections below on "The Challenges" and "International Policy Issues."

The Washington Action Plan from the G-20 Leader's Summit in November 2008 contained specific policy changes that were addressed in the April 2, 2009 Summit in London. The regulatory and other specific changes have been assigned to existing international organizations such as the Financial Stability Forum (now Financial Stability Board) and Bank for International Settlements, as well as international standard setting bodies such as the Basel Committee on Banking Supervision, International Accounting Standards Board, International Organization of Securities Commissions, and International Association of Insurance Supervisors [31].

Effects on Poverty and Flows of Aid Resources

The global crisis is causing huge losses and dislocation in the industrialized countries of the world, but in many of the developing countries it is pushing people deep into poverty. The crisis is being transmitted to the poorer countries through declining exports, falling commodity prices, reverse migration, and shrinking remittances from citizens working overseas. This could have major effects in countries which provide large numbers of migrant workers, including Mexico, Guatemala, El Salvador, India, Bangladesh, and the Philippines.

The decline in tax revenues caused by the slowdown in economic activity also is increasing competition within countries for scarce budget funds and affecting decisions about the allocation of national resources. This relates directly to the ability to finance official development assistance to poorer nations and other programs aimed at alleviating poverty.

In the United States, the economic downturn and the vast resources being committed to provide stimulus to the U.S. economy and rescue trouble financial institutions could clash with some foreign policy priorities of the new Administration. President Obama and top officials in his Administration—including Secretary of State Clinton and Secretary of Defense Gates—have pledged to increase the capacity of civilian foreign policy institutions and levels of U.S. foreign assistance. Financial constraints could impose difficult choices between foreign policy priorities—for example, between boosting levels of non-military aid to Afghanistan and increasing global health programs–or changes to planned levels of increases across the board. The global reach of the economic downturn further complicates the resource problem, as it both limits what other countries can do to address common international challenges and potentially exacerbates the scale of need in conflict areas and the developing world.

New Challenges and Policy in Managing Financial Risk [32]

The Challenges

The actions of the United States and other nations in coping with the global financial crisis first were to contain the contagion, minimize losses to society, restore confidence in financial institutions and instruments, and lubricate the wheels of the system in order for it to return to full operation. Attention now is focused on stimulating the economy and stemming the downturn in macroeconomic conditions that is increasing unemployment and forcing many companies into bankruptcy. As of early 2009, as much as 40% of the world's wealth may have been destroyed since the crisis began, [33] although equity markets have recovered somewhat since then. There still is considerable uncertainty, however, over whether the worst of the crisis has passed and whether monetary and fiscal policies taken so far will be sufficient to cope with the global recession. It also is unknown whether the current crisis is an aberration that can be fixed by tweaking the system, or whether it reflects systemic problems that require major surgery. The challenges of the third phase still remain. They arguably are to change regulatory structure and regulations and the global financial architecture to ensure that future crises do not occur or, at least, to mitigate their effects.

On a more philosophical plane, the fundamental assumption that markets are self-correcting and that individuals pursuing their own financial interests like an "invisible hand" tend also to promote the good of the global community has been questioned. Will the losses of this financial crisis hurt investors and institutions enough that the system will become more prudent in the future? How much further regulation and oversight is necessary to fill gaps in information and technical expertise to compensate for faulty or incomplete methods of modeling risk and to provide more resilience in the system to offset human error? A related question is whether there should be a system of controls on flows of capital during a financial crisis that would be aimed at temporarily calming markets.

At the G-20 Summit on Financial Markets and the World Economy on November 15, 2008, in Washington, DC, the leaders of these nations concluded that major changes are needed in the global financial system. The G-20 recommendations imply that most saw the system as functional but major measures were needed to reduce risk, to provide oversight, and to establish an early warning system of impending financial crises. The G-20 leaders also agreed, however, that "needed reforms will be successful only if they are grounded in a commitment to free market principles, including the rule of law, respect for private property, open trade and investment, competitive markets, and efficient, effectively-regulated financial systems." (See Appendix C and section of this report on the G-20.)

For other nations of the world, what has become clear from the crisis is that U.S. financial ailments can be highly contagious. Foreign financial institutions are not immune to ill health in American banks, brokerage houses, and insurance companies. The financial services industry links together investors and financial institutions in disparate countries around the world. Investors seek higher risk-adjusted returns in any market. In financial markets, moreover, innovations in one market quickly spread to another, and sellers in one country often seek buyers in another. AIG insurance, for example, appears to have been brought down primarily by its Financial Products subsidiary based in London, an operation that engaged heavily in credit default swaps [34]. The revolution in communications, moreover, works both ways. It allows for instant access to information and remote access to market activity, but it also feeds the herd instinct and is susceptible to being used to spread biased or incomplete information.

The linking of economies also transcends financial networks [35]. Flows of international trade both in goods and services are affected directly by macroeconomic conditions in the countries involved. In the second phase of the financial crisis, markets all over the world have been experiencing historic declines. Precipitous drops in stock market values have been mirrored in currency and commodity markets.

Given the international nature of financial markets, the rapid movement of capital and information, and the secondary effects of financial problems on the services-and-production side of the economy, there seems to be no international architecture capable of coping with and preventing global crises from erupting. The financial space above nations basically is anarchic with no supranational authority with firm oversight, regulatory, and enforcement powers. Since financial crises occur even in relatively tightly regulated economies, the likelihood that a supranational authority could prevent an international crisis from occurring is questionable. International norms and guidelines for financial institutions exist, but most are voluntary, and countries are slow to incorporate them into domestic law [36]. As such, the system operates largely on trust and confidence and by hedging financial bets. The financial crisis has been a "wake-up call" for investors who had confidence in, for example, credit ratings placed on securities by credit rating agencies operating under what some have referred to as "perverse incentives and conflicts of interest." After such trusted AAA and AA ratings led to investments of hundreds of billions of dollars in toxic securities, what will be necessary to restore confidence in the system?

The G-20 Summits have taken some steps toward reforming the international financial system. The London Summit called for the regulation of hedge funds, a crack down on tax havens, and for regulatory oversight and registration for Credit Rating Agencies. The new Financial Stability Board is to collaborate with the IMF to provide early warning of macroeconomic and financial risks and actions needed to address them [37]. The leaders agreed that national financial supervisors should establish Colleges of Supervisors consisting of national financial supervisory agencies that oversee globally active financial institutions. These colleges of supervisors, are to meet together to share information and strengthen the surveillance of cross-border firms. In banking, for example, major global banks would meet regularly with their supervisory college for comprehensive discussions of the firm's activities and assessment of the risks it faces. (See Appendix C and section of this report on the G-20.)

Another issue is the mismatch between regulators and those being regulated. The policymakers can be divided between those of national governments and, to an extent, those of international institutions, but the resulting policy implementation, oversight, and regulation almost all rest in national governments (as well as sub-national governments such as states, e.g. New York, for insurance regulation). Yet many of the financial and other institutions that are the object of new oversight or regulatory activity may themselves be international in presence. They tend to operate in all major markets and congregate around world financial centers (i.e., London, New York, Zurich, Hong Kong, Singapore, Tokyo, and Shanghai) where client portfolios often are based and where institutions and qualified professionals exist to support their activities. The major market for derivatives, for example, is London, even though a sizable proportion of the derivatives, themselves, may be issued by U.S. companies based on U.S. assets. Some have suggested that the U.S. Federal Reserve assume the role of a systemic regulator with a global reach that could oversee institutions that are large or interconnected enough to pose a risk to the financial system [38]. A similar issue exists on the tangible product side of the economy. Multinational producers of consumer and industrial goods can transfer production among supply bases all over the world, but most manufacturing is tied to capital equipment that is fixed in place. Financial transactions, in contrast, can nominally occur anywhere. Unless regulations and constraints apply equally to major markets, transactions can, for example, move from New York to London, Zurich, or elsewhere. Tighter regulations in the United States, for instance, could induce transactions to move to London.

A related issue is the functional nature of U.S. regulation and lack of macroprudential or systemic regulation and oversight [39]. Separate regulatory agencies oversee each line of financial service: banking, insurance, securities, and futures. This is microprudential regulation under which no single regulator possesses all of the information and authority necessary to monitor systemic and synergistic risk or the potential that seemingly isolated events could lead to broad dislocation and a financial crisis so widespread that it affects the real economy. Also no single regulator can take coordinated action throughout the financial system.

In a report on systemic regulation, the Council on Foreign Relations explained the problem as follows:

> One regulatory organization in each country should be responsible for overseeing the health and stability of the overall financial system. The role of the systemic regulator should include gathering, analyzing, and reporting information about significant interactions between and risks among financial institutions; designing and implementing systemically sensitive regulations, including capital requirements; and coordinating with the fiscal authorities and other government agencies in managing systemic crises. We argue below that the central bank should be charged with this important new responsibility [40]

Others reportedly also have mentioned the U.S. Federal Reserve as a systemic regulator [41]. Other countries have addressed their own versions of this problem. The United Kingdom, for example, created a tripartite regulatory and oversight system consisting of the Bank of England, the H.M. Treasury, and a Financial Services Agency (a national regulatory agency for all financial services). Australia and the Netherlands have created systems in which one financial regulatory agency is responsible for prudential regulation of relevant financial institutions and a separate and distinct regulatory agency is responsible for business conduct and consumer protection [42]

One early regulatory change was announced on November 14, 2008, by the President's Working Group on Financial Markets (Treasury, Securities and Exchange Commission, Federal Reserve, and the Commodity Futures Trading Commission). The Working Group is undertaking a series of initiatives to strengthen oversight and the infrastructure of the over-the-counter derivatives market. This included the development of credit default swap central counterparties— clearinghouses between parties that own debt instruments and others willing to insure against defaults [43]

For the global banking industry, the Basel II framework from the Bank for International Settlements actually has been on the table for some time awaiting full implementation by countries of the world. Basel II is aimed at providing a more risk-sensitive approach to financial market supervision by better aligning capital charges with the underlying risk that banks take on. It is to help reduce the incentive for banks to shift assets off their balance sheets, and it includes methodologies to arrive at minimum capital requirements for credit risk, operational risk and market risk; the supervisory review process, and market disclosure [44]. On July 20, 2007, the United States began implementing pertinent parts of Basel II. [45] Some analysts assert that the current financial crisis has already made Basel II obsolete and call for a Basel III [46] One analyst considers the Basel capital rules to be an inappropriate basis for an international arrangement among banking supervisors [47].

Policy

As the global financial and economic crisis works its way to the regulatory phase, policy proposals to change the regulatory and oversight structure at both the domestic and international levels have been coming forth through the legislative process, from the Administration, and from recommendations by international organizations such as the IMF, [48] Bank for International Settlements, [49] and Financial Stability Board (Forum) [50] Currently, it appears that the vehicle for forming an international consensus on measures to be taken by individual countries is the G-20. (See Appendix C.)

Table 1. Problems, Targets of Policy, and Actions Taken or Possibly to Take in Response to the Global Financial Crisis

Problem	Targets of Policy	Actions Taken or Possibly To Take
Containing the Contagion and Restoring Market Operations		
Bankruptcy of financial institutions	Financial institution, Financial sector	—Capital injection through loans or stock purchases—Increase capital requirements —Takeover of company by government or other company —Allow to go bankrupt
Excess toxic debt	Capital base of debt holding institution	—Write-off of debt by holding institution —Purchase of toxic debt through Public Private Partnership Investment Program government at a discount (March 23, 2009, Treasury announcement) —Ease mark-to-market accounting requirements (April 2, 2009, Financial Accounting Standards Board) —Restructure mortgages —Nationalize debt holding institutions?
Credit market freeze	Lending institutions	—Coordinated lowering of interest rates by central banks/Federal Reserve —Guarantee short-term, uncollateralized business lending —Capital injection through loans or stock purchases
Consumer runs on deposits in banks and money market funds	Banks Brokerage houses	—Guarantee bank deposits —Guarantee money market accounts —Buy underlying money market securities to cover redemptions
Declining stock markets	Investors Short sellers	—Temporary ban on short sales of stock —Government purchases of stock?
Global recession, rising unemployment, decreasing tax revenues, declining exports	National governments	—Stimulative monetary and fiscal policies —Increased lending by International Financial Institutions —Trade policy? —Support for unemployed
Coping with Long-Term, Systemic Problems		
Poor underwriting standards Overly high ratings of collateralized debt obligations by rating companies Lack of transparency in ratings	Credit rating agencies Bundlers of collateralized debt obligations Corporate leveraged lenders	—More transparency in factors behind credit ratings and better models to assess risk? —Regulation of Credit Rating Agencies (April 2, 2009 London Summit) —Changes to the IOSCO Code of Conduct for Credit Rating Agencies? —Strengthen oversight of lenders? —Strengthen disclosure requirements to make information more easily accessible and usable?
Incentive distortions for originators of mortgages (no penalty for mortgage defaults due to faulty lending practices)	Mortgage originators Fannie Mae/Freddie Mac All participants in the originate-to-distribute chain	—Require loan originators and bundlers to provide initial and ongoing information on the quality and performance of securitized assets? —Strengthened oversight of mortgage originators? —Penalties for malfeasance by originators?
Shortcomings in risk management practices Severe underestimation of risks in the tails of default distributions and insufficient regard for systemic risk Risk models that encourage pro-cyclical risk taking	Investors Banks, securities companies Regulatory agencies	—More prudent oversight of capital, liquidity, and risk management? —Raise capital requirements for complex structured credit products and to account for liquidity risk? —Strengthen authorities' responsiveness to risk? —Set stricter capital and liquidity

Table 1. (Continued)

Problem	Targets of Policy	Actions Taken or Possibly To Take
		buffers for financial institutions?
Banks had weak controls over off-balance sheet risks	Bank structured investment vehicles Bank sponsored conduits Regulatory agencies	—Strengthen accounting and regulatory practices? —Raise capital requirements for off-balance sheet investment vehicles?
Regulators are "stove piped." Do not deal adequately with large complex financial institutions	Financial intermediaries engaged in a combination of banking, securities, futures, or insurance	—create an independent agency to monitor systemic risk (March 20, 2009 Treasury Announcement) —increase coordination and cooperation among regulatory agencies
Hedge funds and private equity are largely unregulated Information on Credit Default Swaps not public	Regulatory agencies	—extend regulation and oversight to hedge funds and private equity (April 2, 2009, London Summit) —create clearing counterparty for credit default swaps (March 26, 2009 Treasury Announcement)
	Problems for International Policy	
Lack of consistency in regulations among nations and need for new regulations to cope with new risks and exposures	National regulatory and oversight authorities Bank for International Settlements International Monetary Fund Financial Stability Board (Financial Stability Forum)	—Implement G-20 Action Plan (November 15, 2008 G-20 Summit) —Implement Basel II (Bank for International Settlements' capital and other requirements for banks) (in process by countries) —Bretton Woods II agreement? —Greater role for the Financial Stability Board/Forum and International Monetary Fund (April 2, 2009 London Summit) —Establish colleges of national supervisors to oversee financial sectors across boundaries (November 15, 2008 G-20 Summit)
Countries unable to cope with financial crisis	IMF, Development Banks National monetary authorities and governments	—Increased resources for the IMF and World Bank (April 2, 2009 London Summit) —Loans and swaps by capital surplus countries —Creation of long-term international liquidity pools to purchase assets?
Countries slow to recognize emerging problems in financial systems	National monetary and banking authorities Governments IMF Regional organizations	—Increased IMF and Financial Stability Board/Forum macroprudential/systemic oversight, surveillance and consultations (April 2, 2009 London Summit) —Build more resilience into the system? —Increase reporting requirements? —Establish colleges of national supervisors to oversee financial sectors across national borders
Problem	**Targets of Policy**	**Actions Taken or Possibly To Take**
		(Nov. 15, 2008, G-20 Summit)
Lack of political support to implement changes in policy	National political leaders	—G-20 international summit meetings —Bilateral and plurilateral meetings and events

Source: Congressional Research Service.

Notes: In the Actions to Take column, a "?" indicates that the action or policy has been proposed but is still in development or not yet taken.

Table 1 lists the major problems raised by the crisis, the targets of policy, and the policies already being taken or possibly to take by various entities in response to the global financial crisis. The long-term policies listed in the table essentially center on issues of transparency, disclosure, risk management, creating buffers to make the system more resilient, dealing with the secondary effects of the crisis, and the interface between domestic and international financial institutions. The length and breadth of the list indicates the extent that the financial crisis has required diverse and draconian action. The number of policies or actions not yet taken and being considered (marked by a "?" in the table) indicate that policymakers may still have a long way to go to rebuild the financial system that has been at the heart of the economic strength of the world. Many of these items are discussed in later sections of this report and are addressed in separate CRS reports [51]

ORIGINS, CONTAGION, AND RISK [52]

Financial crises of some kind occur sporadically virtually every decade and in various locations around the world. Financial meltdowns have occurred in countries ranging from Sweden to Argentina, from Russia to Korea, from the United Kingdom to Indonesia, and from Japan to the United States [53] As one observer noted: as each crisis arrives, policy makers express ritual shock, then proceed to break every rule in the book. The alternative is unthinkable. When the worst is passed, participants renounce crisis apostasy and pledge to hold firm next time [54]

Each financial crisis is unique, yet each bears some resemblance to others. In general, crises have been generated by factors such as an overshooting of markets, excessive leveraging of debt, credit booms, miscalculations of risk, rapid outflows of capital from a country, mismatches between asset types (e.g., short-term dollar debt used to fund long-term local currency loans), unsustainable macroeconomic policies, off-balance sheet operations by banks, inexperience with new financial instruments, and deregulation without sufficient market monitoring and oversight.

As shown in Figure 2, the current crisis harkens back to the 1997-98 Asian financial crisis in which Thailand, Indonesia, and South Korea had to borrow from the International Monetary Fund to service their short-term foreign debt and to cope with a dramatic drop in the values of their currency and deteriorating financial condition. Determined not to be caught with insufficient foreign exchange reserves, countries subsequently began to accumulate dollars, Euros, pounds, and yen in record amounts. This was facilitated by the U.S. trade (current account) deficit and by its low saving rate [55]. By mid-2008, world currency reserves by governments had reached $4.4 trillion with China's reserves alone approaching $2 trillion, Japan's nearly $1 trillion, Russia's more than $500 billion, and India, South Korea, and Brazil each with more than $200 billion [56]. The accumulation of hard currency assets was so great in some countries that they diverted some of their reserves into sovereign wealth funds that were to invest in higher yielding assets than U.S. Treasury and other government securities [57]

Following the Asian financial crisis, much of the world's "hot money" began to flow into high technology stocks. The so-called "dot-com boom" ended in the spring of 2000 as the value of equities in many high-technology companies collapsed.

After the dot-com bust, more "hot investment capital" began to flow into housing markets—not only in the United States but in other countries of the world. At the same time, China and other countries invested much of their accumulations of foreign exchange into U.S. Treasury and other securities. While this helped to keep U.S. interest rates low, it also tended to keep mortgage interest rates at lower and attractive levels for prospective home buyers [58]. This housing boom coincided with greater popularity of the securitization of assets, particularly mortgage debt (including subprime mortgages), into collateralized debt obligations (CDOs) [59]. A problem was that the mortgage originators often were mortgage finance companies whose main purpose was to write mortgages using funds provided by banks and other financial institutions or borrowed. They were paid for each mortgage originated but had no responsibility for loans gone bad. Of course, the incentive for them was to maximize the number of loans concluded.

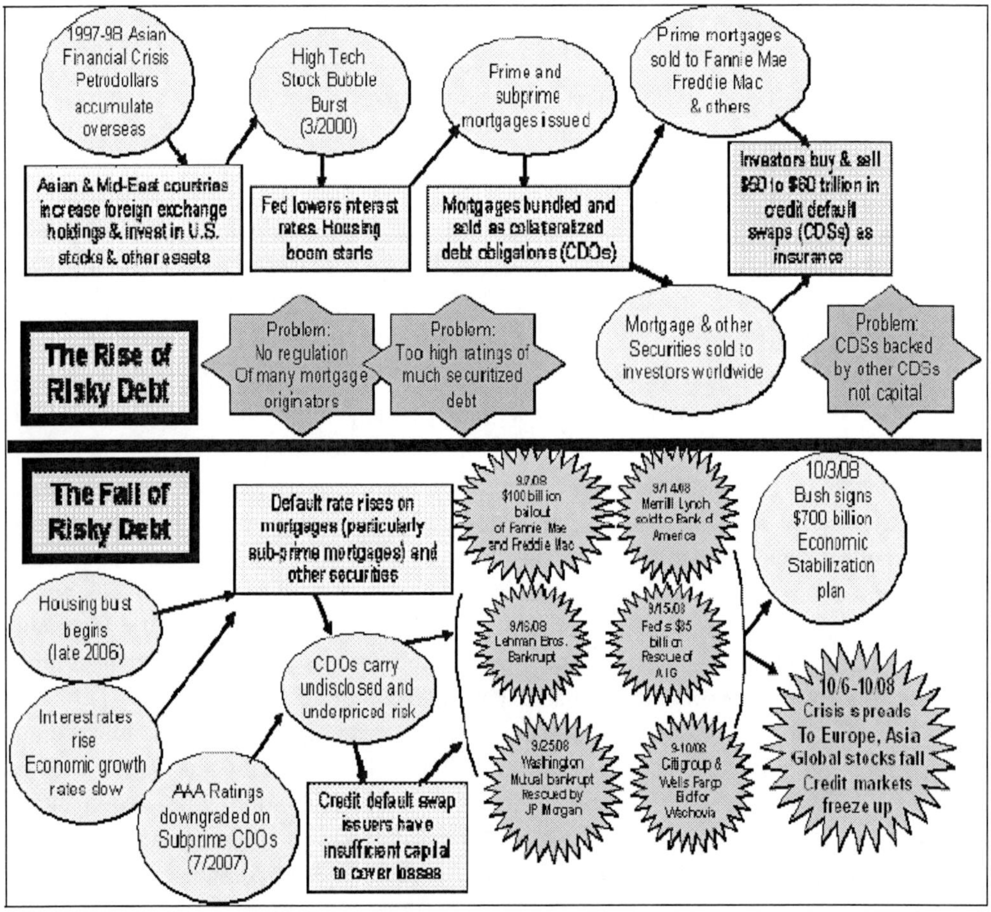

Figure 2. Origins of the Financial Crisis: The Rise and Fall of Risky Mortgage and Other Debt.

This coincided with political pressures to enable more Americans to buy homes, although it appears that Fannie Mae and Freddie Mac were not directly complicit in the loosening of lending standards and the rise of subprime mortgages [60].

In order to cover the risk of defaults on mortgages, particularly subprime mortgages, the holders of CDOs purchased credit default swaps [61] (CDSs). These are a type of insurance contract (a financial derivative) that lenders purchase against the possibility of credit event (a default on a debt obligation, bankruptcy, restructuring, or credit rating downgrade) associated with debt, a borrowing institution, or other referenced entity. The purchaser of the CDS does not have to have a financial interest in the referenced entity, so CDSs quickly became more of a speculative asset than an insurance policy. As long as the credit events never occurred, issuers of CDSs could earn huge amounts in fees relative to their capital base (since these were technically not insurance, they did not fall under insurance regulations requiring sufficient capital to pay claims, although credit derivatives requiring collateral became more and more common in recent years). The sellers of the CDSs that protected against defaults often covered their risk by turning around and buying CDSs that paid in case of default. As the risk of defaults rose, the cost of the CDS protection rose. Investors, therefore, could arbitrage between the lower and higher risk CDSs and generate large income streams with what was perceived to be minimal risk.

In 2007, the notional value (face value of underlying assets) of credit default swaps had reached $62 trillion, more than the combined gross domestic product of the entire world ($54 trillion), [62] although the actual amount at risk was only a fraction of that amount (approximately 3.5%). By July 2008, the notional value of CDSs had declined to $54.6 trillion and by October 2008 to an estimated $46.95 trillion [63] The system of CDSs generated large profits for the companies involved until the default rate, particularly on subprime mortgages, and the number of bankruptcies began to rise. Soon the leverage that generated outsized profits began to generate outsized losses, and in October 2008, the exposures became too great for companies such as AIG.

Risk

The origins of the financial crisis point toward three developments that increased risk in financial markets. The first was the originate-to-distribute model for mortgages. The originator of mortgages passed them on to the provider of funds or to a bundler who then securitized them and sold the collateralized debt obligation to investors. This recycled funds back to the mortgage market and made mortgages more available. However, the originator was not penalized, for example, for not ensuring that the borrower was actually qualified for the loan, and the buyer of the securitized debt had little detailed information about the underlying quality of the loans. Investors depended heavily on ratings by credit agencies.

The second development was a rise of perverse incentives and complexity for credit rating agencies. Credit rating firms received fees to rate securities based on information provided by the issuing firm using their models for determining risk. Credit raters, however, had little experience with credit default swaps at the "systemic failure" tail of the probability distribution.

The models seemed to work under normal economic conditions but had not been tested in crisis conditions. Credit rating agencies also may have advised clients on how to structure securities in order to receive higher ratings. In addition, the large fees offered to credit rating firms for providing credit ratings were difficult for them to refuse in spite of doubts they might have had about the underlying quality of the securities. The perception existed that if one credit rating agency did not do it, another would.

The third development was the blurring of lines between issuers of credit default swaps and traditional insurers. In essence, financial entities were writing a type of insurance contract without regard for insurance regulations and requirements for capital adequacy (hence, the use of the term "credit default swaps" instead of "credit default insurance").

Much risk was hedged rather than backed by sufficient capital to pay claims in case of default. Under a systemic crisis, hedges also may fail. However, although the CDS market was largely unregulated by government, more than 850 institutions in 56 countries that deal in derivatives and swaps belong to the ISDA (International Swaps and Derivatives Association). The ISDA members subscribe to a master agreement and several protocols/amendments, some of which require that in certain circumstances companies purchasing CDSs require counterparties (sellers) to post collateral to back their exposures [64].

It was this requirement to post collateral that pushed some companies toward bankruptcy. The blurring of boundaries among banks, brokerage houses, and insurance agencies also made regulation and information gathering difficult. Regulation in the United States tends to be functional with separate government agencies regulating and overseeing banks, securities, insurance, and futures. There was no suprafinancial authority.

The Downward Slide

The plunge downward into the global financial crisis did not take long. It was triggered by the bursting of the housing bubble and the ensuing subprime mortgage crisis in the United States, but other conditions have contributed to the severity of the situation. Banks, investment houses, and consumers carried large amounts of leveraged debt. Certain countries incurred large deficits in international trade and current accounts (particularly the United States), while other countries accumulated large reserves of foreign exchange by running surpluses in those accounts. Investors deployed "hot money" in world markets seeking higher rates of return. These were joined by a huge run up in the price of commodities, rising interest rates to combat the threat of inflation, a general slowdown in world economic growth rates, and increased globalization that allowed for rapid communication, instant transfers of funds, and information networks that fed a herd instinct. This brought greater uncertainty and changed expectations in a world economy that for a half decade had been enjoying relative stability.

An immediate indicator of the rapidity and spread of the financial crisis has been in stock market values. As shown in Figure 3, as values on the U.S. market plunged, those in other countries were swept down in the undertow. By mid-October 2008, the stock indices for the United States, U.K., Japan, and Russia had fallen by nearly half or more relative to their levels on October 1, 2007.

Declines in stock market values reflected huge changes in expectations and the flight of capital from assets in countries deemed to have even small increases in risk. Many investors, who not too long ago had heeded financial advisors who were touting the long term returns from investing in the BRICs (Brazil, Russia, India, and China), [65] pulled their money out nearly as fast as they had put it in. Dramatic declines in stock values coincided with new accounting rules that required financial institutions holding stock as part of their capital base to value that stock according to market values (mark-to-market). Suddenly, the capital base of banks shrank and severely curtailed their ability to make more loans (counted as assets) and still remain within required capital-asset ratios. Insurance companies too found their capital reserves diminished right at the time they had to pay buyers of or post collateral for credit default swaps. The rescue (establishment of a conservatorship) for Fannie Mae and Freddie Mac in September 2008 potentially triggered credit default swap contracts with notional value exceeding $1.2 trillion.

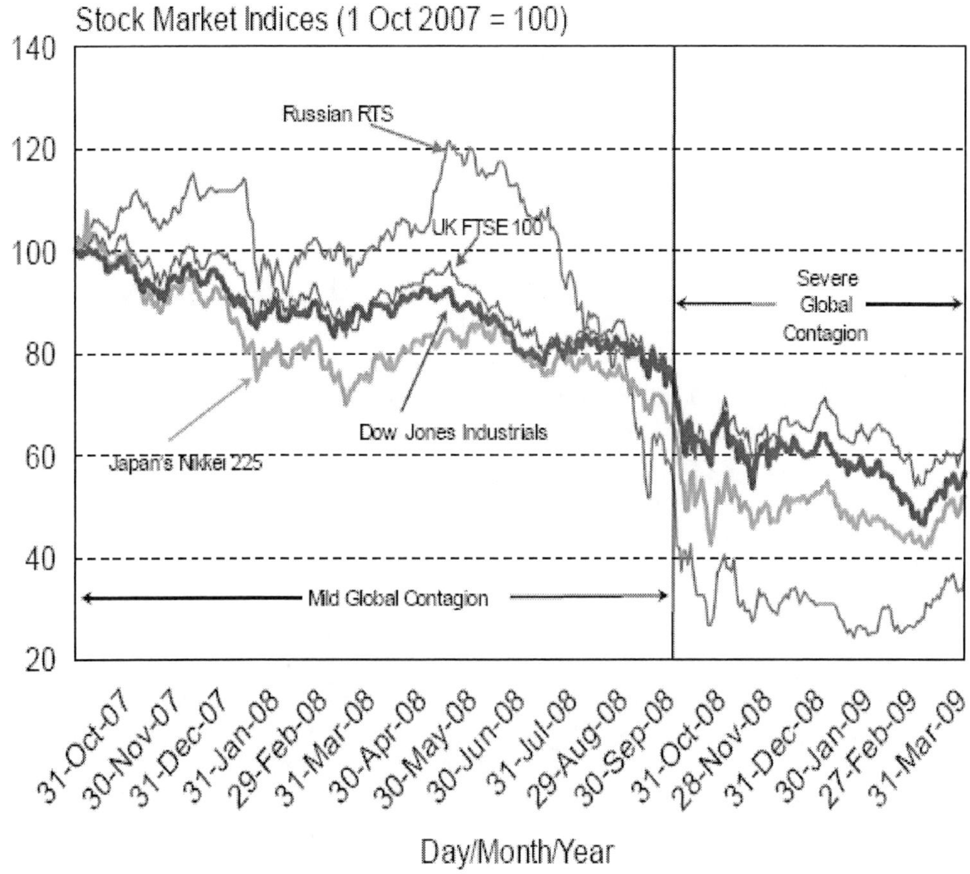

Source: Factiva database.

Figure 3. Selected Stock Market Indices for the United States, U.K., Japan, and Russia.

In addition, the rising rate of defaults and bankruptcies created the prospect that equities would suddenly become valueless. The market price of stock in Freddie Mac plummeted from $63 on October 8, 2007 to $0.88 on October 28, 2008. Hedge funds, whose "rocket scientist" analysts claimed that they could make money whether markets rose or fell, lost vast sums of money. The prospect that even the most seemingly secure company could be bankrupt the next morning caused credit markets to freeze. Lending is based on trust and confidence. Trust and confidence evaporated as lenders reassessed lending practices and borrower risk.

One indicator of the trust among financial institutions is the Libor, the London Inter-Bank Offered Rate. This is the interest rate banks charge for short-term loans to each other. Although it is a composite of primarily European interest rates, it forms the basis for many financial contracts worldwide including U.S. home mortgages and student loans. During the worst of the financial crisis in October 2008, this rate had doubled from 2.5% to 5.1%, and for a few days much interbank lending actually had stopped. The rise in the Libor came at a time when the U.S. monetary authorities were lowering interest rates to stimulate lending. The difference between interest on Treasury bills (three month) and on the Libor (three month) is called the "Ted spread." This spread averaged 0.25 percentage points from 2002 to 2006, but in October 2008 exceeded 4.5 percentage points. By the end of December, it had fallen to about 1.5%. The greater the spread, the greater the anxiety in the marketplace [66]

As the crisis has moved to a global economic slowdown, many countries have pursued expansionary monetary policy to stimulate economic activity. This has included lowering interest rates and expanding the money supply.

Currency exchange rates serve both as a conduit of crisis conditions and an indicator of the severity of the crisis. As the financial crisis hit, investors fled stocks and debt instruments for the relative safety of cash—often held in the form of U.S. Treasury or other government securities. That increased demand for dollars, decreased the U.S. interest rate needed to attract investors, and caused a jump in inflows of liquid capital into the United States. For those countries deemed to be vulnerable to the effects of the financial crisis, however, the effect was precisely the opposite. Demand for their currencies fell and their interest rates rose.

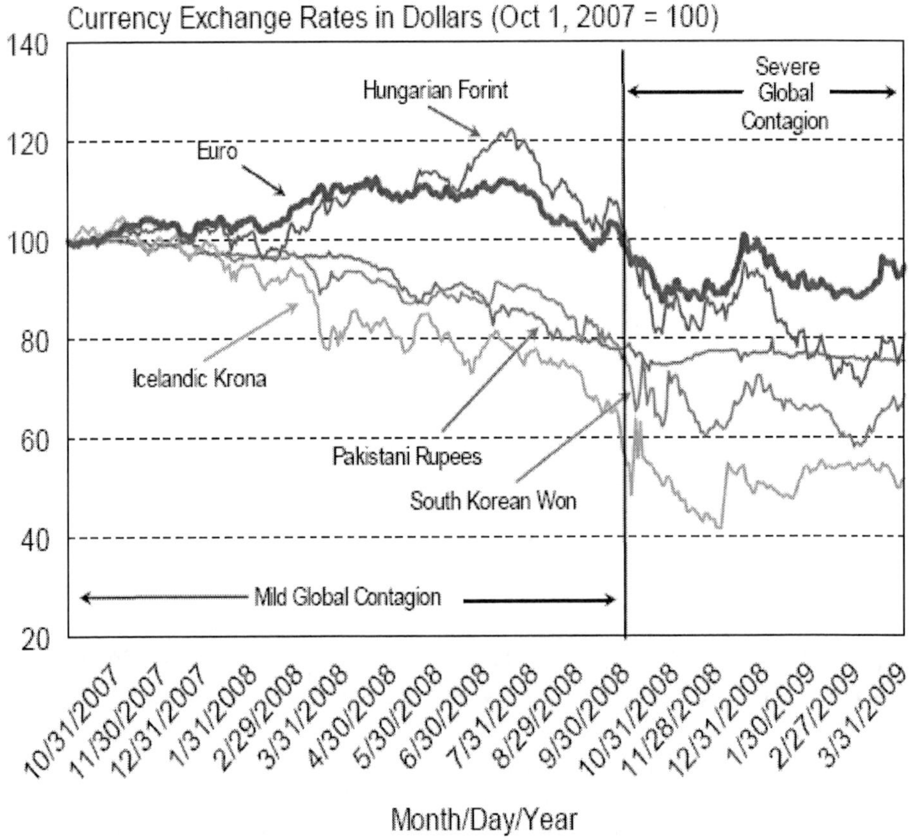

Source: Data from PACIFIC Exchange Rate Service, University of British Columbia.

Figure 4. Exchange Rate Values for Selected Currencies Relative to the U.S. Dollar.

For a country in crisis, a weak currency increases the local currency equivalents of any debt denominated in dollars and exacerbates the difficulty of servicing that debt. The greater burden of debt servicing usually has combined with a weakening capital base of banks because of declines in stock market values to further add to the financial woes of countries. National governments have had little choice but to take fairly draconian measures to cope with the threat of financial collapse. As a last resort, some have turned to the International Monetary Fund for assistance.

As economies weakened, governments moved from shoring up their financial institutions to coping with rapidly developing recessionary economic conditions. While actions to assist banks, insurance companies, and securities firms recover or stave off bankruptcy continued, stimulus packages became policy priorities. In the fourth quarter of 2008, economic growth rates dropped in some countries at rates not seen in decades.(See Figure 1) China alone has estimated that 20 million workers have become unemployed.

Table 2 shows stimulus packages by selected major countries of the world. While the $787 billion package by the United States is the largest, China's $586 billion, the European Union's $256 billion, and Japan's $250 billion packages also are quite large. Appendix A provides a more complete list of stimulus packages by country.

EFFECTS ON EMERGING MARKETS [67]

The global credit crunch that began in August 2007 has led to a financial crisis in emerging market countries (see box) that is being viewed as greater in both scope and effect than the East Asian financial crisis of 1997-98 or the Latin American debt crisis of 200 1-2002, although the impact on individual countries may have been greater in previous crises. Of the emerging market countries, those in Central and Eastern Europe appear, to date, to be the most impacted by the financial crisis.

The ability of emerging market countries to borrow from global capital markets has allowed many countries to experience incredibly high growth rates. For example, the Baltic countries of Latvia, Estonia, and Lithuania experienced annual economic growth of nearly 10% in recent years. However, since this economic expansion was predicated on the continued availability of access to foreign credit, they were highly vulnerable to a financial crisis when credit lines dried up.

Of all emerging market countries, Central and Eastern Europe appear to be the most vulnerable. On a wide variety of economic indicators, such as the total amount of debt in the economy, the size of current account deficits, dependence on foreign investment, and the level of indebtedness in the domestic banking sector, countries such as Hungary, Ukraine, Bulgaria, Kazakhstan, Kyrgyzstan, Latvia, Estonia, and Lithuania, rank among the highest of all emerging markets. Throughout the region, the average current account deficit increased from 2% of GDP in 2000 to 9% in 2008. In some countries, however, the current account deficit is much higher. Latvia's estimated 2008 current account deficit is 22.9% of GDP and Bulgaria's is 21.4%. [68] The average deficit for the region was greater than 6% in 2008 (Figure 5).

Table 2. Stimulus Packages by Selected Countries

Date Announced	Country	$Billion	Status, Package Contents
17-Feb-09	United States	787.00	Infrastructure technology, tax cuts, education, transfers to states, energy, nutrition, health, unemployment benefits. Budget in deficit.
4-Feb-09	Canada	32.00	Two-year program. Infrastructure, tax relief, aid for sectors in peril. Government to run an estimated $1.1 billion budget deficit in 2008 and $52 billion deficit in 2009.
7-Jan-09	Mexico	54.00	Infrastructure, a freeze on gasoline prices, reducing electricity rates, help for poor families to replace old appliances, construction of low-income housing and an oil refinery, rural development, increase government purchases from small- and medium-sized companies. Paid for by taxes, oil revenues, and borrowing.
12-Dec-08	European Union	39.00	Total package of $256 billion called for states to increase budgets by $217 billion and for the EU to provide $39 billion to fund cross-border projects including clean energy and upgraded telecommunications architecture.
13-Jan-09	Germany	65.00	Infrastructure, tax cuts, child bonus, increase in some social benefits, $3,250 incentive for trading in cars more than nine years old for a new or slightly used car.
24-Nov-08	United Kingdom	29.60	Proposed plan includes a 2.5% cut in the value added tax for 13 months, a postponement of corporate tax increases, government guarantees for loans to small and midsize businesses, spending on public works, including public housing and energy efficiency. Plan includes an increase in income taxes on those making more than $225,000 and increase National Insurance contribution for all but the lowest income workers.
5-Nov-08	France	33.00	Public sector investments (road and rail construction, refurbishment and improving ports and river infrastructure, building and renovating universities, research centers, prisons, courts, and monuments) and loans for carmakers. Does not include the previously planned $15 billion in credits and tax breaks on investments by companies in 2009.
16-Nov-08	Italy	52.00	Awaiting final parliamentary approval. Three year program. Measures to spur consumer credit, provide loans to companies, and rebuild infrastructure. February 6, announced a $2.56 billion stimulus package that was part of the three-year program that includes payments of up to $1,950 for trading in an old car for a new, less polluting one and 20% tax deductions for purchases of appliances and furniture.
20-Nov-08	Russia	20.00	Cut in the corporate profit tax rate, a new depreciation mechanism for businesses, to be funded by Russia's foreign exchange reserves and rainy day fund.
10-Nov-08	China	586.00	Low-income housing, electricity, water, rural infrastructure, projects aimed at environmental protection and technological innovation, tax deduction for capital spending by companies, and spending for health care and social welfare.
13-Dec-08	Japan	250.00	Increase in government spending, funds to stabilize the financial system (prop up troubled banks and ease a credit crunch by purchasing commercial paper), tax cuts for homeowners and companies that build or purchase new factories and equipment, and grants to local government. The April 2009 package included increasing the safety net for non-regular workers, supporting small businesses, revitalizing regional economies, promoting solar power and nursing and medical services.
6-Apr-09	Japan	100.00	
3-Nov-08	South Korea	14.64	$11 billion for infrastructure (including roads, universities, schools, and hospitals; funds for small- and medium-business, fishermen, and families with low income) and tax cuts. Includes an October 2008 stimulus package of $3.64 billion to provide support for the construction industry.
9-Feb-09	South Korea	37.87	The government announced its intention to invest $37.87 billion over the next four years in eco-friendly projects including the construction of dams; "green" transportation networks such as low-carbon emitting railways, bicycle roads, and other public transportation systems; and expand existing forest areas.
28-Nov-08	Taiwan	15.60	Shopping vouchers of $108 each for all citizens, construction projects to be carried out over four years include expanding metro systems, rebuilding bridges and classrooms, improving, railway and sewage systems, and renew urban areas.
26-Jan-09	Australia	35.2	$7 billion stimulus package in October 2008 was cash handouts to low income earners and pensioners. January's $28.2 billion package includes infrastructure, schools and housing, and cash payments to low- and middle-income earners. Budget is in deficit.
23-Dec-08	Brazil	5.00	Program established in 2007 to continue to 2010. Tax cuts (exempt capital goods producers from the industrial and welfare taxes, increase the value of personal computers exempted from taxes) and rebates. Funded by reducing the government's budget surplus.

What are Emerging Market Countries?

There is no uniform definition of the term "emerging markets." Originally conceived in the early 1980s, the term is used loosely to define a wide range of countries that have undergone rapid economic change over the past two decades. Broadly speaking, the term is used to distinguish these countries from the long-industrialized countries, on one hand, and less-developed countries (such as those in Sub-Saharan Africa), on the other. Emerging market countries are located primarily in Latin America, Central and Eastern Europe, and Asia.

Since 1999, the finance ministers of many of these emerging market countries began meeting with their peers from the industrialized countries under the aegis of the G-20, an informal forum to discuss policy issues related to global macroeconomic stability. The members of the G-20 are the European Union and 19 countries: Argentina, Australia, Brazil, Canada, China, France, Germany, India, Indonesia, Italy, Japan, Mexico, Russia, Saudi Arabia, South Africa, South Korea, Turkey, the United Kingdom and the United States.

For more information, see "When are Emerging Markets no Longer Emerging?, Knowledge@Wharton, available at http://knowledge.wharton.upenn.edu/article.cfm?articleid=1911.

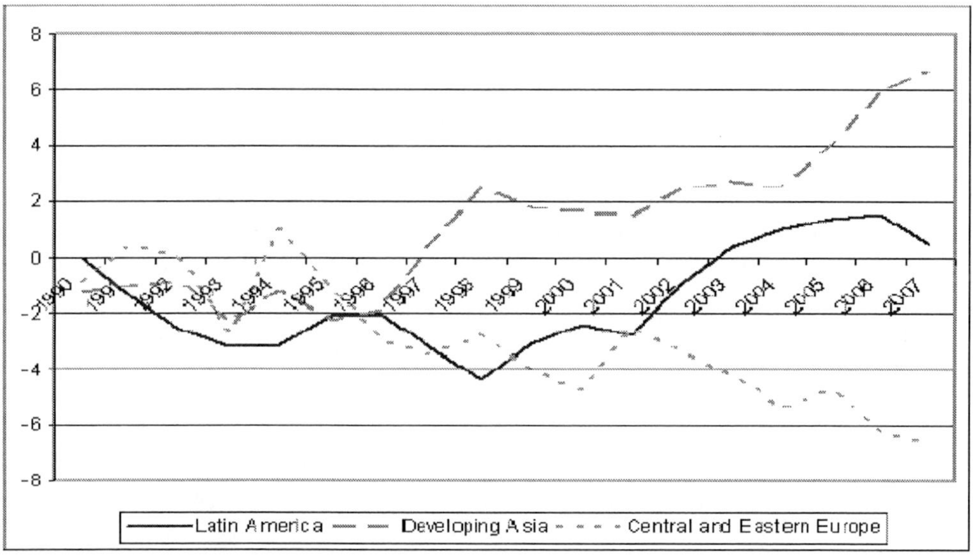

Source: International Monetary Fund.

Figure 5. Current Account Balances (as a percentage of GDP).

Due to the impact of the financial crisis, several Central and Eastern European countries have already sought emergency lending from the IMF to help finance their balance of payments. On October 24, the IMF announced an initial agreement on a $2.1 billion two-year loan with Iceland (approved on November 19). On October 26, the IMF announced a $16.5 billion agreement with Ukraine. On October 28, the IMF announced a $15.7 billion package for Hungary. On November 3, a staff-level agreement on an IMF loan was reached with Kyrgyzstan, [69] and on November 24, the IMF approved a $7.6 billion stand-by arrangement for Pakistan to support the country's economic stabilization [70].

The quickness with which the crisis has impacted emerging market economies has taken many analysts by surprise. Since the Asian financial crisis, many Asian emerging market economies enacted a policy of foreign reserve accumulation as a form of self-insurance in case they once again faced a "sudden stop" of capital flows and the subsequent financial and balance of payments crises that result from a rapid tightening of international credit flows [71]. Two additional factors motivated emerging market reserve accumulation. First, several countries have pursued an export-led growth strategy targeted at the U.S. and other markets with which they have generated trade surpluses [72]. Second, a sharp rise in the price of commodities from 2004 to the first quarter of 2008 led many oil-exporting economies, and other commodity-based exporters, to report very large current account surpluses.

Figure 6 shows the rapid increase in foreign reserve accumulation among these countries. These reserves provided a sense of financial security to EM countries. Some countries, particularly China and certain oil exporters, also established sovereign wealth funds that invested the foreign exchange reserves in assets that promised higher yields [73].

While global trade and finance linkages between the emerging markets and the industrialized countries have continued to deepen over the past decade, many analysts believed that emerging markets had successfully "decoupled" their growth prospects from those of industrialized countries. Proponents of the theory of decoupling argued that emerging market countries, especially in Eastern Europe and Asia, have successfully developed their own economies and intra-emerging market trade and finance to such an extent that a slowdown in the United States or Europe would not have as dramatic an impact as it did a decade ago. A report by two economists at the IMF found some evidence of this theory. The authors divided 105 countries into three groups: developed countries, emerging countries, and developing countries and studied how economic growth was correlated among the groups between 1960 and 2005. The authors found that while economic growth was highly synchronized between developed and developing countries, the impact of developed countries on emerging countries has decreased over time, especially during the past twenty years. According to the authors:

> In particular, [emerging market] countries have diversified their economies, attained high growth rates and increasingly become important players in the global economy. As a result, the nature of economic interactions between [industrialized and emerging market] countries has evolved from one of dependence to multidimensional interdependence [74]

Despite efforts at self-insurance through reserve accumulation and evidence of economic decoupling, the U.S. financial crisis, and the sharp contraction of credit and global capital flows in October 2008 affected all emerging markets to a degree due to their continued dependence on foreign capital flows. According to the Wall Street Journal, in the month of October, Brazil, India, Mexico, and Russia drew down their reserves by more than $75 billion, in attempt to protect their currencies from depreciating further against a newly resurgent U.S. dollar [75]

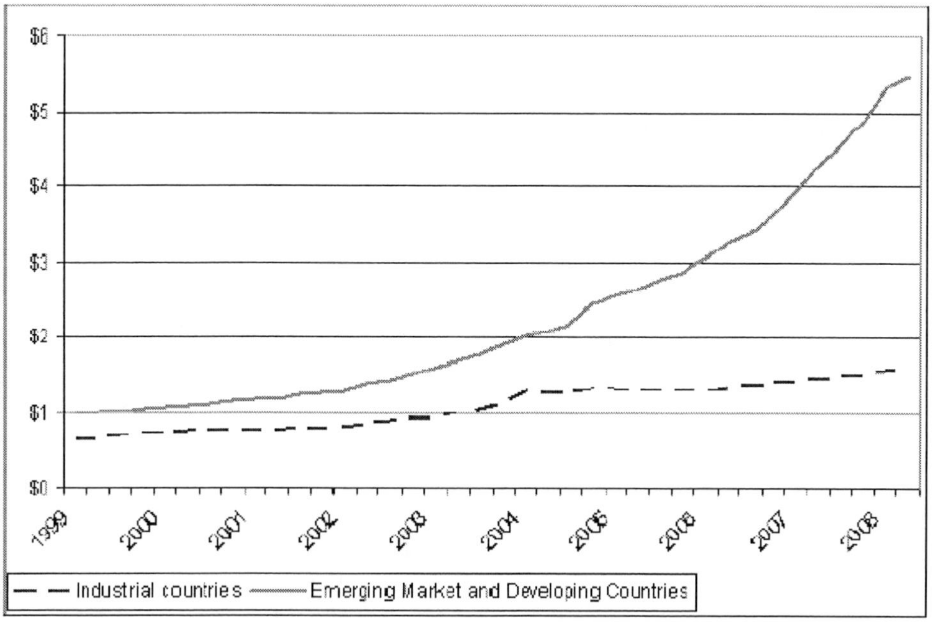

Source: IMF.

Figure 6. Global Foreign Exchange Reserves ($ Trillion).

A key to understanding why emerging market countries have been so affected by the crisis (especially Central and Eastern Europe) is their high dependence on foreign capital flows to finance their economic growth (Figures 7-8). Even though several emerging markets have been able to reduce net capital inflows by investing overseas (through sovereign wealth funds) or by tightening the conditions for foreign investment, the large amount of gross foreign capital flows into emerging markets remained a key vulnerability for them. For countries such as those in Central and Eastern Europe which have both high gross and net capital flows, vulnerability to financial crisis is even higher.

Once the crisis occurred, it became much more difficult for emerging market countries to continue to finance their foreign debt. According to Arvind Subramanian, an economist at the Peterson Institute for International Economics, and formerly an official at the IMF:

> If domestic banks or corporations fund themselves in foreign currency, they need to roll these over as the obligations related to gross flows fall due. In an environment of across-the-board deleveraging and flight to safety, rolling over is far from easy, and uncertainty about rolling over aggravates the loss in confidence [76]

As emerging markets have grown, Western financial institutions have increased their investments in emerging markets. G-10 [77] financial institutions have a total of $4.7 trillion of exposure to emerging markets with $1.6 trillion to Central and Eastern Europe, $1.5 trillion to emerging Asia, and $1.0 trillion to Latin America. While industrialized nation bank debt to emerging markets represents a relatively small percentage (13%) of total cross-border bank lending ($36.9 trillion as of September 2008), this figure is disproportionately high for European financial institutions and their lending to Central and Eastern Europe.

For European and U.K. banks, cross-border lending to emerging markets, primarily Central and Eastern Europe accounts for between 21% and 24% of total lending. For U.S. and Japanese institutions, the figures are closer to 4% and 5%.[78] The heavy debt to Western financial institutions greatly increased central and Eastern Europe's vulnerability to contagion from the financial crisis.

In addition to the immediate impact on growth from the cessation of available credit, a downturn in industrialized countries will likely affect emerging market countries through several other channels. As industrial economies contract, demand for emerging market exports will slow down.

This will have an impact on a range of emerging and developing countries. For example, growth in larger economies such as China and India will likely slow as their exports decrease. At the same time, demand in China and India for raw natural resources (copper, oil, etc) from other developing countries will also decrease, thus depressing growth in commodity-exporting countries [79]

Slower economic growth in the industrialized countries may also impact less developed countries through lower future levels of bilateral foreign assistance. According to analysis by the Center for Global Development's David Roodman, foreign aid may drop precipitously over the next several years. His research finds that after the Nordic crisis of 1991, Norway's aid fell 10%, Sweden's 17%, and Finland's 62%. In Japan, foreign aid fell 44% between 1990 and 1996, and has never returned to pre-crisis assistance levels [80]

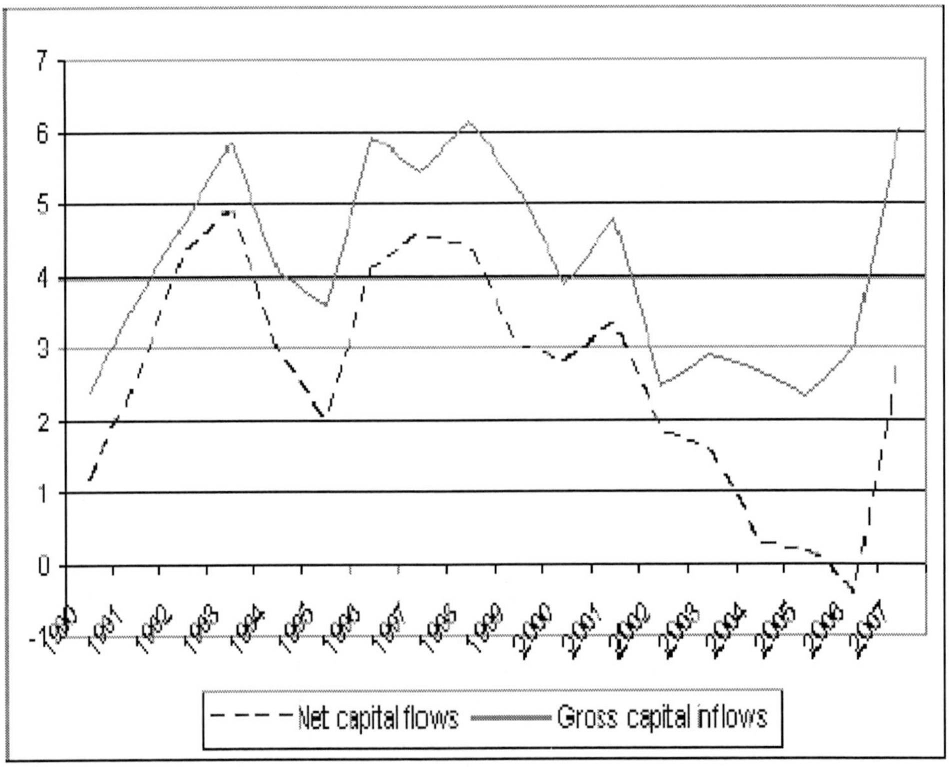

Source: IMF.

Figure 7. Capital Flows to Latin America (in percent of GDP).

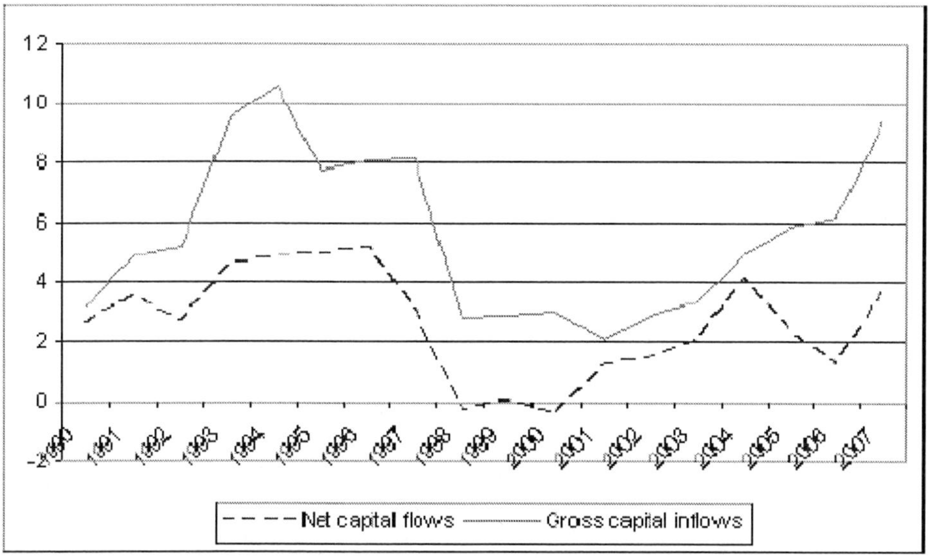

Source: IMF.

Figure 8. Capital Flows to Developing Asia (in percent of GDP).

Latin America [81]

Financial crises are not new to Latin America, but the current one has two unusual dimensions. First, as substantiated earlier in this report, it originated in the United States, with Latin America suffering shocks created by collapses in the U.S. housing and credit markets, despite minimal direct exposure to the "toxic" assets in question. Second, it spread to Latin America in spite of recent strong economic growth and policy improvements that have generally increased economic stability and reduced risk factors, particularly in the financial sector [82] Repercussions from the global financial crisis have varied by country based in part on policy differences, but also exposure to two major risks, the degree of reliance on the U.S. economy, and/or dependence on commodity exports. Nonetheless, investors have been especially hard on the region as a whole, perhaps leery of its capacity to weather short-term financial contagion let alone a protracted global recession.

The economies of Latin America and the Caribbean grew at an average annual rate of nearly 5.5% for the five years 2004-2008, lending credence to the once prominent idea that they were "decoupling" from slower growing developed economies, particularly the United States [83]. Domestic policy reforms have been credited with achieving macroeconomic stability, stronger fiscal positions, sounder banking systems, and lower sovereign debt risk levels. Others note, however, that Latin America's recent growth trend is easily explained by international economic fundamentals, questioning the importance of the decoupling theory. The sharp rise in commodity prices, supportive external financing conditions, and high levels of remittances contributed greatly to the region's improved economic welfare, reflecting gains from a strong global economy. In addition, all three trends reversed even before the financial crisis began, suggesting that Latin America remains very much tied to world markets and trends [84]

Latin America is experiencing two levels of economic problems related to the crisis. First order effects from financial contagion are evident in the high volatility of financial market indicators. All major indicators fell sharply in the second half of 2008, as capital sought safe haven in less risky assets, many of them, ironically, dollar denominated. Regional stock indexes have fallen at one point by half since October 2008, but recovered slightly in many cases. Currencies followed suit in many Latin American countries. They depreciated suddenly from investor flight to the U.S. dollar reflecting a lack of confidence in local currencies, the rush to portfolio rebalancing, and the fall in commodity import revenue related to sharply declining prices and diminished global demand. In at least two countries, Mexico and Brazil, large speculative derivative positions in the currency markets exacerbated the depreciations, compounding losses [85]

Debt markets followed in kind, as credit tightened and international lending contracted, even for short-term needs such as inventory and trade finance. Borrowing has become more expensive, as seen in widening bond spreads. Over the past year, bond spreads in the Emerging Market Bond Index (EMBI) and corporate bond index for Latin America increased by over 600 basis points, half occurring in the fall of 2008. This trend suggests first, that Latin America was already beginning to experience a slowdown prior to the financial crisis, and second, that the crisis itself was a sudden subsequent shock to the region. The full extent of the problem will become clearer in 2009 as the more highly leveraged Latin American countries seek to roll over their public debt. Still, compared to earlier financial crises when bond spreads on average rose by over 1,000 basis points, the Latin America's stronger economic fundamentals and regulatory regimes helped cushion many countries from a more severe reaction in 2008. Many Latin American banks are well capitalized, have sound balance sheets, and continue to lend. The exceptions are in Argentina, Ecuador, and Venezuela, all of which share a heavy dependence on commodity exports and weak economic policy frameworks. In each of these countries, bond spreads have risen by well over 1,500 basis points, reflecting a lack of confidence in their financial future [86]

Second order effects all point to a deterioration of broader economic fundamentals. GDP growth for the region is expected to be a negative 1%-2% in 2009. The fall in global demand, particularly for Latin America's commodity exports, will be a big factor, as already seen in contracting export revenue. Tightening credit markets and the sharp rise in the cost of capital for Latin America is dampening investment. Consumption, trade surpluses, and remittances are also declining, which along with deteriorating public sector budgets, points to the region-wide economic slowdown [87]. Public sector borrowing is expected to rise and budget constraints may threaten spending on social programs, with a predictably disproportional effect on the poor.

Policy responses have materialized from many quarters, including multilateral organizations, which have adopted programs to ameliorate the credit crisis and stimulate demand. The International Monetary Fund (IMF), World Bank, Inter-American Development Bank (IDB), Andean Development Corporation (CAF), and Latin American Reserve Fund (LARF) have all increased lending to the region, particularly on an expedited and short-term basis. The goal is to provide credit to the private sector and to support, in selective cases, bank recapitalization. Funds will also be made available for public sector spending (infrastructure and social programs) as a form of fiscal stimulus, primarily through the World Bank and IDB.

The United States has taken steps to provide dollar liquidity on a temporary bilateral basis to many central banks of "systemically important" countries with sound banking systems. In Latin America, this group includes Mexico and Brazil, each of which has access to a $30 billion currency swap reserve with the U.S. Federal Reserve System through April 30, 2009. The swap arrangement is intended to ensure dollar availability in support of the large trade and investment transactions conducted between the United States and these two countries [88]

National governments are also using monetary, fiscal, and exchange rate policies to stimulate their economies. The capacity to undertake any of these options varies tremendously among the Latin American countries. Fiscal capacity is constrained in many countries by high debt levels. Among the few countries adopting a fiscal stimulus, preliminary estimates of their size suggest they are small, ranging from 1.0% of GDP in Mexico, Brazil, and Argentina, up to 2.5% of GDP in Peru [89] Many countries may also be limited in using monetary policy responses to expand liquidity. In particular, reducing interest rates is difficult for those experiencing significant currency depreciations, which increase inflationary pressures. There is also a growing concern that countries may eventually resort to nationalistic policies that will reduce the flows of goods, services, and capital. Capital controls, increased tariffs, and regulations that hinder trade and capital flows can have debilitating effects on recovery strategies in the long run. The magnitude of the global economic downturn and adequacy of policy responses vary by country as three examples discussed below illustrate.

Mexico

The Mexican economy contracted sharply in the fourth quarter of 2008 and a survey of estimates forecasts that economic growth may fall by 2%-3% in 2009 [90] Declines are seen in both industry and services sectors. In January 2009, automobile production alone fell by 50% and car exports declined by 57% from the year earlier. Mexico faces two problems: one short term, the other long-term, but both tied to its dependence on the U.S. economy. The United States accounts for half of Mexico's imports, 80% of its exports, and most of its foreign investment remittances income. Therefore, Mexico, despite its relatively strong fiscal position and solid macroeconomic fundamentals, has begun to suffer first from direct links to the U.S. financial fallout, and second, from its vulnerability to a protracted U.S. recession.

On the financial side, Mexico experienced a run on the peso in which its value fell at one point by 40% from its August 2008 high (currently down by 37% compared to 17% for the regional currency index). The decline was not related to investments in U.S. mortgage-backed securities, but rather the re-balancing of investor portfolios away from emerging markets, the dramatic fall in commodity prices, and decline in U.S. demand for Mexican exports. The Central Bank of Mexico has responded by purchasing pesos, but currency intervention has only slowed the depreciation trend and there is growing debate over the feasibility of continuing this policy given limited foreign exchange reserves [91]

The peso also suffered because Mexican firms had apparently taken to heart the notion of "decoupling," believing that the peso's strength would not be seriously challenged by the U.S. financial crisis. Many firms had gone beyond hedging in the currency market to bet heavily on the future strength of the peso by taking large derivative positions in the currency. As the peso began to depreciate, companies had to unwind these large speculative (and off balance sheet) positions quickly, accelerating its fall. One large firm had losses exceeding $1.4 billion and filed for bankruptcy, indicative of the severity of the problem. The Mexican government responded by selling billions of dollars of reserves and accepting a temporary currency swap arrangement with the U.S. Federal Reserve to assure liquidity in the currency market [92]

Mexico's long-term economic prospects hinge on U.S. aggregate demand. Because Mexico has a poorly diversified trade regime, the effects of the U.S. downturn are already noticeable, with Mexican exports to the United States on a monthly basis falling 37% from October 2008 to January 2009, reaching the lowest level since January 2005. The trade effect has been compounded by the fall in remittances from Mexican workers living in the United States, which in 2007 amounted to $26 billion, equal to 3% of Mexico's GDP. Employment figures for the formal economy are beginning to register large job losses, but data are sketchy. In the short-term, it will be important to evaluate Mexico's ability to counter the peso's decline and maintain liquidity to support both domestic financing and its trade with the United States. In the medium term, the depth of Mexico's economic slowdown in response to the U.S. recession will be the most telling benchmark of its vulnerability to the global crisis [93]

To date, the Mexican government has adopted a $4.4 stimulus package heavily weighted towards reducing energy costs to consumers. The price of cooking gas has been reduced by 10% and petroleum prices in the domestic market have been frozen. The Mexican government estimates that consumers will benefit by some $45 billion. On the fiscal side, the Mexican Government has announced a small $10.8 billion dollar package (1.1% of GDP), which has yet to begin [94].

Brazil

Brazil entered the financial crisis from a position of relative macroeconomic and fiscal strength, but nonetheless is not immune to the global contraction. Although the economy grew by 5.1% in 2008, it decelerated 3.5% in the fourth quarter relative to the third. Some GDP growth estimates for 2009 call for Brazil to enter a recession, a marked revision downward from 4% growth forecast in late 2008. Investment in both public and private projects appears to be on hold and at the close of 2008, industrial output fell by over 20% in the last two months of 2008, led by a nearly 60% decline in automobile production compared to output a year earlier [95]

Financial repercussions sparked the crisis and affected Brazil in ways similar to Mexico. Brazil's stock market index tumbled by half in 2008 as investors fled both stocks and the Brazilian currency (the real). The Brazilian government sold billions of dollars to fight a rapidly depreciating currency, which fell at one point by over 35% from its August 2008 high. Both indexes have recovered slightly, but remain down by 25%-30% with volatility expected to continue. Brazil also has a large currency derivative market, where speculative trades contributed to the real's decline, although to a lesser degree than in Mexico. Brazil's central bank agreed to the temporary currency swap arrangement with the U.S. Federal Reserve. It also has $188 billion in international reserves (down from a peak of $206 billion in September 2008), a sound and well-regulated banking system, and an experienced central bank staff that has so far helped maintain confidence in the finance [al system [96]

The real economy faces longer-term challenges. The fall in production has led to Brazil shedding 654,000 jobs in December 2008, another critical indicator of the sudden, sharp slowdown in the economy. In addition to the fall in domestic demand, Brazil's exports have suffered in part because over half are commodities, which experienced dramatic price declines in late 2008. Capital inflows, which were strong in 2008, are also expected to slow, despite Brazil's recent solid macroeconomic performance and its investment grade rating. As with other countries, the extent to which global demand diminishes will ultimately affect all these variables. Brazil has a large internal market and is well-positioned on macroeconomic and fiscal fronts, which may soften effects of the global financial crisis, depending, as with other countries, on the severity of the recession [97]

From the policy perspective, Brazil has emphasized enhancing financial sector liquidity through monetary policy over adopting a large fiscal stimulus. The Central Bank has injected billions of dollars into the banking system, lowered reserve requirements, and reduced the key short-term interest rate twice in 2009, from 13.75% to 11.25%. The Brazilian government has authorized state-owned banks to purchase private banks, approved stricter accounting rules for derivatives, extended credit directly to firms through the National Development Bank (BNDES) and the Central Bank, exempted foreign investment firms from the financial transaction tax, and entered into a new $30 billion currency swap arrangement with the U.S. Federal Reserve [98]. Unibanco of Brazil has also procured a $60 million credit extension from the World Bank's International Finance Corporation to support trade financing. On the fiscal side, the government has frozen spending of approximately 6% of the federal budget, preferring to reinforce a policy of fiscal balance, but has also announced a small $16 billion stimulus package (1% of GDP) [99]

Argentina

Argentina, because of its shaky economic and financial position at the outset of the crisis, is poorly positioned to deal with a protracted downturn compared to most other Latin American countries. Although until recently it has experienced dramatic economic growth since 2002, this trend reflects a rebound from the previous severe 2001-2002 financial crisis and rise in commodity prices that benefitted Argentina's large agricultural sector. The collapse of commodity prices in late 2008 has diminished export revenues and Argentina is also experiencing declines in investment, domestic consumer demand, and industrial production. Installed capacity utilization fell from 79% in October 2008 to 67.4% in January 2009. Particularly hard hit has been motor vehicles, metallurgy, and textiles. Economists forecast the economy will grow by less than 1% in 2009, with the possibility of a recession by 2010 [100]

Argentina has been financially isolated from global markets since its 2001 crisis and is also hampered by a litany of questionable policy choices, which combined with the global recession, has further diminished confidence in its financial system. Although the banks remain liquid and solvent, the stock market is down 37% from last fall and the peso has depreciated by 18%. Among the highly questionable policies that have diminished confidence in the country is the 2002 historic sovereign debt default and failure to renegotiate with Paris Club countries and private creditor holdouts. Others include government interference in the supposedly independent government statistics office (particularly with respect to inflation reporting), price controls, high export taxes, and most recently, nationalization of private pension funds to bolster public finances [101] These policies have isolated the economy from international capital markets despite the need to finance a growing debt burden and public and private sector investments. Price controls and export restrictions (quotas and taxes) have led to market distortions, protests over government policies, and declining consumer confidence.

After ten months of steady growth, Argentina's exports declined by 6% in November and an additional 24% in December 2008, which includes key agricultural and energy products [102]. In response to falling demand for Argentine exports and the government's questionable financial policies and position, Argentina's currency has begun to depreciate slowly, but not in line with its neighbors' currencies because of heavy exchange rate intervention. In selling dollars to protect the peso's value, however, Argentina has so far used up over 15% of its one-time $54 billion in foreign reserves, forced interest rates skyward, and made exports less competitive. In recognition that industrial production and exports are falling rapidly, Argentina has also adopted administrative trade restrictions to limit imports. These affect Brazilian goods in particular, including textiles and various machinery exports, raising tensions between the two major trade partners of the regional customs union, Mercosur [103]

Risk assessment has been swift and punishing. Bond ratings have fallen, yields on short-term public debt exceed 30%, and the interest rate spread on Argentina's bonds has risen to over 1,700 basis points. The interest rate spread on credit default swaps peaked at 4,500 basis points in December 2008 before falling to the current level of 3,500 basis points, indicating the high cost required to insure against bond defaults. All these indicators point to a global perception of Argentina as a high-risk country, likely reinforcing its ostracism from international capital markets[104]

Argentina has adopted a number of policies to address the domestic effects of the global economic crisis. The first initiative is a massive $32 billion public works program, which will raise expenditures by 2 percentage points of GDP. It is complemented by a $3.8 billion (1.2% of GDP) fiscal stimulus package comprising reduced interest rate loans for the purchase of durable goods, a 5 percentage point reduction in export taxes on wheat and corn, and subsidized credit extension to industrial sectors, including small- and medium-sized firms [105]

Given Argentina's large expected public spending outlays for the coming year, the high and growing cost of its debt, falling revenues from imports, and its inability to access international credit markets, it had to take dramatic action to finance these programs. It did so by nationalizing, with the approval of the Congress, the private-sector pension system, effective January 1, 2009. The pension system provided $29 billion in assets immediately and access to an estimated $4.6 billion in annual pension contributions. In addition, Argentina has conducted two bond swaps (with 15.4% yields) for guaranteed loans maturing in 2009 to 2011 [106] Although these two moves have provided Argentina with increased fiscal capacity to meet short- and perhaps medium-term financing needs, the costs entail increased fiscal outlays in the future and heightened investor skepticism.

Russia and the Financial Crisis [107]

Russia tends to be in a category by itself. Although by some measures, it is an emerging market, it also is highly industrialized. Until recently, Russia had been experiencing impressive economic success, an average of 7% annual growth in real gross domestic product (GDP). In 2008, however, Russia faced a triple threat with the financial crisis coinciding with a rapid decline in the price of oil and the aftermath of the country's military confrontation with Georgia over the break-away areas of South Ossetia and Abkhazia. These events have exposed three fundamental weaknesses in the Russian economy: substantial dependence on oil and gas sales for export revenues and government revenues; a rise in foreign and domestic investor concerns; and a weak banking system. The economic downturn is showing up in Russia's performance indicators. In January 2009, Russia's industrial production declined 20% from the previous month, the largest drop in at least seven years and indicates a likely drop in overall Russian GDP [108]. The government predicted that Russian GDP will contract 2.2% in 2009, which would be the first annual contraction since 1998 [109].

The decline in world oil prices has hit Russia hard. Oil, natural gas, and other fuels account for about 65% of Russia's export revenues (2007). [110] In addition, the Russian government is dependent on taxes on oil and gas sales for more than half of its revenues. An average price of oil below $60/barrel could put the government budget into deficit [111]. An average price in the $30-$35/barrel range could cause the Russian economy to stop growing, according to one estimate [112]. As of February 9, 2009, the price of Urals-32 was $42.80, a 69.0% drop from its July 4, 2008 peak of $137.61 [113].

Another sign of financial trouble for Russia has been the rapid decline in stock prices on Russian stock exchanges. At the close of business on February 13, 2009, the RTS index had lost 75.0% of its value from its peak reached on May 19, 2008 [114] (The decline was the largest since Russia experienced a financial crisis in August 1998.) On September 16, 2008, alone, the RTS index lost 11.5% of its value leading the government to close stock markets for two days. The overall drop in equity prices has been blamed on the loss of investor confidence in the wake of the August 2008 conflict between Russia and Georgia but also because of the decline in oil prices and as a result of the credit crisis that has affected markets throughout the world. In addition, the ruble has been declining in nominal terms because foreign investors have been pulling capital out of the market to shore up domestic reserves putting downward pressure on the ruble. The ruble had declined 34.8% in terms of the dollar from July 29, 2008, to February 17, 2009 [115]. Russian official reserves have declined substantially in part because of Russian Central Bank intervention to defend the ruble although the government has allowed some gradual depreciation. Between July 31 and January 23, 2009, the reserves declined from $596.6 billion to $386.5 billion, or 35 .2%. [116]

Russia's banking system remains immature, and high interest rates prevail. Russian companies, therefore, have relied on foreign bank loans for financing rather than equity-based financing or domestic bank loans. However, these foreign loans were secured with company stocks as collateral. Because of the drop in stock values and because of the overall tightening of credit availability, foreign banks have declined to rollover loans. The Russian government, led by President Medvedev and Prime Minister Putin, has implemented several packages of measures valued at over $200 billion since September 2008 to prop up the stock market and the banks. The economic crisis is also forcing Russian leaders to confront restructuring of government budget priorities as Russia is expected to face its first budget deficit since 2000 [117]

EFFECTS ON EUROPE AND THE EUROPEAN RESPONSE [118]

Some European countries [119] initially viewed the financial crisis as a purely American phenomenon. That view has changed as economic activity Europe has declined at a fast pace over a short period of time. Making matters worse, global trade has declined sharply, eroding prospects for European exports providing a safety valve for domestic industries that are cutting output. In addition, public protests, sparked by rising rates of unemployment and concerns over the growing financial and economic turmoil, are increasing the political stakes for European governments and their leaders. The global economic crisis is straining the ties that bind together the members of the European Union and could present a significant challenge to the ideals of solidarity and common interests. In addition, the longer the economic downturn persists, the greater the prospects are that international pressure will mount against those governments that are perceived as not carrying their share of the responsibility for stimulating their economies to an extent that is commensurate with the size of their economy.

European countries are also concerned over the impact the financial crisis and the economic recession are having on the economies of East Europe and prospects for political instability [120] as well as future prospects for market reforms. Worsening economic conditions in East European countries could compound the current problems facing financial institutions in the EU. Although mutual necessity may eventually dictate a more unified position among EU members and increased efforts to aid East European economies, some observers are concerned these actions may come too late to forestall another blow to the European economies and to the United States. Governments elsewhere in Europe, such as Iceland and Latvia, have collapsed as a result of public protests over the way their governments have handled their economies during the crisis.

The crisis has underscored the growing interdependence between financial markets and between the U.S. and European economies. As such, the synchronized nature of the current economic downturn probably means that neither the United States nor Europe is likely to emerge from the financial crisis or the economic downturn alone. The United States and Europe share a mutual interest in developing a sound financial architecture to improve supervision and regulation of individual institutions and of international markets. This issue includes developing the organization and structures within national economies that can provide oversight of the different segments of the highly complex financial system. This oversight is viewed by many as critical to the future of the financial system because financial markets generally are considered to play an indispensible role in allocating capital and facilitating economic activity.

Within Europe, national governments and private firms have taken noticeably varied responses to the crisis, reflecting the unequal effects by country. While some have preferred to address the crisis on a case-by-case basis, others have looked for a systemic approach that could alter the drive within Europe toward greater economic integration. Great Britain has proposed a plan to rescue distressed banks by acquiring preferred stock temporarily. Iceland, on the other hand, has had to take over three of its largest banks in an effort to save its financial sector and its economy from collapse. The Icelandic experience raises important questions about how a nation can protect its depositors from financial crisis elsewhere and about the level of financial sector debt that is manageable without risking system-wide failure.

According to reports by the International Monetary Fund (IMF) and the European Central Bank (ECB), many of the factors that led to the financial crisis in the United States created a similar crisis in Europe [121]. Essentially low interest rates and an expansion of financial and investment opportunities that arose from aggressive credit expansion, growing complexity in mortgage securitization, and loosening in underwriting standards combined with expanded linkages among national financial centers to spur a broad expansion in credit and economic growth. This rapid rate of growth pushed up the values of equities, commodities, and real estate. Over time, the combination of higher commodity prices and rising housing costs pinched consumers' budgets, and they began reducing their expenditures. One consequence of this drop in consumer spending was a slowdown in economic activity and, eventually, a contraction in the prices of housing. In turn, the decline in the prices of housing led to a large-scale downgrade in the ratings of subprime mortgage-backed securities and the closing of a number of hedge funds with subprime exposure. Concerns over the pricing of risk in the market for subprime mortgage-backed securities spread to other financial markets, including to structured securities more generally and the interbank money market. Problems spread quickly throughout the financial sector to include financial guarantors as the markets turned increasingly dysfunctional over fears of under-valued assets.

As creditworthiness problems in the United States began surfacing in the subprime mortgage market in July 2007, the risk perception in European credit markets followed. The financial turmoil quickly spread to Europe, although European mortgages initially remained unaffected by the collapse in mortgage prices in the United States. Another factor in the spread of the financial turmoil to Europe has been the linkages that have been formed between national credit markets and the role played by international investors who react to economic or financial shocks by rebalancing their portfolios in assets and markets that otherwise would seem to be unrelated. The rise in uncertainty and the drop in confidence that arose from this rebalancing action undermined the confidence in major European banks and disrupted the interbank market, with money center banks becoming unable to finance large securities portfolios in wholesale markets. The increased international linkages between financial institutions and the spread of complex financial instruments has meant that financial institutions in Europe and elsewhere have come to rely more on short-term liquidity lines, such as the interbank lending facility, for their day-to-day operations. This has made them especially vulnerable to any drawback in the interbank market [122].

Estimates developed by the International Monetary Fund in January 2009 provide a rough indicator of the impact the financial crisis and an economic recession are having on the performance of major advanced countries. Economic growth in Europe is expected to slow by nearly 2% in 2009 to post a 0.2% drop in the rate of economic growth, while the threat of inflation is expected to lessen. Economic growth, as represented by gross domestic product (GDP), is expected to register a negative 1.6% rate for the United States in 2009, while the euro area countries could experience a combined negative rate of 2.0%, down from a projected rate of growth of 1.2% in 2008. The sharp drop in the prices of oil and other commodities in the later part of 2008 may have helped improve the rate of economic growth, but the length and depth of the economic downturn likely will mean that the IMF projections will prove to be too optimistic when the final data for 2009 are known. Indeed, in mid-February, the European Union announced that the rate of economic growth in the EU in the fourth quarter of 2008 had slowed to an annual rate of negative 6%. [123].

Central banks in the United States, the Euro zone, the United Kingdom, Canada, Sweden, and Switzerland staged a coordinated cut in interest rates on October 8, 2008, and announced they had agreed on a plan of action to address the ever-widening financial crisis [124]. The actions, however, did little to stem the wide-spread concerns that were driving financial markets. Many Europeans were surprised at the speed with which the financial crisis spread across national borders and the extent to which it threatened to weaken economic growth in

Europe. This crisis did not just involve U.S. institutions. It has demonstrated the global economic and financial linkages that tie national economies together in a way that may not have been imagined even a decade ago. At the time, much of the substance of the European plan was provided by the British Prime Minister Gordon Brown, [125] who announced a plan to provide guarantees and capital to shore up banks. Eventually, the basic approach devised by the British arguably would influence actions taken by other governments, including that of the United States.

On October 10, 2008, the G-7 finance ministers and central bankers, [126] met in Washington, DC, to provide a more coordinated approach to the crisis. At the Euro area summit on October 12, 2008, Euro area countries along with the United Kingdom urged all European governments to adopt a common set of principles to address the financial crisis [127] The measures the nations supported are largely in line with those adopted by the U.K. and include:

- Recapitalization: governments promised to provide funds to banks that might be struggling to raise capital and pledged to pursue wide-ranging restructuring of the leadership of those banks that are turning to the government for capital.

- State ownership: governments indicated that they will buy shares in the banks that are seeking recapitalization.

- Government debt guarantees: guarantees offered for any new debts, including inter-bank loans, issued by the banks in the Euro zone area.

- Improved regulations: the governments agreed to encourage regulations to permit assets to be valued on their risk of default instead of their current market price.

In addition to these measures, EU leaders agreed on October 16, 2008, to set up a crisis unit and they agreed to a monthly meeting to improve financial oversight [128] Jose Manuel Barroso, President of the European Commission, urged EU members to develop a "fully integrated solution" to address the global financial crisis, consistent with France's support for a strong international organization to oversee the financial markets. The EU members expressed their support for the current approach within the EU, which makes each EU member responsible for developing and implementing its own national regulations regarding supervision over financial institutions. The European Council stressed the need to strengthen the supervision of the European financial sector. As a result, the EU statement urged the EU members to develop a "coordinated supervision system at the European level." [129] This approach likely will be tested as a result of failed talks with the credit derivatives industry in Europe. In early January 2009, an EU sponsored working group reported that it had failed to get a commitment from the credit derivatives industry to use a central clearing house for credit default swaps. As an alternative, the European Commission reportedly is considering adopting a set of rules for EU members that would require banks and other users of the CDS markets to use a central clearing house within the EU as a way of reducing risk [130]

The "European Framework for Action"

On October 29, 2008, the European Commission released a "European Framework for Action" as a way to coordinate the actions of the 27 member states of the European Union to address the financial crisis [131] The EU also announced that on November 16, 2008, the Commission will propose a more detailed plan that will bring together short-term goals to address the current economic downturn with the longer-term goals on growth and jobs in the Lisbon Strategy [132]. The short-term plan revolves around a three-part approach to an overall EU recovery action plan/framework. The three parts to the EU framework are:

> *A new financial market architecture at the EU level.* The basis of this architecture involves implementing measures that member states have announced as well as providing for (1) continued support for the financial system from the European Central Bank and other central banks; (2) rapid and consistent implementation of the bank rescue plan that has been established by the member states; and (3) decisive measures that are designed to contain the crisis from spreading to all of the member states.
>
> *Dealing with the impact on the real economy.* The policy instruments member states can use to address the expected rise in unemployment and decline in economic growth as a second-round effect of the financial crisis are in the hands of the individual member states. The EU can assist by adding short-term actions to its structural reform agenda, while investing in the future through: (1) increasing investment in R&D innovation and education; (1) promoting flexicurity [133] to protect and equip people rather than specific jobs; (3) freeing up businesses to build markets at home and internationally; and (4) enhancing competitiveness by promoting green technology, overcoming energy security constraints, and achieving environmental goals. In addition, the Commission will explore a wide range of ways in which EU members can increase their rate of economic growth.
>
> *A global response to the financial crisis.* The financial crisis has demonstrated the growing interaction between the financial sector and the goods-and services-producing sectors of economies. As a result, the crisis has raised questions concerning global governance not only relative to the financial sector, but the need to maintain open trade markets. The EU would like to use the November 15, 2008 multi-nation G-20 economic summit in Washington, DC, to promote a series of measures to reform the global financial architecture. The Commission argues that the measures should include (1) strengthening international regulatory standards; (2) strengthen international coordination among financial supervisors; (3) strengthening measures to monitor and coordinate macroeconomic policies; and (4) developing the capacity to address financial crises at the national regional and multilateral levels. Also, a financial architecture plan should include three key principles: (1) efficiency; (2) transparency and accountability; and (3) the inclusion of representation of key emerging economies.

European leaders, meeting prior to the November 15, 2008 G-20 economic summit in Washington, DC, agreed that the task of preventing future financial crisis should fall to the International Monetary Fund, but they could not agree on precisely what that role should be [134]. The leaders set a 1 00-day deadline to draw up reforms for the international financial system. British Prime Minister Gordon Brown reportedly urged other European leaders to back fiscal stimulus measure to support the November 6, 2008 interest rate cuts by the European Central Bank, the Bank of England, and other central banks. Reportedly, French Prime Minister Nicolas Sarkozy argued that the role of the IMF and the World Bank needed to be rethought. French and German officials have argued that the IMF should assume a larger role in financial market regulation, acting as a global supervisor of regulators. Prime Minister Sarkozy also argued that the IMF should "assess" the work of such international bodies as the Bank of International Settlements. Other G-20 leaders, however, reportedly have disagreed with this proposal, agreeing instead to make the IMF "the pivot of a renewed international system," working alongside other bodies. Other Ministers also were apparently not enthusiastic toward a French proposal that Europe should agree to a more formalized coordination of economic policy.

In an effort to confront worsening economic conditions, German Chancellor Angela Merkel proposed a package of stimulus measures, including spending for large-scale infrastructure projects, ranging from schools to communications. The stimulus package represents the second multi-billion euro fiscal stimulus package Germany has adopted in less than three months. The plan, announced on January13, 2009, reportedly was doubled from initial estimates to reach more than 60 billion Euros [135] (approximately $80 billion) over two years. The plan reportedly includes a pledge by Germany's largest companies to avoid mass job cuts in return for an increase in government subsidies for employees placed temporarily on short work weeks or on lower wages [136]. Other reports indicate that Germany is considering an emergency fund of up to 100 billion Euros in state-backed loans or guarantees to aid companies having problems getting credit. [137]

Overall, Germany's response to the economic downturn changed markedly between December 2008 and January 2009 as economic conditions continued to worsen. In a December 2008 article, German Finance Minister Peer Steinbruck defended Germany's approach at the time. According to Steinbruck, Germany disagreed with the EU plan to provide a broad economic stimulus plan, because it favored an approach that is more closely tailored to the German economy. He argued that Germany is providing a counter-cyclical stimulus program even though it is contrary to its long-term goal of reducing its government budget deficit. Important to this program, however, are such "automatic stabilizers" as unemployment benefits that automatically increase without government action since such benefits play a larger role in the German economy than in other economies. Steinbruck argued that, "our experience since the 1970s has shown that ... stimulus programs fail to achieve the desired effect.... It is more likely that such large-scale stimulus programs—and tax cuts as well—would not have any effects in real time. It is unclear whether general tax cuts can significantly encourage consumption during a recession, when many consumers are worried about losing their jobs. The history of the savings rate in Germany, points to the opposite." [138]

France, which has been leading efforts to develop a coordinated European response to the financial crisis, has proposed a package of measures estimated to cost over $500 billion. The French government is creating two state agencies that will provide funds to sectors where they are needed. One entity will issue up to $480 billion in guarantees on inter-bank lending issued before December 31, 2009, and would be valid for five years. The other entity will use a $60 billion fund to recapitalize struggling companies by allowing the government to buy stakes in the firms. On January 16, 2009, President Sarkozy announced that the French government would take a tougher stance toward French banks that seek state aid. Up to that point, France had injected $15 billion in the French banking system. In order to get additional aid, banks would be required to suspend dividend payments to shareholders and bonuses to top management and to increase credit lines to such clients as exporters. France reportedly was preparing to inject more money into the banking system [139]

On December 4, 2008, President Sarkozy announced a $33 billion (26 billion euros) package of stimulus measures to accelerate planned public investments [140]. The package is focused primarily on infrastructure projects and investments by state-controlled firms, including a canal north of Paris, renovation of university buildings, new metro cars, and construction of 70,000 new homes, in addition to 30,000 unfinished homes the government has committed to buy in 2009. The plan also includes a 200 Euro payment to low-income households. On December 15, 2008, France agreed to provide the finance division of Renault and Peugeot $1.2 billion in credit guarantees and an additional $250 million to support the car manufacturers' consumer finance division [141]. In an interview on French TV on January 14, 2009, French Prime Minister Francois Fillon indicated that the French government is considering an increase in aid to the French auto industry, including Renault and Peugeot [142]. The auto industry and its suppliers reportedly employ about 10% of France's labor force.

The British Rescue Plan

On October 8, 2008, the British Government announced a $850 billion multi-part plan to rescue its banking sector from the current financial crisis. Details of this plan are presented here to illustrate the varied nature of the plan. The Stability and Reconstruction Plan followed a day when British banks lost £17 billion on the London Stock Exchange. The biggest loser was the Royal Bank of Scotland, whose shares fell 39%, or £10 billion, of its value. In the downturn, other British banks lost substantial amounts of their value, including the Halifax Bank of Scotland which was in the process of being acquired by Lloyds TSB.

The British plan included four parts:

- A coordinated cut in key interest rates of 50 basis, or one-half of one percent (0.5) between the Bank of England, the Federal Reserve, and the European Central Bank.
- An announcement of an investment facility of $87 billion implemented in two stages to acquire the Tier 1 capital, or preferred stock, in "eligible" banks and building societies (financial institutions that specialize on mortgage financing) in order to recapitalize the firms. To qualify for the recapitalization plan, an institution must be incorporated in the UK (including UK subsidiaries of foreign institutions, which have a substantial business in the UK and building societies). Tier 1 capital often is used as measure of the asset strength of a financial institution.
- The British Government agreed to make available to those institutions participating in the recapitalization scheme up to $436 billion in guarantees on new short- and medium-term debt to assist in refinancing maturing funding obligations as they fall due for terms up to three years.
- The British Government announced that it would make available $352 billion through the Special Liquidity Scheme to improve liquidity in the banking industry. The Special Liquidity Scheme was launched by the Bank of England on April 21, 2008 to allow banks to temporarily swap their high-quality mortgage- backed and other securities for UK Treasury bills [143].

On November 24, 2008, Britain's majority Labor party presented a plan to Parliament to stimulate the nation's slowing economy by providing a range of tax cuts and government spending projects totaling 20 billion pounds (about $30 billion) [144] The stimulus package includes a 2.5% cut in the value added tax (VAT), or sales tax, for 13 months, a postponement of corporate tax increases, and government guarantees for loans to small and midsize businesses. The plan also includes government plans to spend 4.5 billion pounds on public works, such as public housing and energy efficiency.

Some estimates indicate that the additional spending required by the plan will push Britain's government budget deficit in 2009 to an amount equivalent to 8% of GDP. To pay for the plan, the government would increase income taxes on those making more than 150,000 pounds (about $225,000) from 40% to 45% starting in April 2011. In addition, the British plan would increase the National Insurance contributions for all but the lowest income workers [145]

On January 14, 2009, British Business Secretary Lord Mandelson unveiled an additional package of measures by the Labor government to provide credit to small and medium businesses that have been hard pressed for credit as foreign financial firms have reduced their level of activity in the UK.

The three measures are: (1) a 10 billion pound (approximately $14 billion) Capital Working Scheme to provide banks with guarantees to cover 50% of the risk on existing and new working capital loans on condition that the banks must use money freed up by the guarantee to make new loans; (2) a one billion pound Enterprise Finance Guarantee Scheme to assist small, credit-worthy companies by providing guarantees to banks of up to 75% of loans to small businesses; and (3) a 75 million pound Capital for Enterprise Fund to convert debt to equity for small businesses [146].

Collapse of Iceland's Banking Sector

The failure of Iceland's banks raises questions of bank supervision and crisis management for governments in Europe and the United States. As Icelandic banks began to default, Britain used an anti-terrorism law to seize the deposits of the banks to prevent the banks from shifting funds from Britain to Iceland [147]. This incident raises questions about how national governments should address the issue of supervising foreign financial firms operating within their borders and whether they can prevent foreign-owned firms from withdrawing deposits in one market to offset losses in another. In addition, the case of Iceland raises questions about the cost and benefits of branch banking across national borders where banks can grow to be so large that disruptions in the financial market can cause defaults that outstrip the resources of national central banks to address.

On November 19, 2008, Iceland and the International Monetary Fund (IMF) finalized an agreement on an economic stabilization program supported by a $2.1 billion two-year standby arrangement from the IMF [148]. Upon approval of the IMF's Executive board, the IMF released $827 million immediately to Iceland with the remainder to be paid in eight equal installments, subject to quarterly reviews. As part of the agreement, Iceland has proposed a plan to restore confidence in its banking system, to stabilize the exchange rate, and to improve the nation's fiscal position. Also as part of the plan, Iceland's central bank raised its key interest rate by six percentage points to 18% on October 29, 2008, to attract foreign investors and to shore up its sagging currency [149]. The IMF 's Executive Board had postponed its decision on a loan to Iceland three times, reportedly to give IMF officials more time to confirm loans made by other nations. Other observers argued, however, that the delay reflected objections by British, Dutch, and German officials over the disposition of deposit accounts operated by Icelandic banks in their countries. Iceland reportedly smoothed the way by agreeing in principle to cover the deposits, although the details had not be finalized. In a joint statement, Germany, Britain, and the Netherlands said on November 20, 2008, that they would "work constructively in the continuing discussions" to reach an agreement [150]. Following the decision of IMF's Executive Board, Denmark, Finland, Norway, and Sweden agreed to provide an additional $2.5 billion in loans to Iceland.

Between October 7 and 9, 2008, Iceland's Financial Supervisory Authority (FSA), an independent state authority with responsibilities to regulate and supervise Iceland's credit, insurance, securities, and pension markets took control, without actually nationalizing them, of three of Iceland's largest banks: Landsbanki, Glitnir Banki, and Kaupthing Bank prior to a scheduled vote by shareholders to accept a government plan to purchase the shares of the banks in order to head off the collapse of the banks. At the same time, Iceland suspended trading on its stock exchange for two days [151]. In part, the takeover also attempted to quell a sharp depreciation in the exchange value of the Icelandic krona.

The demise of Iceland's three largest banks is attributed to an array of events, but primarily stems from decisions by the banks themselves. Some observers argued that the collapse of Lehman Brothers set in motion the events that finally led to the collapse of the banks, [152] but this conclusion is controversial. Some have argued that at the heart of Iceland's banking crisis is a flawed banking model that is based on an internationally active banking sector that is large relative to the size of the home country's GDP and to the fiscal capacity of the central bank [153]. As a result, a disruption in liquidity threatens the viability of the banks and overwhelms the ability of the central bank to act as the lender of last resort, which undermines the solvency of the banking system.

On October 15, 2008, the Central Bank of Iceland set up a temporary system of daily currency auctions to facilitate international trade. Attempts by Iceland's central bank to support the value of the krona are at the heart of Iceland's problems. Without a viable currency, there was no way to support the banks, which have done the bulk of their business in foreign markets. The financial crisis has also created problems with Great Britain because hundreds of thousands of Britons hold accounts in online branches of the Icelandic banks, and they fear those accounts will default. The government of British Prime minister Gordon Brown has used powers granted under antiterrorism laws to freeze British assets of Landsbanki until the situation is resolved.

Impact on Asia and the Asian Response [154]

Many Asian economies have been through wrenching financial crises in the past 10-15 years. Although most observers say the region's economic fundamentals have improved greatly in the past decade, this crisis provides a worrying sense of deja vu, and an illustration that Asian policy changes in recent years—including Japan's slow but comprehensive banking reforms, Korea's opening of its financial markets, China's dramatic economic transformation, and the enormous buildup of sovereign reserves across the region—have not fully insulated (and, so far, cannot fully insulate) Asian economies from global contagion.

In the early months of the crisis, Asian nations did not have to deal with outright bankruptcies or rescues of major financial institutions, as Western governments did. With only a few exceptions— most notably in South Korea—leverage within Asian financial systems was comparatively low and bank balance sheets were comparatively healthy at the outset of the crisis. Nearly all East Asian nations run current account surpluses, a reversal from their state during the Asian financial crisis of the late 1 990s. These surpluses have been one reason for the buildup of enormous government reserves in the region, including China's $1.9 trillion and Japan's $996 billion—the two largest reserve stockpiles in the world. Such reserves give Asian governments resources to provide fiscal stimulus, inject capital into their financial systems, and provide backstop guarantees for private financial transactions where needed. So overall, Asian economies are much healthier than they were before the Asian Financial Crisis of 1997-1998, when several Asian countries burned through their limited reserves quickly trying to defend currencies from speculative selling.

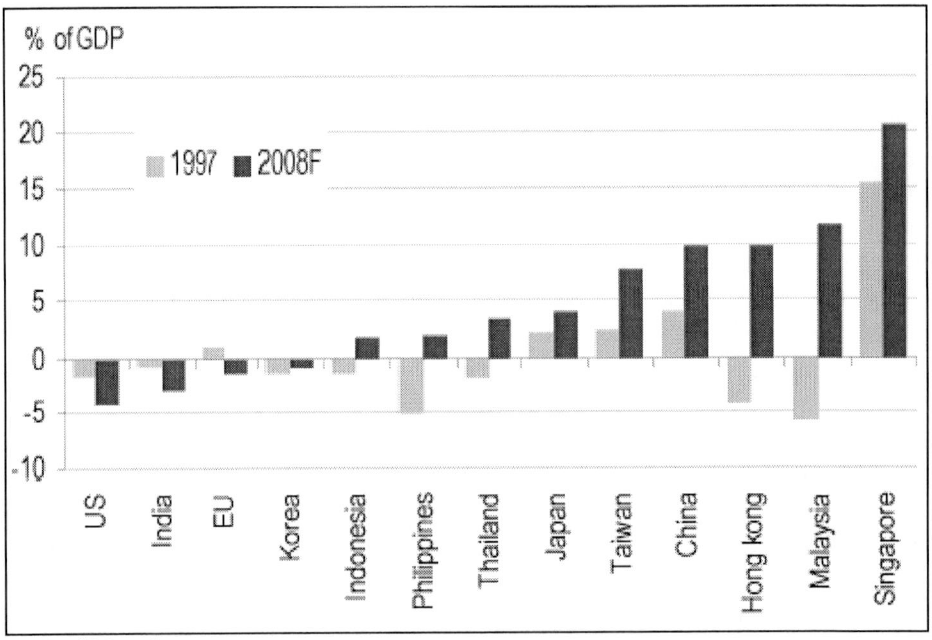

Source: Merrill Lynch.

Figure 10. Asian Current Account Balances are Mostly Healthy.

Still, Asia has not been insulated. The initial stage of the crisis, which centered around losses directly from subprime assets in the United States, has given way to a broader global crisis marked by slowing economies and dried-up liquidity. Asia and the United States are deeply linked in many ways, including trade (primarily Asian exports to the United States), U.S. investments in the region, and financial linkages that entwine Asian banks, companies and governments with U.S. markets and financial institutions. As a result, even though Asian banks disclosed relatively low direct exposures to failed institutions and toxic assets in the United States and Europe, Asian economies appear caught in a second phase of the crisis.

With Western economies slowing and global investors short of cash and pulling back from any markets deemed risky, Asian economies appear extremely vulnerable—and that threatens deeper damage to Asian financial systems and then, in turn, to markets for U.S. exports and investments.

The signs of distress in Asia are legion. Japan's government officially forecasts zero growth for 2009. The Nikkei-225 Index has lost half its value over the course of 2008, exacerbated by a surge by the yen to its highest level against the dollar since 1982. The yen's strength makes Japanese exports more expensive and adds to the damage that slowing economies around the world are already expected to inflict on Japan's export-led economy. Japan entered a recession in the July-September 2008 quarter, contracting for the second straight quarter. And in November, Japanese exports fell by 26.7%, the largest year-on-year decline on record, leaving Japan with a trade deficit for the second straight month—the first time that has happened since 1980 [155].

Meanwhile, South Korea's stock market and currency have plunged precipitously, as South Korean companies have hoarded dollars because of substantial dollar debts. Chinese GDP growth, while still strong, slowed from 10.4% in the April-June quarter to 9.0% in the July- September period. Further slowing in China seems inevitable. In November, Chinese exports dropped 2.2%, the first monthly decline in seven years, while imports plunged by 18% in the month, reflecting a substantial decline in domestic Chinese demand. This has raised concerns that further slowing could lead to unemployment and social unrest, key concerns of the Chinese government. Such concerns prompted the government to announce a $586 billion stimulus package in early November 2008, although the measures included many policies that had previously been announced. Smaller economies dependent on the financial and trading sectors, such as Hong Kong and Singapore, have been hammered—Singapore is already in a recession, and Hong Kong's government has announced it will guarantee all the $773 billion in Hong Kong bank deposits through 2010.

One of the most worrying developments in Asia is that Pakistan, already coping with severe political instability, has been forced to seek emergency loans from the IMF because of dwindling government reserves. This points to the limits of bilateral solutions to the crisis: For much of October and early November, Pakistan reportedly sought support from China, Saudi Arabia and other Middle Eastern states before being forced to the IMF [156]. On November 13, well into discussions with the IMF, Pakistan officials announced they had received a $500 million aid package from Beijing, far short of the $10 billion-$15 billion that Pakistani leaders say they need over the next two years [157]. Then on November 15, Pakistani and IMF officials confirmed that Pakistan would receive $7.6 billion in emergency loans, including $4 billion immediately to avoid sovereign default. But this remains short of what Pakistan says it needs [158]

Since the outset of the crisis, governments in Japan, South Korea, Hong Kong, Singapore, Malaysia, Australia, New Zealand, Indonesia and elsewhere have been forced into a range of moves to support domestic financial systems, pumping money into financial markets, issuing guarantees for bank deposits, and providing fiscal stimulus to shore up economic growth and slow declines in local stock markets. In several instances, including in Japan and South Korea, initial interventions failed to staunch financial market declines, leading authorities to broaden their support moves as the crisis deepened.

So in Asia, a belief that held sway in recent years that Asian economies were starting to "decouple" from the United States and Europe, generating growth that didn't depend on the rest of the world, has given way to a realization that a crisis that originated in the West can sweep up the region as well. Declines in Asian stock markets are similar in scale to, or larger than, those in the U.S. and Europe, despite the lack of bankruptcies and failed institutions in Asia. Throughout the crisis thus far, Asian economies have experienced a so-called "flight to quality," in which lenders and investors have sought safe investments and moved out of those perceived as risky. This has so far included the majority of Asia's emerging economies. Some economists, however, believe that Asia's reserves and current account surpluses may recover more strongly than other emerging markets once the crisis stabilizes [159].

Asian Reserves and Their Impact

Some analysts argue that substantial Asian reserves could be one source of relief for the global economy [160]. Japan has contributed funding for the IMF support package of Iceland, and on November 14, Prime Minister Taro Aso said Japan would lend the IMF $100 billion to support further packages that might be needed before the IMF increases its capital in 2009 [161]. Many wonder if China and other reserve-rich developing nations will find ways to use those reserves to support financially-strapped governments. As noted previously, Pakistan reportedly has approached China and several Gulf states for such support.

One key question is whether Asian countries will seek to play a larger role in setting multilateral moves to shore up regulation, and international support for troubled countries. Five Asian countries—Japan, China, South Korea, India and Indonesia, were present at the G-20 summit. But Asian approaches to multilateral regulation are still unclear. At an October 25-26 meeting of the Asia Europe Forum (ASEM), Chinese Premier Wen Jiabao said China generally agrees with many European governments which seek an expansion of multilateral regulations. "We need financial innovation, but we need financial oversight even more," Wen reportedly told a press conference [162]. In late January, speaking at an annual gathering of economic and political leaders in Davos, Switzerland, Wen blamed the crisis on an "excessive expansion of financial institutions in blind pursuit of profit," a failure of government supervision in the financial sector, and an "unsustainable model of development, characterized by prolonged low savings and high consumption." [163] Many analysts saw this as a criticism of the United States, which has much lower savings and higher consumption rates than China.

Previous Asian attempts to play a leadership role have been unsuccessful. In 1998, in the midst of the Asian Financial Crisis, Japan and the Asian Development Bank proposed the creation of an "Asian Monetary Fund" through which wealthier Asian governments could support economies in financial distress. The proposal was successfully opposed by the U.S. Treasury Department, which argued that it could be a way for countries to bypass the conditions that the IMF demands of its borrowers and go straight to "easier" sources of credit.

Two years later, in 2000, Finance Ministers from the ASEAN+3 nations (the 10 members of the Association of Southeast Asian Nations [164], plus Japan, South Korea and China) announced the Chiang Mai Initiative (CMI), whose primary measure was to provide a swap mechanism that countries could tap to cover shortfalls of foreign reserves. This was a less aggressive proposal than the Asian Monetary Fund. Although a small portion of the swap lines could be tapped in an emergency, most would likely be subject to IMF conditions for recipients [165].

On October 26, Japan, China, South Korea, and ASEAN members agreed to start an $80 billion multilateral swap arrangement in 2009, which would allow countries with substantial balance of payments problems to tap the reserves of larger economies. There remains, however, disagreement within the region about whether the IMF should play an active role in setting conditions for countries that use these swap lines.

Asian leaders have sought to start other regional discussions. On October 22, a Japanese government official floated the idea of a pan-Asian financial stability forum, modeled after the Financial Stability Forum at the BIS, which was discussed in May at a meeting of Finance Ministers from Japan, South Korea and China [166]. On December 13, the leaders of Japan, China, and South Korea held a trilateral summit in Fukuoka, Japan, agreeing on bilateral swap lines between South Korea and the two others – a new renminbi-won swap line worth the equivalent of $28 billion and an expansion of an existing yen-won swap line to the equivalent of $20 billion [167]. Beyond this measure of support for South Korea, however, the summit did not provide broader multilateral initiatives.

National Responses

So far, the national-level responses among Asian governments include the following:

Japan

Japan was part of the early moves among major economies to flood markets with liquidity, in the "crisis containment" part of the global response, and the Bank of Japan has continued its aggressive monetary stimulus in the months since. Alongside other major central banks, the Bank of Japan pumped tens of billions of dollars into financial markets in late September and early October. It followed these moves with an announcement on October 14 that it would offer an unlimited amount of dollars to institutions operating in Japan, to ensure that Japanese interbank credit markets continued to function. The BOJ did not lower interest rates in the crisis's early stages, but on October 31, it joined other global central banks, including the U.S. Federal Reserve, by cutting a key short-term interest rate to 0.3%, from 0.5%, and on December 19 it cut the rate to 0.1%.

For a time, Japan was considered relatively insulated, because of its well capitalized banks, substantial reserves and current account surplus. Japan spent nearly $440 billion between 1998 and 2003 to assist and recapitalize its banking system, and most observers say Japan's financial system emerged from the experience fairly sound. Healthy capital positions helped Mitsubishi UFG Group, Japan's largest bank, and Nomura, the country's largest brokerage, to buy pieces of distressed U.S. investment banks as the crisis was deepening in October. Mitsubishi UFG bought 21% of Morgan Stanley for $9 billion, and Nomura purchased the Asian, European and Middle Eastern operations of Lehman Brothers.

But as Western economies began to slow, Japan's financial insulation thinned. The Japanese economy is highly exposed to slowdowns in export markets, particularly in the U.S. and Europe. The U.S. accounted for 20.1% of Japan's exports in 2007. Japan has sought to provide fiscal stimulus: The government unveiled a $107 billion stimulus package in August, and on January 27, the Japanese parliament passed a second package, valued at $54 billion. The package—and, more broadly, Prime Minister Taro Aso's response to the crisis—has been the subject of severe infighting within Aso's ruling Liberal Democratic Party. Aso's government currently faces extremely low support ratings of around 20%. [168]

There have been signs of stress in the Japanese financial system in the weeks following the Nomura and Mitsubishi UFG purchases. In October, Yamato Insurance, a mid-sized insurance company, filed for bankruptcy, with $2.7 billion in liabilities. Then, in late October, with share prices tumbling, the much larger Mitsubishi UFG Group—which just two weeks earlier was sufficiently capitalized that it had bought the Morgan Stanley stake—said it would raise as much as $10.7 billion to improve its capital base. Many analysts say smaller banks may need direct help from the government. Japan's two largest political parties, the ruling Liberal Democratic Party and the main opposition Democratic Party of Japan, have agreed on the need to re-authorize expired legislation that would allow the government to purchase equity to support private banks, and Japanese media reports say this is expected to be passed in December. This move would restart a program first authorized in 2002 as part of the bank recapitalization process.

China [169]

The extent of China's exposure to the current global financial crisis, in particular from the fallout of the U.S. sub-prime mortgage problem, is mixed but is believed to be relatively small. China's numerous restrictions on capital flows to and from China limit the ability of individual Chinese citizens and many firms to invest their savings overseas. Thus, the exposure of Chinese private sector firms and individual investors to sub-prime U.S. mortgages is likely to be rather small. On the other hand, the exposure of Chinese government entities, such as the State Administration of Foreign Exchange, the China Investment Corporation (a $200 billion sovereign wealth fund created in 2007), [170] state banks, and state owned enterprises), may be more exposed and may have suffered losses from troubled U.S. mortgage securities. The Chinese government generally does not release detailed information on the holdings of its financial entities, although some of its banks have reported on their supposed level of exposure to sub-prime U.S. mortgage securities. Such entities have generally reported that their exposure to troubled sub-prime U.S. mortgages has been minor relative to their total investments, that they have liquidated such assets or have written off losses, and that they continue to earn high profit margins [171].

However, China's economy has not been immune to effects of the global financial crisis, given its heavy reliance on trade and foreign direct investment (FDI) for its economic growth. Numerous sectors have been hard hit. [172] To illustrate:

- The real estate market in several Chinese cities has exhibited signs of a bubble that is bursting, including a slowdown in construction, falling prices and growing levels of unoccupied buildings. This has increased pressure on the banks to lower interest rates further to stabilize the market.
- The value of China's main stock market index, the Shanghai Stock Exchange Composite Index, dropped by 36% from June 2, 2008, to March 18, 2009 [173]
- China's trade has plummeted recent months (see Figure 11). For example, exports and imports in February 2009 were down 25.7% and 24.1%, respectively on a year-on-year basis. The decline in exports was the biggest monthly decline every recorded.

- The level of FDI flows to China has fallen four months in a row (November 2008-February 2009). Monthly FDI flows to China dropped by 15.8% in February 2009 and by 32.6% in January (year-on-year basis).
- Numerous press reports indicate sharp reductions of production and employment in China. The Chinese government in January 2009 estimated that 20 million migrant workers had lost their jobs in 2008.
- Global Insight, an international forecasting firm, estimates that China's real GDP growth would slow to 5.7% in 2009 [174] Some analysts contend annual economic growth of less than 8% could lead to social unrest, given that every year there are 20 million new job seekers in China [175]

China has responded to the crisis on a number of fronts. On September 27, 2008, Chinese Premier Wen Jiabao reportedly stated in a speech that "What we can do now is to maintain the steady and fast growth of the national economy and ensure that no major fluctuations will happen. That will be our greatest contribution to the world economy under the current circumstances."[176]. On October 8, 2008, China's central bank announced plans to cut interest rates and the reserve- requirement ratio in order to help stimulate the economy. The announcement coincided with announcements by the U.S. Federal Reserve and other central banks of major economies around the world to lower their benchmark interest rates, although, neither China's central bank or the media stated that these measures were taken in conjunction with the other major central banks.

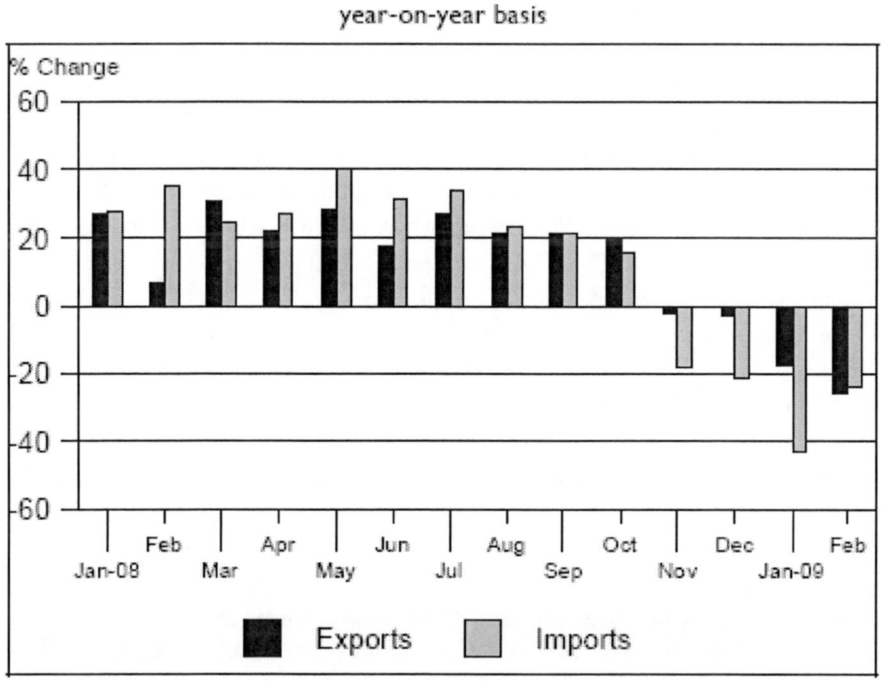

Source: Global Insight and China's Customs Administration.

Figure 11. Changes in China's Monthly Trade Data: January 2008-February 2009.

On October 21, 2008, China's State Council announced it was considering implementing a new economic stimulus package, which would include an acceleration of construction projects, new export tax rebates, a reduction in the housing transaction tax, increased agriculture subsidies, and expanding lending to small and medium enterprises [177]. On November 9, 2008 the Chinese government announced it would implement a two-year $586 billion stimulus package, mainly dedicated to infrastructure projects.

The package would finance programs in 10 major areas, including affordable housing, rural infrastructure, water, electricity, transport, the environment, technological innovation and rebuilding areas hit by disasters (especially, areas that were hit by the May 12, 2998 earthquake) [178]. On November 14, 2008, China reportedly provided $500 million in aid to Pakistan. On November 15, 2008, Chinese President Hu Jintao attended the G-20 summit, calling for reform of the global financial system and stating that growing China's economy was the most important step the government could take to respond to the global financial crisis.

Analysts debate what role China might play in responding to the global financial crisis, given its nearly $2 trillion in foreign exchange reserves. Some have speculated that China could use some of these reserves to shore up troubled financial institutions and companies around the world, such as in the United States. Others have contended that China could, in order to help stabilize its largest export market (the United States), use its reserves to purchase some of the large amount of U.S. debt securities that will need to be issued to help fund the hundreds of billions of dollars in new federal spending on government purchases of troubled assets and programs to stimulate the U.S. economy [179].

China already plays a major role in funding U.S. debt. China's holdings of U.S. securities (which include short term and long term Treasury securities, government agency debt, corporate debt, and equities) are estimated to have totaled $1.4 trillion at the end of December 2008; this figure is equivalent to over $1,000 per Chinese citizen. Over the past few years, China has been the single largest foreign purchaser of U.S. Treasury securities, which are used to fund the federal budget deficit. In September 2008, China overtook Japan to become the largest foreign holder of U.S. Treasury securities, at $585 billion, and these holdings grew to $740 billion as of January 2009 [180]. On September 21, 2008, the White House indicated that President Bush had called President Hu to discuss the global financial crisis and steps the United States planned to take to address the crisis. An unnamed Chinese trade official reportedly stated that "the purpose of that call was to ask for China's help to deal with this financial crisis by urging China to hold even more U.S. Treasury bonds and U.S. assets." The official was further quoted as saying that China recognized that it "has a stake" in the health of the U.S. economy, both as a major market for Chinese exports and in terms of preserving the value of U.S.-based assets held by China." and that a stabilized U.S. economy was in China's own interest. [181]. At a press conference during her visit to China on February 21, 2009, Secretary of State Hillary Rodham Clinton brought up this issue, stating that she appreciated "greatly the Chinese government's continuing confidence in the US treasuries."

There are a number of reasons why China might be reluctant to boost significantly its purchases of U.S. assets. One concern would be whether increased Chinese investments in the U.S. economy would produce long-term economic benefits for China. In March 2009, Chinese Premier Wen Jiabao at a news conference stated: "We lent such huge fund [sic] to the United States and of course we're concerned about the security of our assets and, to speak truthfully, I am a little bit worried." Many analysts (including some in China) have questioned the wisdom of China's policy of investing a large level of foreign exchange reserves in U.S. government securities, which offer a relatively low rate of return, when China has such huge development needs. In addition, some Chinese investments in U.S. financial companies have fared poorly, and Chinese officials might be reluctant to put additional money into investments that were deemed to be too risky. A sharp economic slowdown in the Chinese economy could increase pressure to invest money at home rather than overseas. China may also be reluctant to boost investment in U.S. companies, due to concerns that doing so would be risky or could come under unfavorable scrutiny by Congress.

Some U.S. policymakers have expressed concern that increased Chinese purchases of U.S. debt could give it greater political leverage over the United States. They warn that this would undermine the ability of the United States to press China to reform various aspects of its economy, such as its currency policy. [182] Another major concern for U.S. officials is the extent China may attempt to subsidize industries impacted by the global economic slowdown and whether the pace of China's economic reforms will be slowed. Many U.S. officials have urged China not to try to export its way out of the crisis (especially through the use of subsidies, trade barriers, or a depreciation of its currency), but instead focus on promoting increased domestic consumption, further economic reforms, and continuing the appreciation of its currency (the renminbi) so that greater domestic demand in China will result in higher Chinese demand for imports. On February 19, 2008, the Chinese government stated that it would use its some of its foreign exchange reserves to boost imports, stimulate the domestic economy, and to help Chinese companies boost investment overseas [183]. However, the government has also stated that it intends to assist Chinese export industries as well.

South Korea

South Korea, Asia's fourth largest economy, has been deeply affected by the crisis, with both the South Korean stock market and the won tumbling throughout recent months, sometimes precipitously. On October 28, the won reached its lowest point since 1998, when South Korea was in the middle of its IMF support package. Oxford Analytica estimates that foreign investors withdrew a net $25 billion from the Korean stock market between January and late September [184]. Experts say South Korean banks have large dollar-denominated debts, and therefore need to protect their holdings of dollars. This has contributed to the won's fall, and in early October, President Lee Myung-bak invoked patriotism to encourage Korean banks to stop hoarding dollars and buy won [185].

South Korea has announced several packages to stimulate the economy and shore up the domestic banking industry. The government announced a broad economic rescue package on October 19, 2008, promising to guarantee $100 billion in South Korean banks' foreign-currency debt and provide another $30 billion to directly support South Korean banks. (The total amount was equivalent to 14% of the country's GDP.) Struggling with its plunging stock market and currency, President Lee's government has also announced policies to spend up to $9.2 billion to support real-estate developers struggling with unsold apartments, and to provide further financial support to small businesses. On October 27, Korea's central bank cut its prime interest rate by 0.75 percentage points to 4.25%, the largest cut it has made since it began setting base interest rates in 1999. The rate has since been cut two more times, to 3%. On December 17, the government said it would launch a $15 billion fund to boost the capital of Korean banks.

South Korea has been an enormous economic success, and has bounced back strongly from the Asian Financial Crisis that forced it to turn to the IMF for a $58 billion support package in December 2007. After contracting by 6.9% in 1998, South Korea's GDP bounced back by 9.5% and 8.5% in the ensuing two years. Since 2002, GDP growth has been in the 3%-6% range.

However, President Lee has said the current situation is more severe than the 1997 crisis. Economically, South Korea is an outlier within Asia. It is one of the few Asian countries that is running a current account deficit ($12.6 billion in January-August 2008). Its banks are unusually leveraged, with loan-deposit ratios of more than 130%, higher than that in the United States and the EU, and the only East Asian country over 100%. [186].

Pakistan

Pakistan's economy went into a steady decline in 2008. After several years of strong and comparatively stable growth, Pakistan quickly slid into a severe economic crisis in 2008 [187]. Growth in real GDP declined sharply from about 8% to 3-4%; inflation rose to nearly 24%; and Pakistan's rupee depreciated by over 23% against the U.S. dollar. Pakistans unemployment rate rose, and the United Nations reported that 10 million Pakistanis were undernourished. In the words of Pakistan's President Asif Ali Zardari is, "The greatest challenge this government faces is an economic one" [188].

Rising trade and current account deficits generated a "capital crisis" in the autumn of 2008. Pakistan's foreign reserves slid from $14.2 billion in October 2007 to $4.1 billion at the end of October 2008. According to President Zardari's chief economic advisor, Shaukat Tarin, Pakistan needed $4 to $5 billion by the end of November 2008 to avoid defaulting on maturing sovereign debt obligations. In addition, even if Pakistan does secure the money it needs by the end of November, Tarin stated that Pakistan requires $10 to $15 billion in assistance over the next two to three years to continue to service its account deficits and outstanding debt [189].

Several factors, in addition to the current global financial crisis, are contributing to the recent downturn in Pakistan's economy. Pakistan's continuing struggle against Islamist militancy in its tribal areas along the border with Afghanistan has led to high federal deficits and uncertainty about the stability of the Pakistan government. A recent escalation of bombings and violence in Pakistan has raised the risk for and scared off many foreign investors and businesses. This has worsened the nation's capital shortage. In addition, the flight from risk that has followed the U.S. financial crisis has apparently contributed to some capital flight from Pakistan, especially among overseas Pakistanis and investors from the Middle East.

Pakistan has sought the required assistance from several countries (including China, Saudi Arabia, and the United States), international financial institutions (including the Asian Development Bank (ADB), the International Monetary Fund (IMF), the Islamic Development Bank (IDB), and the World Bank), and an informal group of nations called the "Friends of Pakistan." Although the ADB, the World Bank and others did offer some support, the total amount was insufficient to avoid the default risk. As a consequence, Pakistan reluctantly began negotiating a loan with the IMF. On November 15, Tarin announced that Pakistan had reached a tentative agreement with the IMF to borrow $7.6 billion over the next 23 months [190]. The first installment of the loan—up to $4 billion—was expected by the end of November; Pakistan is to repay the loan by 20 16 [191].

Assuming Pakistan and the IMF formally conclude the agreement, the $7.6 billion loan is well short of the estimated $10 billion to $15 billion Pakistan says it needs over the next two years to avoid a financial crisis. Some observers speculate that the IMF agreement will spur help from other potential donors, such as China, Saudi Arabia, and the United States. However, given the continuing economic problems of the potential donor nations, Pakistan may not be able to secure the full amount of assistance it says it needs. As a result, the IMF loan may end up being only a short-term patch to a long-term economic problem.

In the meantime, Pakistan has announced some changes in economic policy designed to alleviate their capital crisis. On September 19, 2008, acting finance minister Naveed Qamar released new economic policies designed to bring about macroeconomic stability and avoid seeking IMF assistance that included the elimination of fuel, electricity and food subsidies, and a reduction in the government deficit [192]. On November 3, 2008, Tarin announced reforms of Pakistan's tax system, including the politically sensitive taxation of large landowners, to reduce the incidence of tax evasion [193]. There has also been talk of cutting Pakistan's defense budget.

According to some analysts, the new economic policies may foster popular discontent and threaten political stability. The elimination of fuel, electricity and food subsidies may cause significant harm to Pakistan's poor, many of whom are already undernourished. The tax on large landowners may undermine support for Zardari's Pakistan People's Party among its party members and its coalition partners. A cut in Pakistan's defense budget also could harm its military efforts against Islamist militants and weaken the military's political support for the current coalition government.

Other Countries' Moves

Governments around the region have been affected by the crisis, and have issued a range of rescue measures to keep financial markets functioning and shore up economic growth. Other moves include:

Australia, which had seen one of the largest jumps in housing prices in the world in recent years, has seen property prices tumble, leading to a spike in bad loans among Australian banks. Australia's commodities-dependent economy has also been hurt by declining commodities prices, and the Australian dollar has declined substantially in recent weeks. In response, the government issued a full guarantee on all bank deposits in early October, and added a $7 billion fiscal stimulus plan on October 14.

On October 14, The Hong Kong Monetary Authority said it would provide government backing for all of the $773 billion in Hong Kong bank deposits through 2010 as government assistance for banks in Europe and the United States put pressure on Asian regulators to follow suit even though Asian banks tended to be better capitalized. The authority also said that it was prepared to provide capital to the 23 locally incorporated banks if they needed it, following the examples of the United States and Britain.

Many countries have seen trade volumes fall—both because of slowing global demand but also because domestic banks have been wary of issuing trade finance. India's central bank, the Reserve Bank of India, announced emergency measures on November 15 to support Indian banks who issue letters of credit for Indian exporters. The central bank more than doubled the level of funds it makes available for banks to refinance export credits at favorable rates [194].

The availability of trade finance has become a regional problem that further threatens export-led Asian economies, as evidenced by a call from the Asian Development Bank on November 16 for Asian banks to unfreeze credit to borrowers seeking to continue doing business [195]

INTERNATIONAL POLICY ISSUES

In making policy changes, Congress faces several fundamental issues. First is whether any longterm policies should be designed to restore confidence and induce return to the normal functioning of a self-correcting system or whether the policies should be directed at changing a system that may have become inherently unstable, a system that every decade or so creates bubbles and then lurches into crisis. [196] For example, in Congressional testimony on October 23, 2008, former Federal Reserve Chairman Alan Greenspan stated that a "once-in-a-century credit tsunami"' had engulfed financial markets, and he conceded that his free-market ideology shunning regulation was flawed [197]. In a recent book, the financier George Soros stated that the currently prevailing paradigm, that financial markets tend towards equilibrium, is both false and misleading. He asserted that the world's current financial troubles can be largely attributed to the fact that the international financial system has been developed on the basis of that flawed paradigm [198] Could this crisis mark the beginning of the end of "free market capitalism?" On the other hand, the International Monetary Fund has observed that market discipline still works and that the focus of new regulations should not be on eliminating risk but on improving market discipline and addressing the tendency of market participants to underestimate the systemic effects of their collective actions [199].

A second question deals with what level any new regulatory authority should reside. Should it primarily be at the state, national, or international level? If the authority is kept at the national level, how much power should an international authority have? Should the major role of the IMF, for example, be informational, advisory, and technical, or should it have enforcement authority? Should enforcement be done through a dispute resolution process similar to that in the World Trade Organization, or should the IMF or other international institution be ceded oversight and regulatory authority by national governments?

Bretton Woods II

The second question above is central for those calling for a new Bretton Woods conference. U.K. Prime Minister Gordon Brown called for such a conference to have the specific objective of remaking the international financial architecture [200]. In the declaration of the G-20 Summit on Financial Markets and the World Economy, world leaders stated:

We underscored that the Bretton Woods Institutions must be comprehensively reformed so that they can more adequately reflect changing economic weights in the world economy and be more responsive to future challenges. Emerging and developing economies should have greater voice and representation in these institutions. (See Appendix C.)

G-20 Meetings

On November 15, 2008, the G-20 Summit on Financial Markets and the World Economy was held in Washington, DC. This was billed as the first in a series of meetings to deal with the financial crisis, discuss efforts to strengthen economic growth, and to lay the foundation to prevent future crises from occurring. This summit included emerging market economies rather than the usual G-7 or G-8 nations that periodically meet to discuss economic issues. It was not apparent that the agenda of the emerging market economies differed greatly from that of Europe, the United States, or Japan.

The G-20 is an informal forum that promotes open and constructive discussion between industrial and emerging-market countries on key issues related to global economic stability. The members include the finance ministers and central bankers from the member nations. A G-20 leaders' summit is a new development.

The G-20 Washington Declaration to address the current financial crisis was both a laundry list of objectives and steps to be taken and a convergence of attitudes by national leaders that concrete measures had to be implemented both to stabilize national economies and to reform financial markets. The declaration established an Action Plan that included high priority actions to be completed prior to March 31, 2009. Details are to be worked out by the G-20 finance ministers. The declaration also called for a second G-20 summit that was held in London on April 2, 2009. Since the attendees now include the Association for Southeast Asian Nations, the G-20 no longer refers to just 20 nations.

At the April 2009 G-20 London Summit, leaders agreed on establishing a new Financial Stability Board (incorporating the Financial Stability Forum) to work with the IMF to ensure cooperation across borders; closer regulation of banks, hedge funds, and credit rating agencies; and a crackdown on tax havens. The leaders could not agree on the need for additional stimulus packages by nations, but they considered the additional funding for the IMF and multilateral development banks as key stimulus directed at developing and emerging market economies. The leaders reiterated their commitment to resist protectionism and promote global trade and investment. [201]

At the November G-20 summit, the leaders agreed on common principles to guide financial market reform:

- Strengthening transparency and accountability by enhancing required disclosure on complex financial products; ensuring complete and accurate disclosure by firms of their financial condition; and aligning incentives to avoid excessive risk- taking.
- Enhancing sound regulation by ensuring strong oversight of credit rating agencies; prudent risk management; and oversight or regulation of all financial markets, products, and participants as appropriate to their circumstances.
- Promoting integrity in financial markets by preventing market manipulation and fraud, helping avoid conflicts of interest, and protecting against use of the financial system to support terrorism, drug trafficking, or other illegal activities.
- Reinforcing international cooperation by making national laws and regulations more consistent and encouraging regulators to enhance their coordination and cooperation across all segments of financial markets.

- Reforming international financial institutions (IFIs) by modernizing their governance and membership so that emerging market economies and developing countries have greater voice and representation, by working together to better identify vulnerabilities and anticipate stresses, and by acting swiftly to play a key role in crisis response.

At the London Summit, the leaders reviewed progress on the November G-20 Action Plan that set forth a comprehensive work plan to implement the above principles. The Plan included immediate actions to:

- Address weaknesses in accounting and disclosure standards for off-balance sheet vehicles;
- Ensure that credit rating agencies meet the highest standards and avoid conflicts of interest, provide greater disclosure to investors, and differentiate ratings for complex products;
- Ensure that firms maintain adequate capital, and set out strengthened capital requirements for banks' structured credit and securitization activities;
- Develop enhanced guidance to strengthen banks' risk management practices, and ensure that firms develop processes that look at whether they are accumulating too much risk;
- Establish processes whereby national supervisors who oversee globally active financial institutions meet together and share information; and
- Expand the Financial Stability Forum to include a broader membership of emerging economies.

The leaders instructed finance ministers to make specific recommendations in the following areas:

- Avoiding regulatory policies that exacerbate the ups and downs of the business cycle;
- Reviewing and aligning global accounting standards, particularly for complex securities in times of stress;
- Strengthening transparency of credit derivatives markets and reducing their systemic risks;
- Reviewing incentives for risk-taking and innovation reflected in compensation practices; and
- Reviewing the mandates, governance, and resource requirements of the International Financial Institutions.

The leaders agreed that needed reforms will be successful only if they are grounded in a commitment to free market principles, including the rule of law, respect for private property, open trade and investment, competitive markets, and efficient, effectively-regulated financial systems. The leaders further agreed to:

- Reject protectionism, which exacerbates rather than mitigates financial and economic challenges;
- Strive to reach an agreement this year on modalities that leads to an ambitious outcome to the Doha Round of World Trade Organization negotiations;
- Refrain from imposing any new trade or investment barriers for the next 12 months; and
- Reaffirm development assistance commitments and urge both developed and emerging economies to undertake commitments consistent with their capacities and roles in the global economy.

The International Monetary Fund [202]

Policy proposals for changes in the international financial architecture have included a major role for the IMF. As a lender of last resort, coordinator of financial assistance packages for countries, monitor of macroeconomic conditions worldwide and within countries, and provider of technical assistance, the IMF has played an important role during financial crises whether international or confined to one member country.

The financial crisis has shown that the world could use a better early warning system that can detect and do something about stresses and systemic problems developing in world financial markets. It also may need some system of what is being called a macro-prudential framework for assessing risks and promoting sound policies. This would not only include the regulation and supervision of financial instruments and institutions but also would incorporate cyclical and other macroeconomic considerations as well as vulnerabilities from increased banking concentration and inter-linkages between different parts of the financial system [203]. In short, some institution could be charged with monitoring synergistic conditions that arise because of interactions among individual financial institutions or their macroeconomic setting.

However, the IMF 's current system of macroeconomic monitoring tends to focus on the risks to currency stability, employment, inflation, government budgets, and other macroeconomic variables. The IMF, jointly with the Financial Stability Board, has recently stepped up its work on financial markets, macro-financial linkages, and spillovers across countries with the aim of strengthening early warning systems. The IMF has not, however, traditionally pressed countries to counter specific risks such as how macroeconomic variables, potential synergisms and blurring of boundaries among regulated entities, and new investment vehicles affect prudential risk for insurance, banking, and brokerage houses. The Bank for International Settlements makes recommendations to countries on measures to be undertaken (such as Basel II) to ensure banking stability and capital adequacy, but the financial crisis has shown that the focus on capital adequacy has been insufficient to ensure stability when a financial crisis becomes systemic and involves brokerage houses and insurance companies as well as banks.

The International Monetary Fund

The IMF was conceived in July 1944, when representatives of 45 governments meeting in the town of Bretton Woods, New Hampshire, agreed on a framework for international economic cooperation. The IMF came into existence in December 1945 and now has membership of 185 countries.

The IMF performs three main activities:

- monitoring national, global, and regional economic and financial developments and advising member countries on their economic policies (surveillance);
- lending members hard currencies to support policy programs designed to correct balance of payments problems; and
- offering technical assistance in its areas of expertise, as well as training for government and central bank officials.

The financial crisis has created an opportunity for the IMF to reinvigorate itself and possibly play a constructive role in resolving, or at the least mitigating, the effects of the global downturn. It has been operating on two fronts: (1) through immediate crisis management, primarily balance of payments support to emerging-market and less-developed countries, and (2) contributing to longterm systemic reform of the international financial system [204]. The IMF also has a wealth of information and expertise available to help in resolving financial crises and has been providing policy advice to member countries around the world.

IMF rules stipulate that countries are allowed to borrow up to three times their quota [205] over a three-year period, although this requirement has been breached on several occasions in which the IMF has lent at much higher multiples of quota. In response to the current financial crisis, the IMF has activated its Emergency Financing Mechanism to speed the normal process for loans to crisis-afflicted countries. The emergency mechanism enables rapid approval (usually within 48- 72 hours) of IMF lending once an agreement has been reached between the IMF and the national government.

As of April 2009, the IMF, under its Stand-By Arrangement facility, has provided or is in the process of providing financial support packages for Iceland ($2.1 billion), Ukraine ($16.4 billion), Hungary ($25.1 billion), Pakistan ($7.6 billion), Belarus ($2.46 billion), Serbia ($530.3 million), Armenia ($540 million), El Salvador ($800 million), Latvia ($2.4 billion), and Seychelles ($26.6 million). The IMF also created a Flexible Credit Line for countries with strong fundamentals, policies, and track records of policy implementation. Once approved, these loans can be disbursed when the need arises rather than being conditioned on compliance with policy targets as in traditional IMF-supported programs. The IMF board has approved Mexico for $47 billion under this facility. Poland has requested a credit line of $20.5 billion.

The IMF also may use its Exogenous Shocks Facility (ESF) to provide assistance to certain member countries. The ESF provides policy support and financial assistance to low-income countries facing exogenous shocks, events that are completely out of the national government's control. These could include commodity price changes (including oil and food), natural disasters, and conflicts and crises in neighboring countries that disrupt trade. The ESF was modified in 2008 to further increase the speed and flexibility of the IMF's response.

Through the ESF, a country can immediately access up to 25% of its quota for each exogenous shock and an additional 75% of quota in phased disbursements over one to two years.

The increasing severity of the crisis has led world leaders to conclude that the IMF needs additional resources. At the 2009 February G-7 finance ministers summit, the government of Japan lent the IMF $100 billion dollars [206]. At the April 2009 London G-20 summit leaders of the world's major economies agreed to increase resources of the IMF and international development banks by $1.1 trillion including $750 billion more for the International Monetary Fund, $250 billion to boost global trade, and $100 billion for multilateral development banks. For the additional IMF resources, $250 billion was to be made available immediately through bilateral arrangements between the IMF and individual countries, while an additional $250 billion would become available as additional countries pledged their participation. The increased resources include the $100 billion loan from Japan, and the members of the European Union had agreed to provide an additional $100 billion. Subsequently, Canada ($10 billion), South Korea ($10 billion), Norway ($4.5 billion), and Switzerland ($10 billion) agreed to subscribe additional funds. The Obama Administration has asked Congress to approve a U.S. subscription of $100 billion to the IMF 's New Arrangements to Borrow. China reportedly has said it is willing to provide $40 billion through possible purchases of IMF bonds [207] The sources for the remaining $145.5 billion of the planned increase in the NAB have not been announced.

The IMF reportedly is considering issuing bonds, something it has never done in its 60-year history [208] These would be sold to central banks and government agencies and not to the general public. According to economist and former IMF chief economist Michael Mussa, the United States and Europe previously blocked attempts by the IMF to issue bonds since it could potentially make the IMF less dependent on them for financial resources and thus less willing to take policy direction from them [209]. However, several other multilateral institutions such as the World Bank and the regional development banks routinely issue bonds to help finance their lending.

The IMF is not alone in making available financial assistance to crisis-afflicted countries. The International Finance Corporation (IFC), the private-sector lending arm of the World Bank, has announced that it will launch a $3 billion fund to capitalize small banks in poor countries that are battered by the financial crisis. The Inter-American Development Bank (IDB) announced on October 10, 2008 that it will offer a new $6 billion credit line to member governments as an increase to its traditional lending activities. In addition to the IDB, the Andean Development Corporation (CAF) announced a liquidity facility of $1.5 billion and the Latin American Fund of Reserves (FLAR) has offered to make available $4.5 billion in contingency lines. While these amounts may be insufficient should Brazil, Argentina, or any other large Latin American country need a rescue package, they could be very helpful for smaller countries such as those in the Caribbean and Central America that are heavily dependent on tourism and property investments.

Changes in U.S. Regulations and Regulatory Structure

Aside from the international financial architecture, a large question for Congress may be how U.S. regulations might be changed and how closely any changes are harmonized with international norms and standards. Related to that is whether U.S. oversight and regulatory agencies, government sponsored enterprises, credit rating firms, or other related institutions should be reformed, merged, their mandates changed, or rechartered. (Many of these questions are addressed in separate CRS reports.) [210].

As events have developed, policy proposals have been coming forth through the legislative process and from the Administration, but other proposals are emerging from recommendations by international organizations such as the IMF, [211] Bank for International Settlements, [212] and Financial Stability Forum [213].

The IMF has suggested various principles that could guide the scope and design of measures aimed at restoring confidence in the international financial system. They include:

- employ measures that are comprehensive, timely, clearly communicated, and operationally transparent;
- aim for a consistent and coherent set of policies to stabilize the global financial system across countries in order to maximize impact while avoiding adverse effects on other countries;
- ensure rapid response on the basis of early detection of strains;
- assure that emergency government interventions are temporary and taxpayer interests are protected; and
- pursue the medium-term objective of a more sound, competitive, and efficient financial system [214]

LEGISLATION

For legislation related to a fiscal stimulus and monetary policy, see CRS Report R40104, *Economic Stimulus: Issues and Policies*, by Jane G. Gravelle, Thomas L. Hungerford, and Marc Labonte and CRS Report RL34427, *Financial Turmoil: Federal Reserve Policy Responses*, by Marc Labonte.

For a discussion of housing legislation, see CRS Report RL34623, *Housing and Economic Recovery Act of 2008*, coordinated by N. Eric Weiss andCRS Report RL33879, *Housing Issues in the 110th Congress*, coordinated by Libby Perl.

For policy related to the financial sector, see CRS Report R40224, *Troubled Asset Relief Program and Foreclosures*, by N. Eric Weiss et al., and CRS Report RL34730, *Troubled Asset Relief Program: Legislation and Treasury Implementation*, by Baird Webel and Edward V. Murphy.

For policy related to government sponsored enterprises, see CRS Report RS21663, *Government- Sponsored Enterprises (GSEs): An Institutional Overview*, by Kevin R. Kosar.

For policy related to the International Monetary Fund, see CRS Report RS22976, *The Global Financial Crisis: The Role of the International Monetary Fund (IMF)*, by Martin A. Weiss.

Appendix A. Major Recent Actions and Events of the International Financial Crisis [215]

2009

May 7. The government's "stress tests" indicated that ten of the largest U.S. banks would have to raise a combined $74.6 billion in capital to cushion themselves against economic under- performance.

May 5. The European Commission lowered its growth forecast for the European Union to -4% in 2009 and -0.1% in 2010.

May 4. The International Monetary Fund approved a 24-month $17.1 billion Stand-By Arrangement for Romania. The total international financial support package will amount to $26.4 billion, with the European Union providing $6.6 billion, the World Bank $1.3 billion, and the European Bank for Reconstruction and Development, the European Investment Bank, and the International Finance Corporation a combined $1.3 billion.

April 30. Chrysler announced merger with Fiat and filed for bankruptcy. Separately, the Financial Accounting Standards Board changed the mark-to-market accounting rule to give banks more discretion in reporting value of assets.

April 22. The International Monetary Fund projected global economic activity to contract by 1.3% in 2009 with a slow recovery (1.9% growth) in 2010. Overall, the advanced economies are forecast to contract by 3.8% in 2009, with the U.S. economy shrinking by 2.8%.

*April 21.*The IMF estimated that banks and other financial institutions faced aggregate losses of $4.05 trillion in the value of their holdings as a result of the crisis. Of that amount, $2.7 trillion is from loans and assets originating in the United States, the fund said. That estimate is up from $2.2 trillion in the fund's interim report in January, and $1.4 trillion last October.

April 14. The IMF granted Poland a $20.5 billion credit line using a facility intended to backstop countries with sound economic policies that have been caught short by the global financial crisis. On April 1, Mexico said that it was tapping the new credit line for $47 billion.

April 2. At the G-20 London Summit, leaders of the world's largest economies agreed to tackle the global financial crisis with measures worth $1.1 trillion including $750 billion more for the International Monetary Fund, $250 billion to boost global trade, and $100 billion for multilateral development banks. They also agreed on establishing a new Financial Stability Board to work with the IMF to ensure cooperation across borders; closer regulation of banks, hedge funds, and credit rating agencies; and a crackdown on tax havens, but they could only agree on additional stimulus measures through IMF and multilateral development bank lending and not through country stimulus packages. The leaders reiterated their commitment to resist protectionism and promote global trade and investment.

April 1. The U.S. Conference Board's Consumer Confidence Index inched 0.7 of a point higher in March, virtually unchanged from the 42-year low reached in February. The present situation index has fallen from a cyclical peak of 138.3 in July 2007 to 21.5 this month.

Its record low was 15.8 in December 1982, when the unemployment rate stood at a post-war high of 10.8%.

April 1. Japan's economy shrank 3.3%, or by 12.7% in annual terms. This marked the deepest contraction in the economy since the first quarter of 1974, when the global economy was reacting to the oil shock, and the second-biggest decline in growth in the post-war era. Japan has experienced a record decline in exports. Total exports fell 13.9% in quarterly comparisons and by a stunning 45.0% in annual terms. These declines were mirrored by the Bank of Japan's quarterly business confidence survey, or tankan. The tankan results for the first quarter of 2009's headline Diffusion Index (DI) of business conditions for large manufacturing companies dropped to a reading of -58 in the three months through March from the -24 results recorded in the December quarter. The DI surveys respondents' business conditions expectations over the next three to six months. The reading for the first quarter was the worst on record.

April 1. Mexico's President Felipe Calderón claimed yesterday that his country was willing to take up a new credit line from the International Monetary Fund (IMF). He confirmed that government finances were "in order", allowing the country to boost central bank reserves via a new IMF borrowing of some US$30–40 billion as soon as this week. The IMF has failed to attract any borrower for a US$1 00-million loan offering last year. Potential borrowers may be concerned over conditionality requirements for loans and the negative message sent out when any economy requires IMF financing. The new Flexible Credit Line (FCL), launched recently by the IMF to attract developing nations, offers eligible countries easy access to large loans. Countries will be able to either immediately draw funds from the FCL, or keep it as an easily accessibly pool of finance.

March 31. The Organization for Economic Cooperation and Development (OECD) in a new survey reports worsening economic prospects. It is now expected that the global recession will worsen by an average GDP contraction of 4.3% in the OECD area in 2009 before a policy- induced recovery gradually builds strength through 2010. International trade is forecast to fall by more than 13% in 2009 and world economic activity will shrink by 2.7%. Specific forecasts include: U.S.: -4% in 2009 and 0% in 2010; Japan: -6.6% in 2009 and -0.5% in 2010; Eurozone: - 4.1% in 2009 and -0.3% in 2010. Brazil's GDP is expected to decline by 0.3% in 2009 while Russia's is projected to fall 5.6%. Growth in India will ease to 4.3% in 2009 and in China to 6.3%. By the end of 2010 unemployment rates across OECD nations may reach 10.1% from 7.5% in the first quarter of 2009. The unemployed in the 30 advanced OECD countries would increase by about 25 million, the largest and most rapid growth in OECD unemployment in the post-war period.

March 31. U.S. housing prices continue to fall. The Standard & Poor's S&P/Case-Shiller 20-City Composite Index fell 19.0% annually in January 2009, the fastest on record. High inventories and foreclosures continued to drive down prices. All 20 cities covered in the survey showed a decrease in prices, with 9 of the 20 areas showing rates of annual decline of over 20%.

As of January 2009, average home prices are at similar levels to what they were in the third quarter of 2003. From their peaks in mid-2006, the 10-City Composite is down 30.2% and the 20- City Composite is down 29.1%.

March 31. The World Trade Organization (WTO) predicted that the volume of global merchandise trade would shrink by 9% this year. This will be the first fall in trade flows since 1982. Between 1990 and 2006 trade volumes grew by more than 6% a year, easily outstripping the growth rate of world output, which was about 3%. Now the global economic machine has gone into reverse: output is declining and trade is shrinking faster.

March 30. The central banks of China and Argentina reached an agreement for a 70 billion yuan/U.S. $10 billion currency swap for three years, the sixth such swap China has concluded with emerging economies including South Korea, Hong Kong, Indonesia, Belarus and Malaysia. The move may provide capital to these emerging markets and may in the long-term promote the Chinese yuan's international role. For Argentina, these moves may help to offset challenges in securing foreign exchange financing.

March 24. The Executive Board of the International Monetary Fund (IMF) approved a major overhaul of the IMF 's lending framework, including the creation of a new Flexible Credit Line (FCL). The changes to the IMF's lending framework include:

- modernizing IMF conditionality for all borrowers,
- introducing a new Flexible Credit Line,
- enhancing the flexibility of the Fund's traditional stand-by arrangement,
- doubling normal access limits for nonconcessional resources,
- simplifying cost and maturity structures, and
- eliminating certain seldom-used facilities.

"These reforms represent a significant change in the way the Fund can help its member countries—which is especially needed at this time of global crisis," said IMF Managing Director Dominique Strauss-Kahn. "More flexibility in our lending along with streamlined conditionality will help us respond effectively to the various needs of members. This, in turn, will help them to weather the crisis and return to sustainable growth."

March 23. The U.S. Treasury released the details of its Public Private Partnership Investment Program to address the challenge of legacy toxic assets (mortgages and securities backed by loans) being carried by the financial system. The Treasury and the Federal Deposit Insurance Corporation with funding from the TARP and private capital are to purchase eligible assets worth about $500 billion with the potential to expand the program to $1 trillion.

March 20. The European Union announced additional support for the IMF's lending capacity in the form of a loan to the IMF totaling €75 billion, about US$100 billion.. The EU's common strategy is released. It focuses on regulating hedge funds, private equity, credit derivatives and credit rating agencies, and vowed to crack down on tax havens.

March 19. The U.S. Federal Reserve announced a plan to purchase longer-term Treasury securities. The Fed is now trying not just to influence the spread between private interest rates and Treasuries (through its mortgage-backed securities purchases, for example), but also to pull down the entire spectrum of interest rates by driving down the rate on benchmark Treasuries. Key points of yesterday's Fed announcement include:

- The federal funds rate, with a current target range of 0.0%–0.25%, is likely to remain exceptionally low for "an extended period." Last month, the Fed said the low rate would apply "for some time."

The Fed will purchase:

- up to an additional US$750 billion of agency mortgage-backed securities, for a total of US$1.25 trillion, and
- up to an additional US$100 billion of agency debt for a total of up to US$200 billion.
- It followed the central banks of the United Kingdom and Japan by announcing its intention to purchase longer-term Treasury securities (up to US$300 billion worth) over the next six months.
- It has launched its Term Asset-Backed Securities Loan Facility (TALF) program to support credit for households and small businesses, and may expand that program to other lending.
- The Fed anticipates that fiscal and monetary stimulus, plus policies aimed at stabilizing the financial sector, will contribute to a gradual resumption of growth—although it has not said when.

This announcement caused the 10-year Treasury yield to fall from just over 2.9% to under 2.6%. Mortgage rates should follow Treasury yields down and spark another refinancing wave. Economists question whether lower rates will revive home purchases as well as refinancing.

March 18. The Federal Reserve announced that it would buy approximately $1.2 trillion in government bonds and mortgage-related securities in order to lower borrowing costs for home mortgages and other types of loans.

March 11. Chinese total exports experienced their biggest fall on record in February declining 25.7% on the year in February, to US$64.9 billion. Imports also declined 24.1% on the year, And China's trade surplus shrank to a three-year low of US$4.84 billion from US$39.1 billion in January. For the first two months of the year combined, exports fell 21.1% from the same period of 2008. Trade contracted despite investment being supported by the recent rapid expansion of credit and by the release of funds under the government's four trillion yuan/US$580 billion fiscal stimulus package.

March 10. Finance Minister Najib Razak announced a large Malaysian fiscal stimulus package. The 60 billion ringgit/US$ 16.3 billion package is the government's second supplementary budget, after the initial 7 billion ringgit stimulus already implemented. The package equals 9.0% of gross domestic product (GDP).

March 10. Philippines' exports experienced a record contraction in January as global demand continued to decline. Official data showed that total exports fell 41% year-on-year to US$2.49 billion. In December, exports contracted by a revised 40.3% in annual terms. Shipments of electronics, which account for more than half of total exports, almost halved, shrinking 48.4% in annual terms to US$1.35 billion.

March 10. United Kingdom industrial production suffered the largest annual drop since January 1981 in January. Manufacturing output plunged by 2.9% month on month and 12.8% year on year in January 2009, according to the Office for National Statistics (ONS). This followed a drop of 1.9% monthly in December and marked the eleventh successive monthly decline in manufacturing output.

March 10. China's official registered unemployment rate hit a three-year high of 4.2% in 2008. Although during the post-Asian Financial Crisis slowdown, between 1979 and 1982, unemployment was mostly concentrated in the state sector, this time the private sector has experienced worse unemployment, with migrant labor being fired first, with no social programs for relief. The number of business failures is estimated to be 7.5% of the country's Small and Medium sized Enterprises (SMEs), or nearly 500,000 firms.

February 24. U.S. President Barack Obama used his first address to a joint session of Congress to outline how the economic recovery can work. He outlined the rationale behind the economic stimulus and the financial sector rescue plans, conceding costs and risks, but warning of the greater danger of inaction. President Obama promised to reduce the federal budget deficit by half by the end of his first term. On the same day, U.S. Federal Reserve Chairman Ben Bernanke testified to Congress that if the financial system is stabilized soon, the recession will end in 2009 and the economy will grow in 2010.

February 24. The Latvian government fell over fiscal adjustment measures that are required for Latvia to comply with the IMF-led rescue program terms. This caused Standard & Poor's (S&P) to reduce its sovereign rating for Latvia from BBB- to BB+. S&P has thus cut the Baltic State to junk bond status. Latvia's ratings among various rating institutions currently vary significantly, from BB+ to BBB+.

February 23. The Dow Jones Industrial Average lost 3.4% to close at 7113.78, its lowest level in 12 years, and just under half the high it reached 16 months ago. Banking stocks led the index down, and losses were experienced in most sectors. The U.S. market declines have influenced international declines as well. Japan's Nikkei 225 ended down 1.5%, Australia's S&P/ASX 200 was off by 0.6%, Taiwan's Taiex lost 1.1%, and China's Shanghai Composite fell 4.6%. Equities are wiping huge amounts off the market value of companies and investments including pensions worldwide.

February 23. The Chilean Finance Ministry announced that the Central Bank of Chile will conduct U.S. dollar auctions in March 2009, to finance a US$3 billion stimulus plan announced by President Michelle Bachelet in January. US$1 billion will be directed into fiscal spending transactions. These resources will be drawn from the country's sovereign wealth fund, which currently holds around US$20.11 billion.

February 20. Several Netherlands local and provincial councils have announced that they are planning to launch local stimulus packages to combat the country's economic crisis. The Dutch government is planning to invest €94 million in the local economy and infrastructure projects, including new street lighting and an upgrade of the sewage network. Rotterdam is planning to launch further measures to augment the €200 million package announced in January for the construction industry. Amsterdam plans to invest €200 million in its construction industry, while Utrecht is still exploring options.

February 18. The German government agreed on a revised bank bailout plan. The first version, from October 2008, cost 480 billion euro/U.S. $603.7 billion, has not delivered appropriate results. The new text must be ratified by parliament before taking effect. To ensure the stability of the German financial sector the new plan considers three factors. Expropriation would be a last resort only. Acceleration of state holdings of bank shares, changes to current stock corporation regulations are proposed. The stabilization fund for the financial markets would increase its debt guarantee time period.

February 17. President Obama signed a US$787 billion economic stimulus bill, 111th Congress bill H.R. 1, following House and Senate final votes on the conference report on February 13. As passed, the stimulus package includes some US$575 billion in government spending and US$212 billion in tax cuts.

February 17. U.S. automakers General Motors Corp. and Chrysler LLC submitted recovery plans to the U.S. government requesting U.S. $21.6 billion more in loans to enable their recovery.

February 17. Eastern Europe's deepening recession is putting pressure on those West European banks with local subsidiaries, Moody's Investors Service reports. The countries with the deepest fiscal deficits—the Baltic states, Bulgaria, Croatia, Hungary and Romania—have the highest external vulnerability. Moody's says Kazakhstan, Russia and Ukraine are also under pressure despite low public external debt. The Austrian banking system is the most exposed; banks there and in Belgium, France, Germany, Italy and Sweden account for 84% of total West European claims. Exposure is heavily concentrated among certain banking groups: Raiffeisen, Erste, Societe Generale, UniCredit and KBC. Modern banking has just emerged in Eastern Europe. Eastern subsidiaries are more vulnerable in times of stress, with deteriorating asset quality and vulnerable liquidity positions. EU member countries have failed to coordinate national stimulus programs, and there appears to be no willingness to finance large cross-border rescue packages.

February 16. Russian President Dmitry Medvedev replaced the governors of Pskov, Orel and Voronezh, as well as the Nenets Autonomous Region. The terminations suggest that the Kremlin is using the economic crisis as an excuse for getting rid of governors with whom the federal leadership was already unhappy. As local development levels and production profiles vary greatly, the crisis is having diverse effects on Russia's regions. Russian economic activity as a whole may suffer substantially in the crisis, but inequality across Russian regions may be reduced.

February 16. The Japanese economy contracted by 3.3% quarterly in December, the Cabinet Office reported on preliminary figures. At an annual rate, GDP fell by 12.7%, and is now performing at its worst since 1974.

February 16. In preparation for the London Leaders' summit in April, world leaders are drafting responses to the global financial crisis. The extent to which they agree on the causes of the crisis will be critical to policies proposed. Broad consensus on key features of the financial crisis now includes:

- Maturity. It emerged from a market-led process of change that spanned around 30 years, not two or three, and culminated in the long boom that began in the early 1990s.
- Regulatory failure. For many reasons, neither regulation nor regulators policed these processes.
- Opacity. A major contributory factor was the complexity and opacity of the activities and the balance sheets of major financial institutions.
- Credit boom. The boom resulted from countries' competitive deregulation of financial markets over some 30 years.
-

How these ingredients interacted to cause the crisis remains under debate. The G20 are likely to promote global measures that address both the underlying causes and more immediate responses.

February 14. Finance ministers and central bank governors of the Group of Seven (G7) industrialized nations met in Rome to discuss the financial crisis and economic slowdown. In order to prevent a resurgence of protectionism, the G7 communique pledged members to do all they could to combat recession without distorting free trade.

February 13. The U.S. federal government's monthly budget statement reported a deficit of US $83.8 billion in January 2009, compared with a US $17.8-billion surplus a year earlier. Both higher outlays and falling tax receipts led to the deficit. The deficit for the first four months of the 2009 fiscal year ballooned to a record US$569 billion. The Troubled Asset Relief Program (TARP) added about US$42 billion to the deficit in January, bringing TARP spending so far this fiscal year to US$284 billion.

February 13. Eurozone GDP declined by 1.5% quarterly and 1.2% annually in the fourth quarter of 2008, the sharpest contraction since the bloc came into being in January 1999.

February 12. Ukraine's Finance Minister Viktor Pynzenuk resigned; Fitch downgraded its long-term foreign and local currency issuer rating from "B+" to "B"; and an International Monetary Fund (IMF) mission left Ukraine last week. The IMF, which has not concluded its US $1.9 billion part of the Ukrainian aid package, called for immediate and serious crisis management. The IMF mission announced last week that a successful implementation of the financial rescue for the country is in jeopardy.

February 12. The Irish government reported a 7-billion-euro (US$9 billion) bank rescue plan for two of the country's largest banks, the Allied Irish Bank and the Bank of Ireland. Each bank will receive 3.5 billion euro in recapitalization funds. The government attached conditions including preference shares that the government will obtain, with a fixed annual dividend of 8%, partial control over the appointment of the banks' directors, and executive pay reductions with no bonuses.

February 12. China's State Council approved a stimulus plan yesterday for the shipbuilding industry, urging banks to expand trade finance for the export of vessels, and extending fiscal and financial support for domestic buyers of long-range ships until 2012. The government will also encourage industry restructuring, and force the replacement of outdated ships. The funds will facilitate shipping research and technology. Mergers and acquisitions will be encouraged for industry consolidation. This is the latest Chinese industry stimulus plan, following support for textiles, automotive, steel, and machinery industries over the past few weeks.

February 12. Chinalco, the Aluminum Corporation of China, announced an investment of US$19.5 billion in Australian mining group Rio Tinto. This investment is China's largest-ever overseas purchase. Chinalco will buy $7.2-billion worth of convertible bonds as well as Rio Tinto assets worth $12.3 billion. Rio Tinto assumed substantial debt in its purchase of Canadian aluminum maker Alcan in 2007.

February 12. The Swiss government presented a second economic stimulus plan worth 700 million Swiss francs (US$603 million). The funds are directed at infrastructure (390 million francs), regions (100 million francs), environment and energy (80 million francs), research (50 million francs), renovation of state buildings (40 million francs), and the tourism sector (12 million francs). The first rescue package worth some 900 million francs launched in November did not have its desired effectiveness.

February 12. Kuwait's Sovereign Wealth Fund lost 15% in 2008. The emirate's sovereign wealth fund lost nine billion dinars (US$30.9 billion) in 2008 as a result of the global economic downturn. One example of losses was the US$5-billion capital injection into Citibank and Merrill Lynch in 2008, which fell to US$2.2 billion before returning to its current value of US$2.8 billion. These figures come days after the government unveiled a

US$5.14-billion stimulus package which will be funded by the country's foreign-exchange reserves, as well as the Kuwait Investment Authority.

February 12. Australian legislature rejected fiscal stimulus package as Australian unemployment climbed to two-year high. The US$28 billion package failed over environmentalists' objections.

February 5. The Bank of England's Monetary Policy Committee reduced its key interest rate by 50 basis points from 1.50% to 1.00%. Interest rates are now at their lowest level since the Bank of England was founded in 1694.

February 3. British Prime Minister Gordon Brown and Chinese Premier Wen Jiabao said that coordination was necessary in order to avert the global financial crisis, at the end of Premier Wen's five-day tour of Europe. Prime Minister Brown said that the United Kingdom is planning to double annual exports within the coming 18 months, from £5 billion to £10 billion. He stressed that the United Kingdom will benefit from China's recent stimulus packages, particularly the aerospace, hi-tech manufacturing, education, pharmaceuticals, and low-carbon technologies industries. China and the European Union (EU) have agreed to hold summit talks soon to increase economic cooperation.

February 3. Chinese President Hu Jintao will travel to Mali, Senegal, Tanzania, Mauritius, and Saudi Arabia from February 10 to February 17, 2009. Despite the global economic downturn the Chinese government is increasing investment in Africa and the Middle East. Chinese-African trade has been increasing by an average of 30% per year, almost reaching US$107 billion in 2008.

February 3. China will give Senegal several cooperation projects, including a museum, a theater, a children's hospital, and repair of sports stadiums worth some 80 million yuan or U.S. $11.5 million. This brings the total of pledged Chinese investments to Senegal in 2009 to US$117.3 million, including projects for power services, transport equipment and information technology infrastructure.

February 2. The government of Kazakhstan announced nationalization of two banks, BTA Bank, the nation's largest bank, and Alliance Bank, the nations third-largest bank. The government reported it is considering a possible sale of half of its stake in BTA Bank to Russia's Sberbank. The Kazakh government now owns 78.1% of BTA Bank.

February 2. A survey conducted jointly by the Afghan government and the United Nations forecast that opium production in Afghanistan will decline for the second consecutive year in 2009. The report estimates that the total area of poppy fields under cultivation declined to 378,950 acres, a 19% decline from the previous year. The survey also indicated that poppy cultivation in the main producing regions of the south and the southwest fell for the first time in five years. The decline was largely attributable to recent sharp falls in global prices for opiates following saturation of the market and the negative impact of drought. Farmers had also shifted production to staple grains after global prices surged in the first half of 2008. The survey indicates that prices for dry opium tumbled 25% in 2008 while wheat and rice prices rose 49% and 26% respectively. Afghanistan accounts for 90% of the world's supply of opium with proceeds from trafficking providing a main source of income for insurgents in the border regions with Pakistan.

February 2. Ireland average prices for housing declined by 9.1% in 2008 compared with a fall of 7.3% in 2007. Also, Moody's Ratings Services revised its sovereign outlook for Ireland to negative from stable on the basis of mounting fiscal pressures, economic deterioration, and the government's potentially damaging exposure to the banking sector. This follows a similar revision from Standard & Poor's in January.

January 30. The U.S. Bureau of Economic Analysis (BEA) announced that preliminary real gross domestic product (GDP)—the output of goods and services produced by labor and property located in the United States – for 2008 rose 1.3%, down from 2.0% in 2007. Real GDP decreased at an annual rate of 3.8 percent in the fourth quarter of 2008, the largest decline since the first quarter of 1982.

January 30. South Korea reported that industrial output fell 9.6% in December. Total output tumbled by 18.6% in annual terms compared with the 14.0% decline in November, which was the second-largest decrease in production since the series began in 1970.

January 30. Finland reported that industrial output declined by 15.6% year-on-year in December, after falling by a revised rate of more than 9.0% in November. Production decreased in all main industrial sectors. Also, the Finnish government announced an increase in government expenditure of 1.2 billion euro to support the flagging economy. Additional funds are to be allocated to construction, renovation and transport infrastructure projects.

January 29-February 1. The World Economic Forum (WEF) met in Davos, Switzerland. Chinese Premier Wen Jiabao and Russian Premier Vladimir Putin blamed the U.S.-led financial system for the global financial crisis. European Central Bank (ECB), President, Jean-Claude Trichet noted that the ECB is drafting guidelines for European governments' establishment of "bad banks", to consolidate toxic assets.

January 29. Thailand's parliament approved a $3.35 billion stimulus package aimed at boosting its economy battered by months of street protests. Final approval was expected in February.

January 28. The International Monetary Fund (IMF) revised its forecast for world economic growth down to 0.5% for 2009. This would be the lowest level of growth since World War II and down by 1.7 percentage points since the IMF forecast in November 2008. The IMF indicated that despite wide-ranging policy actions by governments and central banks, financial markets are still under stress and the global economy is taking a turn for the worse. The IMF urged governments to take decisive action to restore financial sector health (by providing liquidity and capital and helping to dispose of problem assets) and to provide macroeconomic stimulus (both monetary and fiscal) to support sagging demand.

January 28. Canada announced a $32 billion stimulus package that included infrastructure spending and tax cuts.

January 28. The U.S. House of Representatives passed the American Recovery and Reinvestment Act of 2009 (H.R. 1, Obey). The cost of the bill was estimated at $819 billion.

January 26. Australia announced a $2.6 billion stimulus package.

January 22. Malaysia announced it is preparing a second economic stimulus package to fend off the threat of recession. Singapore unveiled a $13.7 billion stimulus package.

*January 21.*The Philippines announced a $633 million increase to bring its stimulus program to $6.9 billion.

January 15. The U.S. Senate voted to release the second half of the Treasury's Troubled Assets Recovery Package (TARP) to stabilize the U.S. financial system, granting President-elect Barack Obama authority to spend $350 billion to revive credit markets and help homeowners avoid foreclosure. The Treasury Department announced it would fund a rescue of Bank of America which guarantees $118 billion in troubled assets.

January 6. Chile announced a $4 billion stimulus package.

January 1. Belarus devalued its national currency, the Belarusian ruble, by over 20%. The National Bank announced that it will tie its currency immediately to a basket of three currencies—the U.S. dollar, the euro and the Russian ruble.

2008

December 31. The International Monetary Fund (IMF) gave tentative approval to Belarus for a US$2.5 billion 15 month Stand By Arrangement. Final approval will be decided by the IMF executive board in January.

December 30. South Korea reported that the industrial output index declined by 14.1% annually and by 10.7% monthly. The monthly contraction was the largest in 21 years. The slump in production is closely tied with the sharp reverse in exports, which fell by 18.3%.

December 30. Monetary Union Pact approved by Gulf Cooperation Council (GCC)—Bahrain, Kuwait, Qatar, Saudi Arabia, and the United Arab Emirates. Representatives from five of the six members of the GCC approved a draft accord for a monetary union yesterday at a summit in Muscat. GCC finance ministers did not agree on the ultimate location of the future central bank. The draft accord prepares for the creation of a monetary council, and the framework for a future monetary union.

December 26. The Japanese Ministry of Economy, Trade and Industry released preliminary figures showing that industrial production shrank at a record rate and unemployment rose. Total industrial output contracted 8.1% from October to November 2008. This marked the largest decline in industrial production in 55 years.

December 23. Poland's Monetary Policy Council reduced its main policy rate by 75 basis points. The Polish main policy rate has been reduced by 1% in two months, and now stands at 5.00%.

December 23. Japanese Cabinet approves record fiscal plan for FY2009. The ¥88.5 trillion (US$980.6 billion) fiscal package for FY2009, which begins April 1, 2009, marks a 6.6% increase in spending from initial targets.

December 23. After the IMF submitted a positive review of Iraq's economic reconstruction, the Paris Club of sovereign lenders completed the third and final step of debt forgiveness for Iraq, reducing Iraq's public external debt with its members by 20% or US$7.8 billion. Most of Iraq's remaining debt consists of official loans from Gulf Arab states and former communist countries, which may be forgiven or discounted if Iraq's economy continues to improve. Under former President Saddam Hussein, Iraq's debt totaled $125 billion.

December 23. New Zealand Real GDP declined 0.4% in quarterly seasonally adjusted terms. This marks the third consecutive quarterly decline in Real GDP. The economy fell into its first recession in more than a decade in the March, 2008. The rate of contraction deepened from the first two quarters of the year during which growth shrank by 0.3% and 0.2% respectively. In annual terms, the economy grew 1.7% in the year through September 2008.

December 23. The central People's Bank of China lowered interest rates for the fifth time in four months. Benchmark one-year lending and deposit rates were both lowered by 27 basis points to 5.31% and 2.25% respectively. These rates were lowered by their biggest margin in 11 years a month ago, lowered by 108 basis points.

December 22. U.K. Real GDP contracted by 0.6% quarterly in the third quarter of 2008. The Office for National Statistics (ONS) revised the decline in real GDP from its previous estimate of 0.5% quarterly. This marks the first time that the British economy has contracted since the second quarter of 1992. It had stagnated in the second quarter of 2008 and is therefore on the brink of recession, defined as two successive quarters of contracting quarterly GDP. Prior to that, GDP growth had moderated to 0.4% in the first quarter of 2008 from 0.6% in the fourth quarter of 2007 and 0.8% in the third quarter. Annual GDP growth fell to a 16-year low of 0.3% in the third quarter of 2008 from 1.7% in the second quarter and a peak of 3.3% in the second quarter of 2007. Industrial production contracted by 1.4% quarterly, and 2.5% annually in the third quarter, with manufacturing output down by 1.6% quarterly and 2.3% annually. This marks the third successive quarterly decrease in industrial production, meaning that the sector is already in recession.

December 22. Russia reports that industrial output growth slowed to 0.6% annual growth in October, then contracted by 8.7% annually in November, the worst monthly report since the economic collapse which followed the ruble crisis of 1998. Critical to Russia's economic slowdown is the unwillingness of Russian banks, which are heavily exposed to foreign currency denominated external debt, to lend.

December 21. Eurostat reports that Eurozone industrial orders fell 5.4% monthly in September and 4.7% monthly and 15.1% annually in October.

December 21. Canada reports that its federal government and the province of Ontario will contribute some C$4 billion (US$3.3 billion) to the short-term automotive rescue announced by the U.S. administration. The United States will provide US$13.4 billion in emergency loans to General Motors and Chrysler. General Motors is to receive C$3 billion of the Canadian funds, while Chrysler is to receive C$ 1 billion. Ford declines injections. Limits on executive compensation are a requirement for funds.

December 21. Zimbabwe reports its domestic debt level increased from Z$1 trillion on August 8 to Z$ 179.6 trillion (US$194 million at the current official inter-bank exchange rate) on September 8. This represents a monthly increase of 17,800%. Interest payments now account for roughly 90% of total debt.

December 19. President Bush announced an automotive rescue plan for General Motors Corp. and Chrysler LLC that will make $13.4 billion in federal loans available almost immediately. The money will come from the $700 billion fund set aside to rescue banks and investment firms in October. The government attached several conditions to the three-year loans and set a deadline of March 31 for the automakers to prove they can restructure enough to ensure their survival or recall the loans. As part of the rescue, GM is required to reduce debt by two-thirds via debt-forequity swaps, pay half of the contributions to a retiree health care trust using stock, make union workers' wages competitive with foreign automakers and eliminate the union jobs bank, which pays laid-off workers.

December 19. An international rescue package of 7.5 billion euro (US$ 10.6 billion) for Latvia was announced. The IMF reports a 27-month stand by arrangement between Latvia and the IMF, worth 1.7 billion euro (US$2.4 billion). The remainder of the rescue package includes 3.1 billion euro from the European Union (EU), 1.8 billion euro from Nordic countries, 400 million euro from the World Bank, 200 million euro from the Czech Republic, and 100 million euro each from the European Bank of Reconstruction and Development, Estonia and Poland. Latvia nationalized its second largest bank, Parex Bank. Latvia will implement measures to tighten fiscal policy and stabilize its economy.

December 19. The Bank of Japan lowered the benchmark rate by 20 basis points to 0.3%. This marks the second consecutive monthly cut.

December 18. Turkey reduces rates for the second consecutive month. The Central Bank of the Republic of Turkey (CBRT) announced a 125-basis-point cut to their overnight borrowing rate from 16.25% to 15.00%, and their overnight lending rate by 125 basis points, from 18.75% to 17.50%. Turkish interest rates are the highest in Europe, even after the rate cuts.

December 18. Mexican industrial output decreased an annual 2.7% in October, the sixth consecutive monthly decline. More than 80% of Mexico's exports go to the United States.

December 18. Norwegian Central Bank cut its main policy interest rate by 175 basis points to 3.0%, the third decrease since October.

December 17. U.S. housing starts plummeted 18.9% in November, to a seasonally adjusted annual rate of 625,000 units. This was a record monthly low.

December 16. The U.S. Federal Open Market Committee (FOMC) voted unanimously to lower its target for the federal funds rate more than 75 basis points, to a range of 0.0% to 0.25%. Long term bond yields dropped from 2.50% to 2.35%.

December 15. The Bank of Japan's tankan survey of business confidence fell from minus 3 in the third quarter to minus 24 points in the fourth quarter of the year. The 21 point contraction was the steepest in the index since the oil shocks of the 197 0s, and marked the lowest level in the index since 2002.

December 12. Ecuador's President Rafael Correa announced that Ecuador will stop honoring its external debt; the country should expect lawsuits from bondholders in the short term. This is not the same as declaring the entire Ecuadorean economy in default.

December 11. 27 European Union (EU) governments' leaders approved a 200 billion euro (US$269 billion) economic stimulus package. The cost is approximately 1.5% of the EU's total GDP. Member states will pay major shares; supranational EU institutions, such as the European Investment Bank (EIB), will contribute the remaining 30 billion euro.

December 11. Taiwan's central bank cut its leading discount rate by three quarters of a percentage point to 2.0%, marking the biggest reduction since 1982. It was also the fifth rate cut in two-and-a-half months.

December 11. The central Bank of Korea reduced the seven-day repurchase rate by one percentage point to a record low of 3.00%. Interest rates have been reduced by 225 basis points in two months, 100 basis points in October and 125 basis points in November.

December 5. November U.S. nonfarm employment loss of 533,000 jobs was the largest in 34 years, compared with the 602,000 decline in December 1974. The U.S. Bureau of Labor Statistics also reported the unemployment rate rose from 6.5 to 6.7 percent. November's drop in payroll employment followed declines of 403,000 in September and 320,000 in October, as revised.

November 25. U.S. real GDP fell 0.5% in the third quarter of 2008. The announcement by the U.S. Bureau of Economic Analysis also reported U.S. second quarter GDP increased 2.8%. BEA attributed the third quarter decline to a contraction in consumer spending and deceleration in exports.

November 24. The U.K. announced a fiscal stimulus package valued at £20 billion (US$30.2 billion) aimed at limiting the length and depth of the apparent U.K. recession. The package included a temporary reduction of value-added tax from 17.5% to 15.0%.

November 24. The IMF Executive Board approved a 23-month Stand-By Arrangement for Pakistan in the amount of $7.6 billion to support the country's economic stabilization program.

November 24. The Central Bank of Iceland's currency swap arrangement with Sweden, Norway, and Denmark is extended through December 2009. On the same date, Standard & Poor's Ratings Services, S&P, reduced its long-term Iceland sovereign credit rating from BBB to BBB-, while maintaining its short-term Iceland sovereign currency rating at A-3.

November 24. The U.S. Treasury, Federal Reserve, and Federal Deposit Insurance Corp. said that they will protect Citigroup against certain potential losses and invest an additional $20 billion (on top of the previous $25 billion) in the company. The government is to receive $7 billion in preferred shares in the company.

November 15. At a G-20 (including the G-8, 10 major emerging economies, Australia and the European Union) summit in Washington, the G-20 leaders agreed to continue to take steps to stabilize the global financial system and improve the international regulatory framework.

November 15. Japan announced that it would make $100 billion from its foreign exchange reserves available to the IMF for loans to emerging market economies. This was in addition to $2 billion that Japan is to invest in the World Bank to help recapitalize banks in smaller, emerging market economies. Also, the IMF and Pakistan agreed in principle on a $7.6 billion loan package aimed at preventing the nation from defaulting on foreign debt and restoring investor confidence.

November 14. The President's Working Group on Financial Markets (Treasury, Securities and Exchange Commission, Federal Reserve, and the Commodity Futures Trading Commission) announced a series of initiatives to strengthen oversight and the infrastructure of the over-the- counter derivatives market. This included the development of credit default swap central counterparties—clearinghouses between parties that own debt instruments and others willing to insure against defaults.

November 13. The African Development bank conference on the financial crisis ended with a pessimistic outlook for Sub-Saharan Africa, due to declines in foreign capital, export markets and commodity-based exports.

November 13. Eurostat declared that Eurozone GDP declined by 0.2% in the third quarter of 2008, as well as the second quarter. Since recession is defined as two successive quarters of contracting GDP, this means that the Eurozone is technically in recession.

November 12. United States Treasury Secretary Paulson announced a change in priorities for the US$700 billion Troubled Asset Relief Program (TARP) approved by Congress in early October. The first priority remains to provide direct equity infusions to the financial sector. Roughly US$250 billion has been allocated to this sector. This scope was broadened to include non-banks, particularly insurance companies such as AIG, which provide insurance for credit defaults. Paulson noted that TARP would be used to purchase bank stock, not toxic assets. Paulson's new plan also would provide support for the asset-backed commercial paper market, particularly securitized auto loans, credit card debt, and student loans. Between August and November 2007 asset-backed commercial paper outstanding contracted by nearly US$400 billion. Paulson rejected suggestions that TARP funds be made available to the U.S. auto industry.

November 12. The Central Bank of Russia raised key interest rates by 1%. Swiss Economics Minister announced the Swiss government would inject 341 million Swiss Francs/US$286.6 million for economic stimulus. The State Bank of Pakistan raised interest rates by 2%, to reduce inflation. It also injected 320 billion rupees/US$4 billion into the Pakistan banking system.

November 11. IMF deferred their decision to approve US$2.1 billion loan for Iceland. This was the third time the IMF board scheduled then failed to discuss the Iceland proposal. The tentative Iceland package required Iceland to implement economic stabilization. That economic stabilization was the required trigger for implementation of EU loans to Iceland from Norway, Poland and Sweden. Iceland is reportedly involved in disputes over deposit guarantees with British and Dutch depositors in Icelandic banks.

November 10. The United States government announced further aid to American International Group, AIG. AIG's September $85 billion loan was reduced to $60 billion; the government bought $40 billion of preferred AIG shares, and $52.5 billion of AIG mortgage securities. The U.S. support of AIG increased from September's $85 billion to $150 billion.

November 7. Iceland's President Grimsson reportedly offered the use of the former U.S. Air Force base at Keflavik to Russia. The United States departed Keflavik in 2006.

November 3. IMF announced agreement with Kyrgyzstan on arrangement under the Exogenous Shocks Facility to provide at least U.S. $60 million. The agreement requires the approval of the IMF Executive Board to become final.

November 9. G-20 meeting of finance ministers and central bank governors in Sao Paulo, Brazil, concluded with a communiqué calling for increased role of emerging economies in reform of Bretton Woods financial institutions, including the World Bank and the International Monetary Fund.

November 9. China announced a 4 trillion Yuan/U.S. $587 billion domestic stimulus package. primarily aimed at infrastructure, housing, agriculture, health care, and social welfare spending. This program represents 16% of China's 2007 GDP, and roughly equals total Chinese central and local government outlays in 2006.

November 8. Latvian government took over Parex Bank, the second-largest bank in Latvia.

November 7. United States October employment report revealed a decline of 240,000 jobs in October, and September job losses revised from 159,000 to 284,000. The U.S. unemployment rate rose from 6.1% to 6.5%, a 14-year high.

November 7. Moody's sovereign rating for Hungary is reduced from A2 to A3. Despite IMF assistance, financial instability may require "severe macroeconomic and financial adjustment." Moody's reduced its ratings of Latvia from A3 to A2, before the Latvian statistical office announced Latvian GDP fell at a 4.2% annual rate in the third quarter of 2008. Moody's also announced an outlook reduction for Estonia and Lithuania.

November 6. IMF approved SDR 10.5 billion/U.S. $15.7 billion Stand-By Arrangement for Hungary. U.S. $6.3 billion is to be immediately available.

November 6. International Monetary Fund announced its updated World Economic Outlook. Main findings include that "global activity is slowing quickly", and "prospects for global growth have deteriorated over the past month." The IMF now projects global GDP growth for 2009 at 2.2% , 3/4 of a percentage point lower than projections announced in October, 2008. It projects U.S. GDP growth at 1.4% in 2008 and -0.7% in 2009.

November 6. The European Central Bank, ECB, reduced its key interest rate from 3.75% to 3.25%. In two months the ECB has reduced this rate from 4.25% to 3.25%. The Danish Central Bank lowered its key lending rate from 5.5% to 5%. The Czech National Bank reduced its interest rate from 3.5% to 2.75%. In South Korea, the Bank of Korea reduced its key interest rate from 4.25% to 4%. During October the Bank of Korea reduced its rate from 5.25% to 4.25%.

November 4. United States Institute of Supply Management's manufacturing index fell 4.6 points in October to 38.9, after previously falling in September. The export orders component of the manufacturing index fell 11 points in October to 41, following a drop of 5 points in September. 41 is the lowest level in this export index in 20 years. Exports have been the strongest sector in U.S. manufacturing during the past year.

November 4. Australia. Reserve Bank of Australia lowered its overnight cash rate by 75 basis points to 5.25%, the lowest Australian rate since March 2005.

November 4. Indian Prime Minister Manmohan Singh established a Cabinet-level committee to evaluate the effect of the financial crisis on India's economy and industries. This follows the November 2 Indian and Pakistani Central banks' actions to boost liquidity. India cut its short- term lending rate by 50 basis points to 7.5% and reduced its cash reserve ratio by 100 basis points to 5.5%.

November 4. Chilean President Michelle Bachelet announced a U.S. $1.15 billion stimulus package to boost the housing market and channel credit into small and medium businesses.

November 3. Russian Prime Minister Vladimir Putin reported measures to support the real economy. The measures will include temporary preferences for domestic producers for state procurement contracts, subsidizing interest rates for loans intended to modernize production; and tariff protection for a number of industries such as automobiles and agriculture. The new policy aims to support exporters.

October 31. Three of the six Gulf Cooperation Council, GCC, countries, Bahrain, Kuwait and Saudi Arabian central banks reduced interest rates to follow the actions of the U.S. Federal Reserve and other central banks.

October 31. Kazakhstan government will make capital injections into its top four banks, Halyk Bank, Kazkommertsbank, Alliance Bank and BTA Bank.

October 31. The U.S. Commerce Department reported that consumer spending fell 0.3% in September after remaining flat in the previous month. On a year-to-year basis, spending was down 0.4%, the first such drop since the recession of 1991. Consumer spending has not grown since June.

October 30. The U.S. Bureau of Economic Analysis reported that U.S. real gross domestic product decreased 0.3 per cent in the third quarter of 2008 after increasing 2.8 per cent in the second quarter of 2008.

October 29. The U.S. Federal Reserve lowered its target for the federal funds rate 50 basis points to 1 per cent. It also approved a 50 basis point decrease in the discount rate to 1.25 per cent. The Federal Reserve also announced establishment of temporary reciprocal currency arrangements, or swap lines, with the Banco Central do Brasil, the Banco de Mexico, the Bank of Korea, the Monetary Authority of Singapore, and the Reserve Bank of New Zealand. Swap lines are designed to help improve liquidity conditions in global financial markets.

October 29. IMF approved the creation of a Short-Term Liquidity Facility, established to support countries with strong policies which face temporary liquidity problems.

October 28. The IMF, the European Union, and the World Bank announced a joint financing package for Hungary totaling $25.1 billion to bolster its economy. The IMF is to lend Hungary $15.7 billion, the EU $8.1 billion, and the World Bank $1.3 billion.

October 28. The U.S. Conference Board said that its consumer confidence index has dropped to an all-time low, from 61.4 in September to 38 in October.

October 27. Iceland's Kaupthing Bank became the first European borrower to default on yen- denominated bonds issued in Japan (samurai bonds).

October 26. The IMF announced it is set to lend Ukraine $16.5 Billion.

October 24. IMF announced an outline agreement with Iceland to lend the country $2.1 billion to support an economic recovery program to help it restore confidence in its banking system and stabilize its currency.

October 23. President Bush called for the G-20 leaders to meet on November 15 in Washington, DC to deal with the global financial crisis.

October 22. Pakistan sought help from the IMF to meet balance of payments difficulties and to avoid a possible economic meltdown amid high fuel prices, dwindling foreign investment and soaring militant violence.

G-20. The Group of 20 Finance Ministers and Central Bank Governors from industrial and emerging-market countries is to meet in Sao Paulo, Brazil on November 8-9, 2008, to discuss key issues related to global economic stability.

October 20. The Netherlands agreed to inject €10 billion ($13.4 billion) into ING Groep NV, a global banking and insurance company. The investment is to take the form of nonvoting preferred shares with no maturity date (ING can repay the money on its own schedule and will have the right to buy the shares back at 150% of the issue price or convert them into ordinary shares in three years). The government is to take two seats on ING's supervisory board; ING's executive- board members are to forgo 2008 bonuses; and ING said it would not pay a dividend for the rest of 2008.

October 20. Sweden proposed a financial stability plan, which includes a 1.5 trillion Swedish kronor ($206 billion) bank guarantee, to combat the impact of the economic crisis.

October 20. The U.N.'s International Labor Organization projects that the global financial crisis could add at least 20 million people to the world's unemployed, bringing the total to 210 million by the end of 2009.

October 19. South Korea announced that it would guarantee up to $100 billion in foreign debt held by its banks and would pump $30 billion more into its banking sector.

October 18. President Bush, President Nicolas Sarkozy of France, and the president of the European Commission issued a joint statement saying they agreed to "reach out to other world leaders" to propose an international summit meeting to be held soon after the U.S. presidential election, with the possibility of more gatherings after that. The Europeans had been pressing for a meeting of the Group of 8 industrialized nations, but President Bush went one step further, calling for a broader global conference that would include "developed and developing nations"—among them China and India.

October 17. The Swiss government said it would take a 9% stake ($5.36 billion) in UBS, one of the country's leading banks, and set up a $60 billion fund to absorb the bank's troubled assets. UBS had already written off $40 billion of its $80 billion in "toxic American securities." The Swiss central bank was to take over $31 billion of the bank's American assets (much of it in the form of debt linked to subprime and Alt-A mortgages, and securities linked to commercial real estate and student loans).

October 15. The G8 leaders (Canada, France, Germany, Italy, Japan, Russia, the United Kingdom and the United States, and the European Commission) stated that they were united in their commitment to resolve the current crisis, strengthen financial institutions, restore confidence in the financial system, and provide a sound economic footing for citizens and businesses. They stated that changes to the regulatory and institutional regimes for the world's financial sectors are needed and that they look forward to a leaders' meeting with key countries at an appropriate time in the near future to adopt an agenda for reforms to meet the challenges of the 21st century.

October 14. In coordination with European monetary authorities, the U.S. Treasury, Federal Reserve, and Federal Deposit Insurance Corporation announced a plan to invest up to $250 billion in preferred securities of nine major U.S. banks (including Citigroup, Bank of America, Wells Fargo, Goldman Sachs and JPMorgan Chase). The FDIC also became able to temporarily guarantee the senior debt and deposits in non-interest bearing deposit transaction accounts (used mainly by businesses for daily operations) [216]

October 12-13. Several European countries (Germany, France, Italy, Austria, Netherlands, Portugal, Spain, and Norway) announced rescue plans for their countries worth as much as $2.7 trillion. The plans were largely consistent with a U.K. model that includes concerted action, recapitalization, state ownership, government debt guarantees (the largest component of the plans), and improved regulations.

October 8. In a coordinated effort, the U.S. Federal Reserve, the European Central Bank, the Bank of England and the central banks of Canada and Sweden all reduced primary lending rates by a half percentage point. Switzerland also cut its benchmark rate, while the Bank of Japan endorsed the moves without changing its rates. The Chinese central bank also reduced its key interest rate and lowered bank reserve requirements. The Federal Reserve's benchmark short- term rate stood at 1.5% and the European Central Bank's at 3.75%.

October 5. The German government moved to guarantee all private savings accounts and arranged a bailout for Hypo Real Estate, a German lender. A week earlier, Fortis, a large banking and insurance company based in Belgium but active across much of Europe, had received €11.2 billion ($8.2 billion) from the governments of the Netherlands, Belgium and Luxembourg. On October 3, the Dutch government seized its Dutch operations and on October 5, the Belgian government helped to arrange for BNP-Paribas, the French bank, to take over what was left of the company.

October 3. U.S. House of Representatives passes 110th Congress bill H.R. 1424, Financial Institutions Rescue bill, clearing it for Presidential signing or veto. President signs bill into law, P.L. 110-343, the Emergency Economic Stabilization Act of 2008, sometimes referred to as the Troubled Assets Relief Program, TARP. The new bill's title includes its purpose:

> "A bill to provide authority for the Federal Government to purchase and insure certain types of troubled assets for the purposes of providing stability to and preventing disruption in the economy and financial system and protecting taxpayers ... "

October 3. Britain's Financial Services Authority said it had raised the amount guaranteed in savings accounts to £50,000 ($88,390) from £35,000. Greece also stated that it would guarantee savings accounts regardless of the amount.

October 3. Wells Fargo Bank announced a takeover of Wachovia Corp, the fourth-largest U.S. bank. (Previously, Citibank had agreed to take over Wachovia.)

October 1. U.S. Senate passed H.R. 1424, amended, Financial Institutions Rescue bill.

September/October. On September 30, Iceland's government took a 75% share of Glitnir, Iceland's third-largest bank, by injecting €600 million ($850 million) into the bank. The following week, it took control of Landsbanki and soon after placed Iceland's largest bank, Kaupthing, into receivership as well.

September 26. Washington Mutual became the largest thrift failure with $307 billion in assets. JPMorgan Chase agreed to pay $1.9 billion for the banking operations but did not take ownership of the holding company.

September 22. Ireland increased the statutory limit for the deposit guarantee scheme for banks and building societies from €20,000 ($26,000) to €100,000 ($130,000) per depositor per institution.

September 21. The Federal Reserve approved the transformation of Goldman Sachs and Morgan Stanley into bank holding companies from investment banks in order to increase oversight and allow them to access the Federal Reserve's discount (loan) window.

September 18. Treasury Secretary Paulson announced a $700 billion economic stabilization proposal that would allow the government to buy toxic assets from the nation's biggest banks, a move aimed at shoring up balance sheets and restoring confidence within the financial system. An amended bill to accomplish this was passed by Congress on October 3.

September 16. The Federal Reserve came to the assistance of American International Group, AIG, an insurance giant on the verge of failure because of its exposure to exotic securities known as credit default swaps, in an $85 billion deal (later increased to $123 billion).

September 15. Lehman Brothers bankruptcy at $639 billion is the largest in the history of the United States.

September 14. Bank of America said it will buy Merrill Lynch for $50 billion.

September 7. U.S. Treasury announced that it was taking over Fannie Mae and Freddie Mac, two government-sponsored enterprises that bought securitized mortgage debt.

August 12. According to Bloomberg, losses at the top 100 banks in the world from the U.S. subprime crisis and the ensuing credit crunch exceeded $500 billion as write downs spread to more asset types.

May 4. Finance ministers of 13 Asian nations agreed to set up a foreign exchange pool of at least $80 billion to be used in the event of another regional financial crisis. China, Japan and South Korea are to provide 80% of the funds with the rest coming from the 10 members of ASEAN.

March. The Federal Reserve staved off a Bear Stearns bankruptcy by assuming $30 billion in liabilities and engineering a sale of Bear Sterns to JPMorgan Chase for a price that was less than the worth of Bear's Manhattan office building.

February 17. The British government decided to "temporarily" nationalize the struggling housing lender, Northern Rock. A previous government loan of $47 billion had proven ineffective in helping the company to recover.

January. Swiss banking giant UBS reported more than $18 billion in writedowns due to exposure to U.S. real estate market. Bank of America acquired Countrywide Financial, the largest mortgage lender in the United States.

Appendix B. Stimulus Packages Announced by Governments

Date Announced	Country	$Billion	Status, Package Contents
17-Feb-09	United States	787.00	Infrastructure technology, tax cuts, education, transfers to states, energy, nutrition, health, unemployment benefits. Budget in deficit.
4-Feb-09	Canada	32.00	Two-year program. Infrastructure, tax relief, aid for sectors in peril. Government to run an estimated $1.1 billion budget deficit in 2008 and $52 billion deficit in 2009.
7-Jan-09	Mexico	54.00	Infrastructure, a freeze on gasoline prices, reducing electricity rates, help for poor families to replace old appliances, construction of low-income housing and an oil refinery, rural development, increase government purchases from small- and medium-sized companies. Paid for by taxes, oil revenues, and borrowing.
12-Dec-08	European Union	39.00	Total package of $256 billion called for states to increase budgets by $217 billion and for the EU to provide $39 billion to fund cross-border projects including clean energy and upgraded telecommunications architecture.
13-Jan-09	Germany	65.00	Infrastructure, tax cuts, child bonus, increase in some social benefits, $3,250 incentive for trading in cars more than nine years old for a new or slightly used car.
24-Nov-08	United Kingdom	29.60	Proposed plan includes a 2.5% cut in the value added tax for 13 months, a postponement of corporate tax increases, government guarantees for loans to small and midsize businesses, spending on public works, including public housing and energy efficiency. Plan includes an increase in income taxes on those making more than $225,000 and increase National Insurance contribution for all but the lowest income workers.
5-Nov-08	France	33.00	Public sector investments (road and rail construction, refurbishment and improving ports and river infrastructure, building and renovating universities, research centers, prisons, courts, and monuments) and loans for carmakers. Does not include the previously planned $15 billion in credits and tax breaks on investments by companies in 2009.
16-Nov-08	Italy	52.00	Awaiting final parliamentary approval. Three year program. Measures to spur consumer credit, provide loans to companies, and rebuild infrastructure. February 6, announced a $2.56 billion stimulus package that was part of the three-year program that includes payments of up to $1,950 for trading in an old car for a new, less polluting one and 20% tax deductions for purchases of appliances and furniture.
22-Nov-08	Netherlands	7.50	Tax deduction to companies that make large investments, funds to companies that hire temporary workers, and creation of a program to find jobs for the unemployed.
11-Dec-08	Belgium	2.60	Increase in unemployment benefits, lowering of the value added tax on construction, abolishing taxes on energy, energy checks for families, faster payments of invoices by the government, faster government investment in railroads and buildings, and lowering of employer's fiscal contributions.
27-Nov-08	Spain	14.30	Public works, help for automobile industry, environmental projects, research and development, restoring residential and military housing, and funds to support the sick.
14-Jan-09	Portugal	2.89	Funds to be provided to medium and small-sized businesses, money for infrastructure, particularly schools, and investment in technological improvement.

Appendix B. (Continued)

Date Announced	Country	$Billion	Status, Package Contents
20-Nov-08	Israel	5.40	Public works to include desalination plants, doubling railway routes, adding R&D funding, increasing export credits, cutting assorted taxes, and aid packages for employers to hire new workers.
21-Dec-08	Switzerland	0.59	Public works spending on flood defense, natural disaster and energy-efficiency projects.
5-Dec-08	Sweden	2.70	Public infrastructure and investment in human capital, including job training, vocational workshops, and workplace restructuring.; extension of social benefits to part-time workers.
26-Jan-09	Norway	2.88	Investment in construction, infrastructure, and renovation of state-owned buildings, tax breaks for companies.
20-Nov-08	Russia	20.00	Cut in the corporate profit tax rate, a new depreciation mechanism for businesses, to be funded by Russia's foreign exchange reserves and rainy day fund.
3-Dec-08	Egypt	8.51	Infrastructure, Industrial Development Authority, Export Development Fund, investment funds for small- and medium-sized enterprises, funds for industrial modernization, training, technology transfer centers, export promotion, land development
10-Nov-08	China	586.00	Low-income housing, electricity, water, rural infrastructure, projects aimed at environmental protection and technological innovation, tax deduction for capital spending by companies, and spending for health care and social welfare.
13-Dec-08	Japan	250.00	Increase in government spending, funds to stabilize the financial system (prop up troubled banks and ease a credit crunch by purchasing commercial paper), tax cuts for homeowners and companies that build or purchase new factories and equipment, and grants to local government.
6-Apr-09	Japan	100.00	Increasing safety net for non-regular workers, support for small businesses, revitalizing regional economies, promoting solar power and nursing and medical services.
3-Nov-08	South Korea	14.64	$11 billion for infrastructure (including roads, universities, schools, and hospitals; funds for small- and medium-business, fishermen, and families with low income) and tax cuts. Includes an October 2008 stimulus package of $3.64 billion to provide support for the construction industry.
9-Feb-09	South Korea	37.87	The government announced its intention to invest $37.87 billion over the next four years in eco-friendly projects including the construction of dams; "green" transportation networks such as low-carbon emitting railways, bicycle roads, and other public transportation systems; and expand existing forest areas.
16-Dec-08	Vietnam	6.00	Tax cuts, spending on infrastructure, housing, schools, and hospitals.
28-Jan-09	Indonesia	6.32	(Proposed) Tax incentives for companies and individuals, cuts in fuel and electricity prices, spending on infrastructure.
21-Jan-09	Philippines	7.01	Stimulus package wrapped into the current budget. More spending on infrastructure, agriculture, education, and health, cash for poor households, and tax cuts. Partial funding by borrowing from government corporations and from the nation's social security system.
29-Jan-09	Thailand	3.35	Cash for low earners, tax cuts, expanded free education, subsidies for transport and utilities.

Date Announced	Country	$Billion	Status, Package Contents
22-Jan-09	Singapore	13.70	Personal income tax rebate; cut in maximum corporate tax rate; subsidies for employee wages; training; cash handouts to low-income workers; increase in public sector hiring; assuming 80% of the risk on private bank loans; boosting aid to welfare recipients, government pensioners, and students; invest in infrastructure.
30-Nov-08	Malaysia	1.93	High impact infrastructure projects including roads, schools, and housing. Government budget in deficit. Expect a second, larger stimulus package in February or March 2009.
8-Dec-08	India	4.00	Stimulus package includes $70 million to finance exports of textiles and handicrafts; value added tax rate cut at different levels and across products. Public works spending includes funding for various sectors, including: housing, automobile, infrastructure, power, and medium and small industries. In addition, import duties on naptha was revoked, export duty on iron ore was removed, levy on exports of iron were reduced.
28-Nov-08	Taiwan	15.60	Shopping vouchers of $108 each for all citizens, construction projects to be carried out over four years include expanding metro systems, rebuilding bridges and classrooms, improving, railway and sewage systems, and renew urban areas.
31-Dec-08	Sri Lanka	0.14	Cuts in prices for diesel, kerosene, and furnace oil; lifting of surcharge on electricity, incentive for exporters not to retrench workers, lifting of tax on rubber exports, and subsidies for tea farmers.
26-Jan-09	Australia	35.2	$7 billion stimulus package in October 2008 was cash handouts to low income earners and pensioners. January's $28.2 billion package includes infrastructure, schools and housing, and cash payments to low- and middle-income earners. Budget is in deficit.
7-Jan-09	Mexico	54.00	Infrastructure, a freeze on gasoline prices, reducing electricity rates, help for poor families to replace old appliances, construction of low-income housing and an oil refinery, rural development, increase government purchases from small- and medium-sized companies. Paid for by taxes, oil revenues, and borrowing.
23-Dec-08	Brazil	5.00	Program established in 2007 to continue to 2010. Tax cuts (exempt capital goods producers from the industrial and welfare taxes, increase the value of personal computers exempted from taxes) and rebates. Funded by reducing the government's budget surplus.
5-Dec-08	Argentina	3.80	Low-cost loans to farmers, automakers, or other exporters.
6-Jan-09	Chile	4.00	Infrastructure, subsidies for copper producer, lower employer contributions for small- and medium-sized companies, and income tax rebates. Funded from copper windfall earnings saved in sovereign wealth funds and by issuing bonds.

2007

July/August. German banks with bad investments in U.S. real estate are caught up in the evolving crisis, These include IKB Deutsche Industriebank, Sachsen LB (Saxony State Bank) and BayernLB (Bavaria State Bank).

July 18. Two battered hedge funds worth an estimated $1.5 billion at the end of 2006 were almost entirely worthless. They had been managed by Bear Stearns and were invested heavily in subprime mortgages.

July 12. The Federal Deposit Insurance Corp. took control of the $32 billion IndyMac Bank (Pasadena, CA) in what regulators called the second-largest bank failure in U.S. history.

March/April. New Century Financial corporation stopped making new loans as the practice of giving high risk mortgage loans to people with bad credit histories becomes a problem. The International Monetary Fund warned of risks to global financial markets from weakened US home mortgage market.

APPENDIX C. LONDON SUMMIT – LEADERS' STATEMENT

2 April 2009

1. We, the Leaders of the Group of Twenty, met in London on 2 April 2009.
2. We face the greatest challenge to the world economy in modern times; a crisis which has deepened since we last met, which affects the lives of women, men, and children in every country, and which all countries must join together to resolve. A global crisis requires a global solution.
3. We start from the belief that prosperity is indivisible; that growth, to be sustained, has to be shared; and that our global plan for recovery must have at its heart the needs and jobs of hardworking families, not just in developed countries but in emerging markets and the poorest countries of the world too; and must reflect the interests, not just of today's population, but of future generations too. We believe that the only sure foundation for sustainable globalisation and rising prosperity for all is an open world economy based on market principles, effective regulation, and strong global institutions.
4. We have today therefore pledged to do whatever is necessary to:
   - restore confidence, growth, and jobs;
   - repair the financial system to restore lending;
   - strengthen financial regulation to rebuild trust; fund and reform our international financial institutions to overcome this crisis and prevent future ones;
   - promote global trade and investment and reject protectionism, to underpin prosperity; and
   - build an inclusive, green, and sustainable recovery.

By acting together to fulfill these pledges we will bring the world economy out of recession and prevent a crisis like this from recurring in the future.

5. The agreements we have reached today, to treble resources available to the IMF to $750 billion, to support a new SDR allocation of $250 billion, to support at least $100 billion of additional lending by the MDBs, to ensure $250 billion of support for trade finance, and to use the additional resources from agreed IMF gold sales for concessional finance for the poorest countries, constitute an additional $1.1 trillion programme of support to restore credit, growth and jobs in the world economy. Together with the measures we have each taken nationally, this constitutes a global plan for recovery on an unprecedented scale.

Restoring Growth and Jobs

6. We are undertaking an unprecedented and concerted fiscal expansion, which will save or create millions of jobs which would otherwise have been destroyed, and that will, by the end of next year, amount to $5 trillion, raise output by 4 per cent, and accelerate the transition to a green economy. We are committed to deliver the scale of sustained fiscal effort necessary to restore growth.
7. Our central banks have also taken exceptional action. Interest rates have been cut aggressively in most countries, and our central banks have pledged to maintain expansionary policies for as long as needed and to use the full range of monetary policy instruments, including unconventional instruments, consistent with price stability.
8. Our actions to restore growth cannot be effective until we restore domestic lending and international capital flows. We have provided significant and comprehensive support to our banking systems to provide liquidity, recapitalise financial institutions, and address decisively the problem of impaired assets. We are committed to take all necessary actions to restore the normal flow of credit through the financial system and ensure the soundness of systemically important institutions, implementing our policies in line with the agreed G20 framework for restoring lending and repairing the financial sector.
9. Taken together, these actions will constitute the largest fiscal and monetary stimulus and the most comprehensive support programme for the financial sector in modern times. Acting together strengthens the impact and the exceptional policy actions announced so far must be implemented without delay. Today, we have further agreed over $1 trillion of additional resources for the world economy through our international financial institutions and trade finance.
10. Last month the IMF estimated that world growth in real terms would resume and rise to over 2 percent by the end of 2010. We are confident that the actions we have agreed today, and our unshakeable commitment to work together to restore growth and jobs, while preserving long-term fiscal sustainability, will accelerate the return to trend growth. We commit today to taking whatever action is necessary to secure that outcome, and we call on the IMF to assess regularly the actions taken and the global actions required.
11. We are resolved to ensure long-term fiscal sustainability and price stability and will put in place credible exit strategies from the measures that need to be taken now to support the financial sector and restore global demand. We are convinced that by implementing our agreed policies we will limit the longer-term costs to our economies, thereby reducing the scale of the fiscal consolidation necessary over the longer term.
12. We will conduct all our economic policies cooperatively and responsibly with regard to the impact on other countries and will refrain from competitive devaluation of our currencies and promote a stable and well-functioning international monetary system. We will support, now and in the future, to candid, even-handed, and independent IMF surveillance of our economies and financial sectors, of the impact of our policies on others, and of risks facing the global economy.

Strengthening Financial Supervision and Regulation

13. Major failures in the financial sector and in financial regulation and supervision were fundamental causes of the crisis. Confidence will not be restored until we rebuild trust in our financial system. We will take action to build a stronger, more globally consistent, supervisory and regulatory framework for the future financial sector, which will support sustainable global growth and serve the needs of business and citizens.
14. We each agree to ensure our domestic regulatory systems are strong. But we also agree to establish the much greater consistency and systematic cooperation between countries, and the framework of internationally agreed high standards, that a global financial system requires. Strengthened regulation and supervision must promote propriety, integrity and transparency; guard against risk across the financial system; dampen rather than amplify the financial and economic cycle; reduce reliance on inappropriately risky sources of financing; and discourage excessive risk-taking. Regulators and supervisors must protect consumers and investors, support market discipline, avoid adverse impacts on other countries, reduce the scope for regulatory arbitrage, support competition and dynamism, and keep pace with innovation in the marketplace.
15. To this end we are implementing the Action Plan agreed at our last meeting, as set out in the attached progress report. We have today also issued a Declaration, Strengthening the Financial System. In particular we agree:

- to establish a new Financial Stability Board (F SB) with a strengthened mandate, as a successor to the Financial Stability Forum (FSF), including all G20 countries, FSF members, Spain, and the European Commission;
- that the FSB should collaborate with the IMF to provide early warning of macroeconomic and financial risks and the actions needed to address them;
- to reshape our regulatory systems so that our authorities are able to identify and take account of macro-prudential risks;
- to extend regulation and oversight to all systemically important financial institutions, instruments and markets. This will include, for the first time, systemically important hedge funds;
- to endorse and implement the FSF's tough new principles on pay and compensation and to support sustainable compensation schemes and the corporate social responsibility of all firms;
- to take action, once recovery is assured, to improve the quality, quantity, and international consistency of capital in the banking system. In future, regulation must prevent excessive leverage and require buffers of resources to be built up in good times;
- to take action against non-cooperative jurisdictions, including tax havens. We stand ready to deploy sanctions to protect our public finances and financial systems. The era of banking secrecy is over. We note that the OECD has today published a list of countries assessed by the Global Forum against the international standard for exchange of tax information;

- to call on the accounting standard setters to work urgently with supervisors and regulators to improve standards on valuation and provisioning and achieve a single set of high-quality global accounting standards; and
- to extend regulatory oversight and registration to Credit Rating Agencies to ensure they meet the international code of good practice, particularly to prevent unacceptable conflicts of interest.

16. We instruct our Finance Ministers to complete the implementation of these decisions in line with the timetable set out in the Action Plan. We have asked the FSB and the IMF to monitor progress, working with the Financial Action Taskforce and other relevant bodies, and to provide a report to the next meeting of our Finance Ministers in Scotland in November.

Strengthening Our Global Financial Institutions

17. Emerging markets and developing countries, which have been the engine of recent world growth, are also now facing challenges which are adding to the current downturn in the global economy. It is imperative for global confidence and economic recovery that capital continues to flow to them. This will require a substantial strengthening of the international financial institutions, particularly the IMF. We have therefore agreed today to make available an additional $850 billion of resources through the global financial institutions to support growth in emerging market and developing countries by helping to finance counter-cyclical spending, bank recapitalisation, infrastructure, trade finance, balance of payments support, debt rollover, and social support. To this end:

- we have agreed to increase the resources available to the IMF through immediate financing from members of $250 billion, subsequently incorporated into an expanded and more flexible New Arrangements to Borrow, increased by up to $500 billion, and to consider market borrowing if necessary; and
- we support a substantial increase in lending of at least $100 billion by the Multilateral Development Banks (MDBs), including to low income countries, and ensure that all MDBs, including have the appropriate capital.

18. It is essential that these resources can be used effectively and flexibly to support growth. We welcome in this respect the progress made by the IMF with its new Flexible Credit Line (FCL) and its reformed lending and conditionality framework which will enable the IMF to ensure that its facilities address effectively the underlying causes of countries' balance of payments financing needs, particularly the withdrawal of external capital flows to the banking and corporate sectors. We support Mexico's decision to seek an FCL arrangement.
19. We have agreed to support a general SDR allocation which will inject $250 billion into the world economy and increase global liquidity, and urgent ratification of the Fourth Amendment.

20. In order for our financial institutions to help manage the crisis and prevent future crises we must strengthen their longer term relevance, effectiveness and legitimacy. So alongside the significant increase in resources agreed today we are determined to reform and modernise the international financial institutions to ensure they can assist members and shareholders effectively in the new challenges they face. We will reform their mandates, scope and governance to reflect changes in the world economy and the new challenges of globalisation, and that emerging and developing economies, including the poorest, must have greater voice and representation. This must be accompanied by action to increase the credibility and accountability of the institutions through better strategic oversight and decision making. To this end:

- we commit to implementing the package of IMF quota and voice reforms agreed in April 2008 and call on the IMF to complete the next review of quotas by January 2011;
- we agree that, alongside this, consideration should be given to greater involvement of the Fund's Governors in providing strategic direction to the IMF and increasing its accountability;
- we commit to implementing the World Bank reforms agreed in October 2008. We look forward to further recommendations, at the next meetings, on voice and representation reforms on an accelerated timescale, to be agreed by the 2010 Spring Meetings;
- we agree that the heads and senior leadership of the international financial institutions should be appointed through an open, transparent, and merit-based selection process; and
- building on the current reviews of the IMF and World Bank we asked the Chairman, working with the G20 Finance Ministers, to consult widely in an inclusive process and report back to the next meeting with proposals for further reforms to improve the responsiveness and adaptability of the IFIs.

21. In addition to reforming our international financial institutions for the new challenges of globalisation we agreed on the desirability of a new global consensus on the key values and principles that will promote sustainable economic activity. We support discussion on such a charter for sustainable economic activity with a view to further discussion at our next meeting. We take note of the work started in other fora in this regard and look forward to further discussion of this charter for sustainable economic activity.

Resisting Protectionism and Promoting Global Trade and Investment

22. World trade growth has underpinned rising prosperity for half a century. But it is now falling for the first time in 25 years. Falling demand is exacerbated by growing protectionist pressures and a withdrawal of trade credit. Reinvigorating world trade and investment is essential for restoring global growth. We will not repeat the historic mistakes of protectionism of previous eras. To this end:

- we reaffirm the commitment made in Washington: to refrain from raising new barriers to investment or to trade in goods and services, imposing new export restrictions, or implementing World Trade Organisation (WTO) inconsistent measures to stimulate exports. In addition we will rectify promptly any such measures. We extend this pledge to the end of 2010;
- we will minimise any negative impact on trade and investment of our domestic policy actions including fiscal policy and action in support of the financial sector. We will not retreat into financial protectionism, particularly measures that constrain worldwide capital flows, especially to developing countries;
- we will notify promptly the WTO of any such measures and we call on the WTO, together with other international bodies, within their respective mandates, to monitor and report publicly on our adherence to these undertakings on a quarterly basis;
- we will take, at the same time, whatever steps we can to promote and facilitate trade and investment; and
- we will ensure availability of at least $250 billion over the next two years to support trade finance through our export credit and investment agencies and through the MDBs. We also ask our regulators to make use of available flexibility in capital requirements for trade finance.

23. We remain committed to reaching an ambitious and balanced conclusion to the Doha Development Round, which is urgently needed. This could boost the global economy by at least $150 billion per annum. To achieve this we are committed to building on the progress already made, including with regard to modalities.
24. We will give renewed focus and political attention to this critical issue in the coming period and will use our continuing work and all international meetings that are relevant to drive progress.

Ensuring a Fair and Sustainable Recovery for All

25. We are determined not only to restore growth but to lay the foundation for a fair and sustainable world economy. We recognise that the current crisis has a disproportionate impact on the vulnerable in the poorest countries and recognise our collective responsibility to mitigate the social impact of the crisis to minimise long-lasting damage to global potential. To this end:

- we reaffirm our historic commitment to meeting the Millennium Development Goals and to achieving our respective ODA pledges, including commitments on Aid for Trade, debt relief, and the Gleneagles commitments, especially to sub-Saharan Africa;
- the actions and decisions we have taken today will provide $50 billion to support social protection, boost trade and safeguard development in low income countries, as part of the significant increase in crisis support for these and other developing countries and emerging markets;

- we are making available resources for social protection for the poorest countries, including through investing in long-term food security and through voluntary bilateral contributions to the World Bank's Vulnerability Framework, including the Infrastructure Crisis Facility, and the Rapid Social Response Fund;
- we have committed, consistent with the new income model, that additional resources from agreed sales of IMF gold will be used, together with surplus income, to provide $6 billion additional concessional and flexible finance for the poorest countries over the next two to three years. We call on the IMF to come forward with concrete proposals at the Spring Meetings;
- we have agreed to review the flexibility of the Debt Sustainability Framework and call on the IMF and World Bank to report to the IMFC and Development Committee at the Annual Meetings; and
- we call on the UN, working with other global institutions, to establish an effective mechanism to monitor the impact of the crisis on the poorest and most vulnerable.

26. We recognise the human dimension to the crisis. We commit to support those affected by the crisis by creating employment opportunities and through income support measures. We will build a fair and family-friendly labour market for both women and men. We therefore welcome the reports of the London Jobs Conference and the Rome Social Summit and the key principles they proposed. We will support employment by stimulating growth, investing in education and training, and through active labour market policies, focusing on the most vulnerable. We call upon the ILO, working with other relevant organisations, to assess the actions taken and those required for the future.
27. We agreed to make the best possible use of investment funded by fiscal stimulus programmes towards the goal of building a resilient, sustainable, and green recovery. We will make the transition towards clean, innovative, resource efficient, low carbon technologies and infrastructure. We encourage the MDBs to contribute fully to the achievement of this objective. We will identify and work together on further measures to build sustainable economies.
28. We reaffirm our commitment to address the threat of irreversible climate change, based on the principle of common but differentiated responsibilities, and to reach agreement at the UN Climate Change conference in Copenhagen in December 2009.

Delivering Our Commitments

29. We have committed ourselves to work together with urgency and determination to translate these words into action. We agreed to meet again before the end of this year to review progress on our commitments.

Source: http://www.londonsummit.gov.uk/resources/en/PDF/final-communique.

APPENDIX D. COMPARISON SELECTED FINANCIAL REGULATORY REFORM PROPOSALS [217]

This appendix provides a comparison, in graphic form, of selected proposals for regulatory reform that have been put forward in the wake of the global financial crisis. Seven such proposals are covered in the table below. They are, in chronological order:

U.S. Department of the Treasury, Blueprint for a Modernized Financial Regulatory Structure, March 2008. (This study was completed under Secretary Henry Paulson, during the Bush Administration.)

Counterparty Risk Management Policy Group (CRMPG), Containing Systemic Risk: The Road to Reform, Aug. 6, 2008. (The CRMPG, a group of commercial and investment bankers, began this study at the suggestion of the President's Working Group on Financial Markets. Its focus is on market participants, rather than regulators.)

Congressional Oversight Panel (COP), Special Report on Regulatory Reform: Modernizing the American Financial Regulatory System: Recommendations for Improving Oversight, Protecting Consumers, and Ensuring Stability, January 2009. (The COP was created by the Emergency Economic Stabilization Act of 2008 (P.L. 110-343) to oversee the Troubled Asset Relief Program.)

Group of Thirty, Financial Reform: A Framework for Financial Stability, January 15, 2009. (The Group of Thirty is a private, nonprofit body composed of senior representatives of the private and public sectors and academia, which aims to deepen understanding of international economic and financial issues.)

Group of 20 (G-20), G-20 Working Group on Enhancing Sound Regulation and Strengthening Transparency: Final Report (Draft), February 2009. (The G-20 is made up of the finance ministers and central bank governors of 19 countries: Argentina, Australia, Brazil, Canada, China, France, Germany, India, Indonesia, Italy, Japan, Mexico, Russia, Saudi Arabia, South Africa, South Korea, Turkey, the U.K., and the United States, and also the European Union.)

Financial Services Authority (FSA), The Turner Review: A Regulatory Response to the Global Banking Crisis, March 2009. (The FSA is the UK regulatory agency with jurisdiction over banking, securities, insurance, and derivatives. Adair Turner has been FSA chairman since September 2008.)

U.S. Department of the Treasury, Framework for Regulatory Reform: New Rules of the Road, March 26, 2009. (Only a four-page summary of these proposals is available.)

The table below lists a number of specific recommendations contained in the above reports and studies, and indicates by an "X" which ones contain each recommendation. The absence of an "X" does not necessarily mean that the authors of the report oppose the recommendation—each study has its own scope and focus. In some cases, studies identify issues as needing further study; in others, an issue may be identified as a problem contributing to the financial crisis without a specific recommendation for reform being made. (In neither of these cases would an "X" appear in the table.)

Appendix E. British, U.S., and European Central Bank Operations, April to Mid-October 2008

(An "X" indicates that a report includes the recommendation at the left)

Recommendation	Treasury (2009)	FSA	G-20	Group of 30	COP	CRMPG	Treasury (2008)
Systemic Risk							
Create (or designate) a single regulator with responsibility over all systemically-important financial institutions, regardless of their legal form.	X				X		X
All systemically-important financial institutions should be subject to an appropriate degree of regulation.	X	X	X	X	X		X
The systemic risk regulator should have prompt corrective action powers with regard to failing systemically-important firms.	X				X		X
Firms' internal risk controls should be made more robust and should take systemic risk into account. Corporate boards should assume more responsibility for their firms' risk management practices.		X		X		X	
Systemically-important banks should be restricted in certain risky activities, such as affiliation with non-financial firms, proprietary trading, etc.		X		X	X		
Financial institutions' use of stress testing should be more rigorous.	X		X	X		X	
Regulation of critical payment systems should be strengthened.	X						X
International monitoring for systemic risk should be enhanced, and a more formal mechanism should be created.		X	X	X	X		
Capital Standards							
Large complex systemically-important financial institutions should be subject to more stringent capital regulation than other firms.	X		X		X		X
Minimum capital standards should be raised throughout the banking system, or for all financial institutions.		X	X	X	X		
Capital standards should be adjusted to avoid procyclicality, that is, firms should be required to build up capital during good times, and be allowed to hold less capital during cyclical contractions.		X	X	X	X	X	

Recommendation	Treasury (2009)	FSA	G-20	Group of 30	COP	CRMPG	Treasury (2008)
Regulators' and firms' capital decisions should make greater provision against liquidity risk.	X	X	X	X	X	X	
Hedge Funds and Other Private Pools of Capital							
Hedge funds should be required to register with the Securities and Exchange Commission (SEC) or other national securities regulator.	X		X	X	X		X
Systemically-important hedge funds should be subject to prudential regulation.	X		X	X	X		X
Hedge funds should provide information on a confidential basis to regulators about their strategies and positions.	X	X	X		X		X
Over-the-Counter (OTC) Derivatives							
Credit default swaps should be processed through a regulated centralized counterparty (CCP) or clearing house.	X	X	X	X	X	X	
All standardized OTC derivatives should be processed through a regulated CCP or clearing house.	X				X		
OTC derivatives dealers should be subject to a strong regulatory regime.	X						
Non-standard (or customized) OTC derivatives should be reported to a central trade repository or to a regulator.	X				X		
Resolution Authority for Non-Bank Financial Institutions							
To avoid disorderly liquidations, a government agency should have authority to take over a failing, systemically-important non-bank institution, and place it in conservatorship or receivership, outside the bankruptcy system.	X			X			
Money Market Funds							
SEC (or other national regulator) should impose limits on risk-taking to make money market funds less vulnerable to runs.	X			X			
Funds that offer bank-like services should be chartered as special purpose banks, insured, and regulated.				X			
Compensation Structures in Financial Firms							
Pay practices should discourage excessive risk-taking, via incentives for fostering long-term stability rather than maximizing annual performance bonuses.		X	X		X	X	

Appendix (Continued)

Recommendation	Treasury (2009)	FSA	G-20	Group of 30	COP	CRMPG	Treasury (2008)
Regulators should consider compensation structures when assessing firms' risk management practices.			X				
Credit Rating Agencies							
Credit rating agencies (CRAs) should be registered and regulated with the appropriate government agency.		X	X		X		
CRAs should be held more accountable for the accuracy of their ratings, through after-the-fact audits or independent evaluations.				X	X		
The rating process for complex financial instruments, such as structured securitized products, should be made more transparent, or such instruments should be subject to additional mandatory risk disclosures.		X				X	
CRA revenues (especially when securities issuers pay for ratings) should be subject to oversight or limits.				X	X		
Accounting Standards							
Fair value, or mark-to-market, accounting standards should be modified to reduce their procyclical impact.			X	X			
Current rules for accounting consolidation (specifying when assets and liabilities may be held off the balance sheet) should be replaced by a principles-based standard reflecting the concepts of control and risk exposure.						X	
Other Regulatory Structure Issues							
There should be a single banking regulator for prudential supervision.				X			X
There should be a single regulator for consumer financial products.					X		X
Financial regulators should play a greater role in macroeconomic policy-making.		X	X				
Insurance companies should be chartered and regulated at the federal level.				X			X
Government-sponsored enterprises—a clear line should be drawn between public and private firms.				X			
Minimum international standards—a regulatory floor—should apply in all countries, including tax havens and offshore banking centers.	X	X		X	X		

Source: Prepared by CRS.

REFERENCES

[1] For a more complete list of major developments and actions, see Appendix A.

[2] Prepared by Dick K. Nanto, Specialist in Industry and Trade, Foreign Affairs, Defense, and Trade Division.

[3] International Monetary Fund, 2009 *Global Financial Stability Report: Responding to the Financial Crisis and Measuring systemic Risks*, Summary Version, Washington, DC, April 2009, p. 1ff.

[4] See Jochen Andritzky, John Kiff, Laura Kodres, Pamela Madrid, and Andrea Maechler, *Policies to Mitigate Procyclicality*, International Monetary Fund, IMF Staff Position Note SPN/09/09, Washington, DC, May 7, 2009.

[5] A moral hazard is created if a government rescue of private companies encourages those companies and others to engage in comparable risky behavior in the future, since the perception arises that they will again be rescued if necessary and not have to carry the full burden of their losses.

[6] See, for example, Friedman, George and Peter Zeihan. "The United States, Europe and Bretton Woods II." A Strafor Geopolitical Intelligence Report, October 20, 2008.

[7] See CRS Report RL34412, *Containing Financial Crisis*, by Mark Jickling

[8] See Board of Governors of the Federal Reserve System, *Federal Reserve Press Release*, March 18, 2009. U.S. Department of the Treasury, *U.S. Treasury and Federal Reserve Board Announce Launch of Term Asset-Backed Securities Loan Facility (TALF)*, Press Release tg-45, March 3, 2009. CRS Report RL3 1416, *Monetary Aggregates: Their Use in the Conduct of Monetary Policy*, by Marc Labonte.

[9] Eric S. Rosengren, *Addressing the Credit Crisis and Restructuring the Financial Regulatory System: Lessons from Japan*, Federal Reserve Bank of Boston, Paper given at the Institute of International Bankers Annual Washington Conference, Boston, MA, March 2, 2009.

[10] Thomas F. Cooley, "Swedish Banking Lessons," Forbes.com, January 28, 209.

[11] For details, see CRS Report RL34730, *Troubled Asset Relief Program: Legislation and Treasury Implementation*, by Baird Webel and Edward V. Murphy

[12] U.S. Department of the Treasury, *Treasury Department Releases Details on the Public Private Partnership Investment Program*, Press Release tg-65, March 23, 2009.

[13] For details, see CRS Report RL34427, *Financial Turmoil: Federal Reserve Policy Responses*, by Marc Labonte. "The Fed's Trillion," *The Washington Post*, May 5, 2009, p. A14.

[14] Camilla Anderson, *IMF Spells Out Need for Global Fiscal Stimulus*, International Monetary Fund, IMF Survey Magazine: Interview, Washington, DC, December 28, 2008.

[15] David Saha and Jakob von Weizsäcker, *Estimating the size of the European stimulus packages for 2009*, Brugel, JVW/ DS, 12 December 2008.

[16] Charles Freedman, Michael Kumhof, Douglas Laxton, and Jaewoo Lee, *The Case for Global Fiscal Stimulus*, International Monetary Fund, IMF Staff Position Note SPN/09/03, March 6, 2009.

[17] Steven Pearlstein, "Asia, Europe Find Their Supply Chains Yanked. Beware the Backlash," *The Washington Post*, February 20, 2009, pp. D1, D3.

[18] The Bretton Woods Agreements in 1944 established the basic rules for commercial and financial relations among the world's major industrial states and also established what has become the World Bank and International Monetary Fund.

[19] Information on the London G-20 Summit is available at http://www. londonsummit. gov.uk/en/.

[20] Group of Twenty Nations. "London Summit – Leaders' Statement," 2 April 2009 http://www.londonsummit.gov.uk/ resources/en/PDF/final-communique.

[21] Friedman, George and Peter Zeihan. "The United States, Europe and Bretton Woods II." A Strafor Geopolitical Intelligence Report, October 20, 2008.

[22] Dennis C. Blair, *Annual Threat Assessment of the Intelligence Community for the Senate Select Committee on Intelligence*, Director of National Intelligence, Washington, DC, February 12, 2009. See also, U.S. Senate, Committee on Foreign Relations, "Foreign Policy Implications Of The Global Economic Crisis," Roundtable before the Committee On Foreign Relations, February 11, 2009.

[23] Johnston, Tim. "Asia Nations Join to Prop Up Prices," *Washington Post*, November 1, 2008, p. A10. "Record Fall in NZ Commodity Price Gauge," *The National Business Review*, November 5, 2008.

[24] Joby Warrick, "Experts See Security Risks in Downturn, Global Financial Crisis May Fuel Instability and Weaken U.S. Defenses," *Washington Post*, November 15, 2008. P. A01. Bokhari, Farhan, "Pakistan's War On Terror Hits Roadblock, Global Economic Crisis Prompts Military To Consider Spending Cutbacks," CBS News (online version), October 28, 2008.

[25] Bureau of National Affairs, "WTO Report Finds 'Limited' Impact So Far of Financial Crisis on Higher Trade Barriers," *International Trade Reporter*, 26 ITR 143, January 29, 2009. Report by the World Trade Organization quoted in: Chris Nelson, *The Nelson Report,* Samuels International Associates, Inc., January 15, 2009

[26] H.R. 1 (P.L. 111-5) Sec. 1605 provides that none of the funds appropriated or otherwise made available by the act may be used for a project for the construction, alteration, maintenance, or repair of a public building or public work unless all of the iron, steel, and manufactured goods used in the project are produced in the United States provided that such action would not be inconsistent with the public interest, such products are not produced in the United States, and would not increase the cost of the overall project by more than 25%.

[27] "Europe Warns against 'Buy American' Clause," *Spiegel Online International*, February 3, 2009, Internet edition.

[28] For details, see CRS Report RL34314, *China's Holdings of U.S. Securities: Implications for the U.S. Economy*, by Wayne M. Morrison and Marc Labonte.

[29] The G-7 includes Canada, France, Germany, Italy, Japan, United Kingdom, and the United States. The G-8 is the G-7 plus Russia. The G-20 adds Argentina, Australia, Brazil, China, India, Indonesia, Mexico, Saudi Arabia, South Africa, South Korea, and Turkey.

[30] See CRS Report R40417, *Macroprudential Oversight: Monitoring the Financial System*, by Darryl E. Getter.

[31] Progress on these items as of mid-March 2009 is summarized in: U.K. Chair of the G20, *Progress Report on the Immediate Actions of the Washington Action Plan*, Annex

to the G20 Finance Ministers' and Central Bank Governors' Communique - 14 March, London, March 14, 2009.

[32] Prepared by Dick K. Nanto, Specialist in Industry and Trade, Foreign Affairs, Defense, and Trade Division.

[33] Edmund Conway, "WEF 2009: Global crisis 'has destroyed 40pc of world wealth'," Telegraph.co.uk, January 29, 2009, Internet edition.

[34] Morgenson, Gretchen, "Behind Insurer's Crisis, Blind Eye to a Web of Risk," *The New York Times* (Internet edition), S'/eptember 27, 2008.

[35] For an analysis of global production networks, see CRS Report R40 167, *Globalized Supply Chains and U.S. Policy*, by Dick K. Nanto.

[36] For example, see CRS Report RL34485, *Basel II in the United States: Progress Toward a Workable Framework*, by Walter W. Eubanks.

[37] In addition to the mandate of the Financial Stability Forum (to assess vulnerabilities affecting the financial system, identify and oversee action needed to address them, and promote coordination and information exchange among authorities responsible for financial stability), the Financial Stability Board is to (1) monitor and advise on market developments and their implications for regulatory policy; (2) advise on and monitor best practice in meeting regulatory standards; (3) undertake joint strategic reviews of the policy development work of the international standard setting bodies to ensure their work is timely, coordinated, focused on priorities and addressing gaps; (4) set guidelines for and support the establishment of supervisory colleges; (5) manage contingency planning for cross-border crisis management, particularly with respect to systemically important firms; and (6) collaborate with the IMF to conduct Early Warning Exercises.

[38] "Fed's Rosengren: Systemic regulator needs global reach," Reuters, May 5, 2009, Online at http://www.reuters.com.

[39] See CRS Report R40417, *Macroprudential Oversight: Monitoring the Financial System*, by Darryl E. Getter.

[40] Squam Lake Working Group on Financial Regulation, *A Systemic Regulator for Financial Markets*, Council on Foreign Relations, Center for Geoeconomic Studies, Working Paper, May 2009, p. 2.

[41] Kara Scannell, "Frank Backs Regulator for Systemic Risk," The Wall Street Journal, February 4, 2009, Internet edition.

[42] U.S. Department of the Treasury. *The Department of the Treasury Blueprint for a Modernized Financial Regulatory Structure.* March 2008. 217 p.

[43] U.S. Treasury, "PWG Announces Initiatives to Strengthen OTC Derivatives Oversight and Infrastructure," Press Release HP-1271, November 14, 2008.

[44] Board of Governors of the Federal Reserve System, Federal Deposit Insurance Corporation, Office of the Comptroller of the Currency, and Office of Thrift Supervision. "Banking Agencies Reach Agreement on Basel II Implementation." July 20, 2007.

[45] For details on U.S. implementation, see U.S. Federal Reserve, "Basel II Capital Accord, Basel I Initiatives, and Other Basel-Related Matters." http://www.federalreserve.gov/generalinfo/basel2/USImplementation.htm#Current.

[46] See, for example, Caprio, Gerald, Jr., Ash Demirguc-Kunt, and Edward J. Kane, "The 2007 Meltdown in Structured Securitization: Searching for Lessons Not Scapegoats," World Bank Working Paper, September 5, 2008.

[47] Tarullo, Daniel K. *Banking on Basel, the Future of International Financial Regulation* (Peterson Institute for International Economics, 2008). p. 5.

[48] For analysis and recommendations by the International Monetary Fund, see "Global Financial Stability Report, Financial Stress and Deleveraging, Macro-Financial Implications and Policy," October 2008. 246 p.

[49] For information on Basel II, see CRS Report RL34485, *Basel II in the United States: Progress Toward a Workable Framework*, by Walter W. Eubanks.

[50] Now called the Financial Stability Board. For recommendations by the Financial Stability Forum, see "Report of the Financial Stability Forum on Enhancing Market and Institutional Resilience, Follow-up on Implementation," October 10, 2008. 39 p.

[51] See, for example, CRS Report RL34730, *Troubled Asset Relief Program: Legislation and Treasury Implementation*, by Baird Webel and Edward V. Murphy; CRS Report RL34412, *Containing Financial Crisis*, by Mark Jickling; CRS Report RL33775, *Alternative Mortgages: Causes and Policy Implications of Troubled Mortgage Resets in the Subprime and Alt-A Markets*, by Edward V. Murphy; CRS Report RL34657, *Financial Institution Insolvency:Federal Authority over Fannie Mae, Freddie Mac, and Depository Institutions*, by David H. Carpenter and M. Maureen Murphy; CRS Report RL34427, *Financial Turmoil: Federal Reserve Policy Responses*, by Marc Labonte; CRS Report RS22099, *Regulation of Naked Short Selling*, by Mark Jickling; and CRS Report RS22932, *Credit Default Swaps: Frequently Asked Questions*, by Edward V. Murphy.

[52] Prepared by Dick K. Nanto. See also, CRS Report RL34730, *Troubled Asset Relief Program: Legislation and Treasury Implementation*, by Baird Webel and Edward V. Murphy.

[53] For a review of past financial crises, see Luc Laeven and Fabian Valencia. "Systemic Banking Crises: A New Database," International Monetary Fund Working Paper WP/08/224, October 2008. 80p.

[54] Gelpern, Anna. "Emergency Rules," The Record (Bergen-Hackensack, NJ), September 26, 2008.

[55] From 2005-2007, the U.S. current account deficit (balance of trade, services, and unilateral transfers) was a total of $2.2 trillion.

[56] Reuters. Factbox—Global foreign exchange reserves. October 12, 2008.

[57] See CRS Report RL34336, *Sovereign Wealth Funds: Background and Policy Issues for Congress*, by Martin A. Weiss.

[58] See U.S. Joint Economic Committee, "Chinese FX Interventions Caused international Imbalances, Contributed to U.S. Housing Bubble," by Robert O'Quinn. March 2008.

[59] For further analysis, see CRS Report RL34412, *Containing Financial Crisis*, by Mark Jickling, U.S. Joint Economic Committee, "The U.S. Housing Bubble and the Global Financial Crisis: Vulnerabilities of the Alternative Financial System," by Robert O'Quinn. June 2008.

[60] Fannie Mae (Federal National Mortgage Association) is a government-sponsored enterprise (GSE) chartered by Congress in 1968 as a private shareholder-owned company with a mission to provide liquidity and stability to the U.S. housing and

mortgage markets. It operates in the U.S. secondary mortgage market and funds its mortgage investments primarily by issuing debt securities in the domestic and international capital markets. Freddie Mac (Federal Home Loan Mortgage Corp) is a stockholder-owned GSE chartered by Congress in 1970 as a competitor to Fannie Mae. It also operates in the secondary mortgage market. It purchases, guarantees, and securitizes mortgages to form mortgage- backed securities. For an analysis of Fannie Mae and Freddie Mac's role in the subprime crisis, see David Goldstein and Kevin G. Hall, "Private sector loans, not Fannie or Freddie, triggered crisis," McClatchy Newspapers, October 12, 2008.

[61] A credit default swap is a credit derivative contract in which one party (protection buyer) pays a periodic fee to another party (protection seller) in return for compensation for default (or similar credit event) by a reference entity. The reference entity is not a party to the credit default swap. It is not necessary for the protection buyer to suffer an actual loss to be eligible for compensation if a credit event occurs. The protection buyer gives up the risk of default by the reference entity, and takes on the risk of simultaneous default by both the protection seller and the reference credit. The protection seller takes on the default risk of the reference entity, similar to the risk of a direct loan to the reference entity. See CRS Report RS22932, *Credit Default Swaps: Frequently Asked Questions*, by Edward V. Murphy.

[62] Notional value is the face value of bonds and loans on which participants have written protection. World GDP is from World Bank. Development Indicators.

[63] International Swaps and Derivatives Association, ISDA Applauds $25 Trn Reductions in CDS Notionals, Industry Efforts to Improve CDS Operations. *News Release*, October 27, 2008.

[64] For information on the International Swaps and Derivatives Association, see http://www.isda.org. In 2008, credit derivatives had collateralized exposure of 74%. See ISDA, *Margin Survey 2008*. Collateral calls have been a major factor in the financial difficulties of AIG insurance.

[65] Thomas M. Anderson, "Best Ways to Invest in BRICs," Kiplinger.com, October 18, 2007.

[66] For these and other indicators of the crisis in credit, see http://www.nytimes.com/ interactive/2008/10/08/business/ economy/2008 1008-credit-chart-graphic.html

[67] Prepared by Martin A. Weiss, Specialist in International Trade and Finance, Foreign Affairs, Defense, and Trade Division

[68] Mark Scott, "Economic Problems Threaten Central and Eastern Europe," Business Week, October 17, 2008.

[69] Information on ongoing IMF negotiations is available at http://www.imf.org.

[70] International Monetary Fund, "IMF Executive Board Approves Stand-by Arrangement for Pakistan." *Press Release* No. 08/303, November 24, 2008.

[71] Reinhart, Carmen and Calvo, Guillermo (2000): When Capital Inflows Come to a Sudden Stop: Consequences and Policy Options. Published in: in Peter Kenen and Alexandre Swoboda, eds. Reforming the International Monetary and Financial System (Washington DC: International Monetary Fund, 2000) (2000): pp. 175-20 1.

[72] "New paradigm changes currency rules," *Oxford Analytica*, January 17, 2008.

[73] See CRS Report RL34336, *Sovereign Wealth Funds: Background and Policy Issues for Congress*, by Martin A. Weiss.

[74] Cigdem Akin and M. Ayhan Kose, "Changing Nature of North-South Linkages: Stylized Facts and Explanations." International Monetary Fund Working Paper 07/280. Available at http://www.imf.org/external/pubs/ft/wp/2007/ wp07280.pdf.

[75] Joanna Slater and Jon Hilsenrath, "Currency-Price Swings Disrupt Global Markets ," Wall Street Journal, October 25, 2008.

[76] Arvind Subramanian , "The Financial Crisis and Emerging Markets," Peterson Institute for International Economics, Realtime Economics Issue Watch, October 24, 2008.

[77] The Group of Ten is made up of eleven industrial countries (Belgium, Canada, France, Germany, Italy, Japan, the Netherlands, Sweden, Switzerland, the United Kingdom, and the United States).

[78] Stephen Jen and Spyros Andreopoulos, "Europe More Exposed to EM Bank Debt than the U.S. or Japan," Morgan Stanley Research Global, October 23, 2008.

[79] Dirk Willem te Velde, "The Global Financial Crisis and Developing Countries," *Overseas Development Institute*, October 2008.

[80] David Roodman, "History Says Financial Crisis Will Suppress Aid," *Center for Global Development*, October 13, 2008.

[81] Prepared by J. F. Hornbeck, Specialist in International Trade and Finance, Foreign Affairs, Defense, and Trade Division.

[82] United Nations. Economic Commission on Latin America and the Caribbean. *Latin America and the Caribbean in the World Economies, 2007. Trends 2008*. Santiago: October 2008. p. 28.

[83] Decoupling generally refers to economic growth trends in one part of the world, usually smaller emerging economies, becoming less dependent (correlated) with trends in other parts of the world, usually developed economies. See Rossi, Vanessa. *Decoupling Debate Will Return: Emergers Dominate in Long Run*. London: Chatham House, 2008. p. 5.

[84] Ocampo, Jose Antonio. The Latin American Boom is Over. *REG Monitor*. November 2, 2008.

[85] Latin American Newsletters. *Latin American Economy and Business*. London: October 2008. pp. 1-3 and Fidler, Stephen. Going South. *Financial Times*. January 9, 2009. p. 7.

[86] International Monetary Fund. Regional Economic Outlook. *Western Hemisphere: Grappling with the Global Financial Crisis*. Washington, D.C. October 2008. pp. 7-10.

[87] A summary of these trends is presented in: United Nations. Economic Commission on Latin America and the Caribbean. *Preliminary Overview of the Economies of Latin America and the Caribbean 2008*. Santiago, 2008.

[88] Board of Governors of the Federal Reserve System. *Federal Reserve Press Release*. October 29, 2008.

[89] Loser, Claudio. Stimulus Packages: How Much Can the Region Afford? *Latin American Advisor*. Inter-American Dialogue. January 29, 2009.

[90] Global Outlook. *Mexico*. March 17, 2009.

[91] International Monetary Fund. *Global Markets Monitor*. March 16, 2009.

[92] The Wall Street Journal. *Mexico and Brazil Step In to Fight Currency Declines*, October 24, 2008 and *Latin America Monitor: Mexico*. December 2008.

[93] Latin American Newsletters. *Latin American Mexico and NAFTA Report*, March 2009, p. 10 and *Latin America Monitor: Mexico*, March 2009, p. 3.
[94] Latin American Newsletters. *Latin American Economy & Business,* February 2009, pp. 4-6 and Loser, Claudio. *Stimulus Packages: How Much Can the Region Afford?*, January 29, 2009.
[95] Business Monitor International. *Latin American Monitor: Brazil*. March 2009
[96] Ibid., and Canuto, Otaviano. Emerging Markets and the Systemic Sudden Stop. *RGE Monitor*. November 12, 2008.
[97] *Latin American Brazil & Southern Cone Report*, January 2009, p. 12.
[98] Brazil-U.S. Business Council. *Brazil Bulletin*. October 27, 2008 and December 8, 2008.
[99] Soliani, Andre and Iuri Dantas. Brazil Freezes 37.2 Billion Reais of 2009 Budget. *Bloomberg Press*. January 27, 2009 and Loser, Claudio. *Stimulus Packages: How Much Can the Region Afford?*, January 29, 2009
[100] Latin American Newsletters. *Latin American Economy & Business,* January 2009, pp. 10-11 and Republica Argentina. Ministerio de Economia y Finanzas Publicas. Instituto Nacional de Estadistica y Censos (INDEC). *Utilizacion de la Capacidid Instalada en la Industria*. Buenos Aires. January 2009.
[101] Benson, Drew and Bill Farles. Argentine Bonds, Stocks Tumble on Pension Fund Takeover Plan. *Bloomberg*. October 21, 2008 and International Monetary Fund. *Global Markets Monitor*. March 17, 2009.
[102] Republica Argentina. Ministerio de Economia y Finanzas Publicas. Instituto Nacional de Estadistica y Censos. *Intercambio Comercial Argentino*. Buenos Aires, January 28, 2009.
[103] Global Insight. *Argentina: S&P Lowers Argentina's Rating to B-*. November 3, 2008 and Latin America Weekly Report. *Lula May Accept Argentine Protectionism*. March 12, 2009. p. 8.
[104] International Monetary Fund. Regional Economic Outlook. *Western Hemisphere: Grappling with the Global Financial Crisis*. Washington, DC. October 2008. p. 8ff.
[105] *Latin American Brazil & Southern Cone Report*, February 2009, p. 3.
[106] Ibid., *Latin American Brazil & Southern Cone Report*, January 2009, p. 10, and IMF. *Global Markets Monitor*. March 2, 2009.
[107] Prepared by William H. Cooper, Specialist in International Trade and Finance, Foreign Affairs, Defense, and Trade Division.
[108] *Financial Times*. February 16, 2009.
[109] *Financial Times*. February 18, 2009.
[110] Economist Intelligence Unit.
[111] Open Source Center. *Government Bails Out Oil Companies Suffering From World Financial Crisis*. October 30, 2008.
[112] Economist Intelligence Unit. *Monthly Report—Russia*. October 2008. p. 7.
[113] U.S. Department of Energy. Energy Information Administration.
[114] RTS.
[115] http://www.quote.ru.
[116] Central Bank of Russia.
[117] *Financial Times*.

[118] Prepared by James K. Jackson, Specialist in International Trade and Finance, Foreign Affairs, Defense, and Trade Division.

[119] For additional information, see CRS Report R40415, *The Financial Crisis: Impact on and Response by The European Union*, by James K. Jackson.

[120] Pan, Phillip P., Economic Crisis Fuels Unrest in E. Europe, *The Washington Post*, January 26, 2009, p, A1.

[121] *Regional Economic Outlook: Europe*, International Monetary Fund, April, 2008, p. 19-20; and *EU Banking Structures*, European Central Bank, October 2008, p. 26

[122] Frank, Nathaniel, Brenda Gonzalez-Hermosillo, and Heiko Hesse, *Transmission of Liquidity Shocks: Evidence from the 2007 Subprime Crisis*, IMF Working Paper #WP/08/200, August 2008, the International Monetary Fund.

[123] Flash Estimates for the Fourth Quarter of 2008, Eurostat news release, STAT/09/19, February 13, 2009.

[124] Hilsenrath, Jon, Joellen Perry, and Sudeep Reddy, Central Banks Launch Coordinated Attack; Emergency Rate Cuts Fail to Halt stock Slide; U.S. Treasury Considers Buying Stakes in Banks as Direct Move to Shore Up Capital, the *Wall Street Journal*, October 8, 2008, p. A1.

[125] Castle, Stephen, British Leader Wants Overhaul of Financial System, *The New York Times*, October 16, 2008.

[126] The G-7 consists of Canada, France, Germany, Italy, Japan, the United Kingdom, and the United States.

[127] *Summit of the Euro Area Countries: Declaration on a Concerted European Action Plan of the Euro Area Countries*, European union, October 12, 2008.

[128] *EU Sets up Crisis Unit to Boost Financial Oversight*, Thompson Financial News, October 16, 2008.

[129] *Ibid.*

[130] Bradbury, Adam, EU Eyes Next Step on Clearing, *The Wall Street Journal Europe*, January 7, 2009. p. 21.

[131] Communication From the Commission, From Financial Crisis to Recovery: A European Framework for Action, European Commission, October 29, 2008.

[132] The Lisbon Strategy was adopted by the EU member states at the Lisbon summit of the European Union in March 2001 and then recast in 2005 based on a consensus among EU member states to promote long-term economic growth and development in Europe.

[133] The combination of labor market flexibility and security for workers.

[134] Hall, Ben, George Parker, and Nikki Tait, European Leaders Decide on Deadline for Reform Blueprint, *Financial Times*, November 8, 2008, p. 7.

[135] Benoit, Bernard, Germany Doubles Size of Stimulus, *Financial Times*, January 6, 2009, p. 10; Walker, Marcus, Germany's Big Spending Plans, *The Wall Street Journal Europe*, January 13, 2009, p. 3.

[136] Benoit, Bernard, German Stimulus Offers Job Promise, *Financial Times*, December 16, 2008. p. 1.

[137] Walker, Marcus, Germany Mulls $135 Billion in Rescue Loans, *The Wall Street Journal Europe*, January 8, 2009. p. 1.

[138] Steinbruck, Peer, Germany's Way Out of the Crisis, *The Wall Street Journal*, December 22, 2008.

[139] Parussini, Gabrielle, France to Give Banks Capital, With More Strings Attached, *The Wall Street Journal Europe*, January 16, 2009, p. A17.
[140] Gauthier-Villars, David, Leading News: France Sets Stimulus Plan, *The Wall Street Journal Europe*, December 5, 2008, p. 3.
[141] Hall, Ben, France Gives Renault and Peugeot E.U.R 779m, *Financial Times*, December 16, 2008, p. 4.
[142] Abboud, Leila, France Considers New Measures to Aid Auto Companies, *The Wall Street Journal Europe*, January 15, 2009, p. 4.
[143] The Bank of England, *Financial Stability Report*, April 2008, p. 10.
[144] Scott, Mark, Is Britain's Stimulus Plan a Wise Move? Business Week, November 24, 2008; Werdigier, Julia, Britain Offers $30 Billion Stimulus Plan, *The New York Times*, November 25, 2008.
[145] Falloon, Matt, and Mike Peacock, UK Government to Borrow Record Sums to Revive Economy, *The Washington Post*, November 24, 2008.
[146] *Real Help for Business*, press release, Department for Business, Enterprise and Regulatory Reform, January 14, 2009; Mollenkamp, Carrick, Alistair MacDonald, and Sara Schaefer Munoz, Hurdles rise as U.K. Widens Stimulus Plan, *The Wall Street Journal Europe*, January 14, 2009, p. 1.
[147] Benoit, Bertrand, Tom Braithwaaite, Jimmy Burns, Jean Eaglesham, et. al., Iceland and UK clash on Crisis, *Financial Times*, October 10, 2008, p. 1.
[148] Anderson, Camilla, Iceland Gets Help to Recover From Historic Crisis, *IMF Survey Magazine*, November 19, 2008.
[149] Iceland Raises Key Rate by 6 Percentage Points, *The New York Times*, October 29, 2008.
[150] Jolly, David, Nordic Countries Add $2.5 Billion to Iceland's Bailout, *The New York Times*, November 20, 2008.
[151] Wardell, Jane, Iceland's Financial Crisis Escalates, BusinessWeek, October 9, 2008; Pfanner, Eric, Meltdown of Iceland's Financial system Quickens, *The New York Times*, October 9, 2008.
[152] Portes, Richard, The Shocking Errors Behind Iceland's Meltdown, *Financial Times*, October 13, 2008, p. 15.
[153] Buiter, Willem H., and Anne Sibert, *The Icelandic Banking Crisis and What to Do About it: The Lender of Last Resort Theory of Optimal Currency Areas*. Policy Insight No. 26, Centre for Economic Policy Research, October 2008. p. 2.
[154] Prepared by Ben Dolven, Asia Section Research Manager, Foreign Affairs, Defense, and Trade Division.
[155] Japan Logs Trade Deficit on Slumping World Demand, *Reuters,* November 22, 2008.
[156] Despite Ambivalence, Pakistan May Wrap Deal by Next Week, *The Wall Street Journal*, October 28, 2008.
[157] IMF 'Has Six Days to Save Pakistan,' *Financial Times*, October 28, 2008.
[158] Pakistan Says it will Need Financing Beyond IMF Deal, *The Wall Street Journal,* November 17, 2008.
[159] See, for instance, Morgan Stanley report, "EM Currencies, No Differentiation in the Sell-Off," October 23, 2008.
[160] See, for instance, Jeffrey Sachs, The Best Recipe for Avoiding a Global Recession, *Financial Times*, October 27, 2008.

[161] The moved was announced in a November 14 opinion piece by Japanese Prime Minister Taro Aso, Restoring Financial Stability, printed in *The Wall Street Journal.*

[162] Leaders of Europe and Asia Call for Joint Economic Action, *New York Times*, October 25, 2008.

[163] Chinese Premier Blames Recession on U.S. Actions, *Wall Street Journal,* January 29, 2009.

[164] ASEAN's members are Indonesia, Singapore, Malaysia, Thailand, the Philippines, Brunei, Vietnam, Cambodia, Laos and Burma (Myanmar).

[165] For a fuller discussion of the Chiang Mai Initiative, see East Asian Cooperation, Institute of International Economics, http://www.iie.com/publications/ chapters_ preview/345/3iie3381.pdf.

[166] Japan, China, S. Korea Eye Financial Stability Forum, *Reuters*, October 20, 2008.

[167] Asian Leaders See Growth Driver, *The Wall Street Journal,* December 15, 2008.

[168] Japan Passes Contentious Stimulus Budget, *Associated Press,* January 27, 2009.

[169] The section on China was prepared by Wayne M. Morrison, Specialist in Asian Trade and Finance, Foreign Affairs, Defense, and Trade Division.

[170] For an overview of the China Investment Corporation, see CRS Report RL34337, *China's Sovereign Wealth Fund*, by Michael F. Martin.

[171] China's holdings of Fannie Mae and Freddie Mac securities are likely to be more substantial, but less risky (compared to other sub-prime securities), especially after these two institutions were placed in conservatorship by the Federal Government in September 2008.

[172] China's economy was already slowing down before the global financial crisis hit. This was in large part the result of government efforts to slow the rate of inflation. China's real GDP growth fell from 13% in 2007 to 9% in 2008. The global financial crisis has sharply diminished economic growth. Thus, the Chinese government has abandoned its anti- inflation policies and instead has sought to stimulate the economy.

[173] However, the Shanghai Index is one of the few global indexes to experience positive growth in 2009; from January 5, 2009, to March 18, 2009, it was up 18%.

[174] Global Insight, *China*, March 18, 2009.

[175] According to *Xinhua Net* (March 9, 2008), China's Labor and Social Security Minister Tian Chengping warned that the employment situation in China in 2008 was expected to be "very severe," noting that towns and cities would be able to provide only 12 million new jobs.

[176] *Chinaview*, September 27, 2008.

[177] Global Insight, *Country Intelligence Analysis, China*, October 20, 2008.

[178] China *Xinhua News Agency*, November 12, 2008.

[179] Such a move would help keep U.S. interest rates relatively low. If China decided not to sharply increase its purchases of U.S. securities, U.S. interest rates could go up.

[180] See CRS Report RL343 14, *China's Holdings of U.S. Securities: Implications for the U.S. Economy*, by Wayne M. Morrison and Marc Labonte.

[181] Inside U.S. Trade, *China Trade Extra*, September 24, 2008.

[182] For additional information, see CRS Report RS22984, *China and the Global Financial Crisis: Implications for the United States*, by Wayne M. Morrison.

[183] People's Daily Online, February 19, 2009.

[184] SOUTH KOREA: Seoul Faces Growth and Liquidity Tests, *Oxford Analytica*, October 8, 2008.
[185] Lee Warns Against Dollar Hoarding, *Korea Times*, October 8, 2008.
[186] See Merrill Lynch, "Asia: Risks Rising", October 3, 2008.
[187] For more information about Pakistan's economic crisis, see CRS Report RS22983, *Pakistan's Capital Crisis: Implications for U.S. Policy*, by Michael F. Martin and K. Alan Kronstadt.
[188] "Pakistan's Zardari to Give Up Powers," *AFP*, September 20, 2008.
[189] Simon Cameron-Moore, "Pakistan Needs $ 10-15 Bln Fast, Says PM's Adviser," *Reuters*, October 21, 2008.
[190] "IMF Okays $7.6 Bln Package for Pakistan: Tareen," *Associated Press of Pakistan*, November 15, 2008.
[191] Jamie Anderson, "Pakistan Turns to IMF for Financial Aid," *Money Times*, November 16, 2008.
[192] "Pakistan Unveils Package for Economic Stability," *Reuters*, September 19, 2008.
[193] Farhan Bokhari, "Pakistan Vows to Target Rich Tax Evaders as IMF Concludes Talks on Vital Loan," *Financial Times*, November 3, 2008.
[194] India Acts to Avert Liquidity Crunch, *Financial Times,* November 16, 2008.
[195] Ibid.
[196] For an analysis of bubbles, see CRS Report RL33666, *Asset Bubbles: Economic Effects and Policy Options for the Federal Reserve*, by Marc Labonte.
[197] Lanman, Scott and Steve Matthews. "Greenspan Concedes to 'Flaw' in His Market Ideology," *Bloomberg News Service*, October 23, 2008.
[198] Soros, George. *The New Paradigm for Financial Markets: The Credit Crisis of 2008 and What it Means* (PublicAffairs, 2008) p. i. Soros proposes a new paradigm that deals with the relationship between thinking and reality and accounts for misconceptions and misinterpretations.
[199] International Monetary Fund. "The Recent Financial Turmoil—Initial Assessment, Policy Lessons, and Implications for Fund Surveillance," April 9, 2008.
[200] Gerstenzang, James. "Bush will Meet with G-20 After Election," *Los Angeles Times*, October 23, 2008.
[201] G-20, *Meeting of Finance Ministers and Central Bank Governors, United Kingdom, 14 March 2009*, Communiqué, March 14, 2009
[202] Prepared by Dick K. Nanto and Martin A. Weiss. For further information see CRS Report RS22976, *The Global Financial Crisis: The Role of the International Monetary Fund (IMF)*, by Martin A. Weiss.
[203] Lipsky, John. "Global Prospects and Policies," Speech by John Lipsky, First Deputy Managing Director, International Monetary Fund, at the Securities Industries and Financial Markets Association, New York, October 28, 2008. World Bank. "The Unfolding Crisis, Implications for Financial Systems and Their Oversight," October 28, 2008. p. 8.
[204] See CRS Report RS22976, *The Global Financial Crisis: The Role of the International Monetary Fund (IMF)*, by Martin A. Weiss.
[205] Each member country of the IMF is assigned a quota, based broadly on its relative size in the world economy. A member's quota determines its maximum financial

commitment to the IMF and its voting power. The U.S. quota of about $58.2 billion is the largest.

[206] IMF Signs $100 Billion Borrowing Agreement with Japan, *IMF Survey Magazine: In the News*, February 13, 2009.

[207] "China Urges World Monetary Systems Diversification ," Dow Jones Newswire , April 2, 2009, http://www.djnewswires.com/eu.

[208] Timothy R. Homan, "IMF Plans to Issue Bonds to Raise Funds for Lending Programs ," Bloomberg.com, April 25, 2009.

[209] Bob Davis, "IMF Considers Issuing Bonds to Raise Money," *Wall Street Journal*, February 1, 2009.

[210] See, for example, CRS Report RL34730, *Troubled Asset Relief Program: Legislation and Treasury Implementation*, by Baird Webel and Edward V. Murphy; CRS Report RL34412, *Containing Financial Crisis*, by Mark Jickling; CRS Report RL33775, *Alternative Mortgages: Causes and Policy Implications of Troubled Mortgage Resets in the Subprime and Alt-A Markets*, by Edward V. Murphy; CRS Report RL34657, *Financial Institution Insolvency:Federal Authority over Fannie Mae, Freddie Mac, and Depository Institutions*, by David H. Carpenter and M. Maureen Murphy; CRS Report RL34427, *Financial Turmoil: Federal Reserve Policy Responses*, by Marc Labonte; CRS Report RS22099, *Regulation of Naked Short Selling*, by Mark Jickling; and CRS Report RS22932, *Credit Default Swaps: Frequently Asked Questions*, by Edward V. Murphy.

[211] For analysis and recommendations by the International Monetary Fund, see "Global Financial Stability Report, Financial Stress and Deleveraging, Macro-Financial Implications and Policy," October 2008. 246 p.

[212] For information on Basel II, see CRS Report RL34485, *Basel II in the United States: Progress Toward a Workable Framework*, by Walter W. Eubanks.

[213] For recommendations by the Financial Stability Forum, see "Report of the Financial Stability Forum on Enhancing Market and Institutional Resilience, Follow-up on Implementation," October 10, 2008. 39 p.

[214] International Monetary fund. "Global Financial Stability Report: Financial Stress and Deleveraging, Macrofinancial Implications and Policy" (Summary version), October 2008. pp. ix-x.

[215] Prepared by J. Michael Donnelly, Information Research Specialist, Knowledge Services Group. Source: Various news reports and press releases.

[216] U.S. Treasury. "Joint Statement by Treasury, Federal Reserve and FDIC." Press Release HP-1206, October 14, 2008.

[217] Prepared by Mark Jickling, Specialist in Financial Economics.

In: The Global Financial Crisis: Policies and Implications ISBN 978-1-61470-317-4
Editor: J. P. Gallagher and E. C. Wilkins © 2012 Nova Science Publishers, Inc.

Chapter 4

China and the Global Financial Crisis: Implications for the United States*

Wayne M. Morrison

Abstract

Over the past several years, China has enjoyed one of the world's fastest growing economies and has been a major contributor to world economic growth. However, the current global financial crisis threatens to significantly slow China's economy. Several Chinese industries, particularly the export sector, have been hit hard by crisis, and millions of workers have reportedly been laid off. This situation is of great concern to the Chinese government, which views rapid economic growth as critical to maintaining social stability. China is a major economic power and holds huge amounts of foreign exchange reserves, and thus its policies could have a major impact on the global economy. For example, the Chinese government in November 2008 announced plans to implement a $586 billion package to help stimulate the domestic economy. If successful, this plan could also boost Chinese demand for imports. In addition, in an effort to help stabilize the U.S. economy, China might boost its holdings of U.S. Treasury securities, which would help fund the Federal Government's borrowing needs to purchase troubled U.S. assets and to finance economic stimulus packages. However, some U.S. policymakers have expressed concerns over the potential political and economic implications of China's large and growing holdings of U.S. Government debt securities. This report will be updated as events warrant.

China's Stake in the Current Crisis

China's economy is heavily dependent on global trade and investment flows. In 2007, China overtook the United States to become the world's second largest merchandise exporter after the European Union (EU). China's net exports (exports minus imports) contributed to one-third of its GDP growth in 2007. The Chinese government estimates that

* This is an edited, reformatted and augmented version of CRS Report RS22984, dated April 2, 2009.

the foreign trade sector employs more than 80 million people, of which 28 million work in foreign-invested enterprises [1]. Foreign direct investment (FDI) flows to China have been a major factor behind its productivity gains and rapid economic growth. FDI flows to China in 2007 totaled $75 billion, making it the largest FDI recipient among developing countries and the third largest overall, after the EU and the United States. A global economic slowdown (especially among its major export markets—the United States, the EU, and Japan) could have a significant negative impact on China's export sector and industries that depend on FDI flows. There are indications that the Chinese economy is already slowing down. Chinese real annual GDP growth slowed from 13.0% in 2007 to 9.0% in 2008. China's year-on-year fourth quarter GDP growth was 6.8%. Some analysts contend that China's real GDP growth from the third quarter of 2008 to the fourth quarter of 2008 on an annualized basis was near zero [2]. Some analysts contend annual economic growth of less than 8% could lead to social unrest in China, given that an estimated 20 million people seek jobs every year (including migrant workers that move to urban centers and high school and college graduates) [3]. According to the International Monetary Fund (IMF), China was the single most important contributor to world economic growth in 2007 [4]. Thus, a Chinese economic slowdown would not only affect China, but could also have global implications as well.

CHINA'S EXPOSURE TO THE GLOBAL FINANCIAL CRISIS

The extent of China's exposure to the current global financial crisis, in particular from the fallout of the U.S. sub-prime mortgage problem, is unclear [5]. On the one hand, China places numerous restrictions on capital flows, particularly outflows, in part so that it can maintain its managed float currency policy [6]. These restrictions limit the ability of Chinese citizens and many firms to invest their savings overseas, compelling them to invest those savings domestically, (such as in banks, the stock markets, real estate, and business ventures), although some Chinese attempt to shift funds overseas illegally. Thus, the exposure of Chinese private sector firms and individual Chinese investors to sub-prime U.S. mortgages is likely to be small.

Moreover, Chinese government entities, such as the State Administration of Foreign Exchange, the China Investment Corporation (a $200 billion sovereign wealth fund created in 2007), [7] state banks, and state-owned enterprises, may have been more exposed to troubled U.S. mortgage securities. Chinese government entities account for the lion's share of China's (legal) capital outflows, much of which derives from China's large and growing foreign exchange reserves. These reserves rose from $403 billion in 2003 (year end) to $1.95 trillion as of December 2008 [8]. In order to earn interest on these holdings. the Chinese government invests in overseas assets. A large portion of China's reserves are believed to be invested in U.S. securities, such as long-term (LT) Treasury debt (used to finance the federal deficit), LT U.S. agency debt (such as Freddie Mac and Fannie Mae mortgage-backed securities), LT U.S. corporate debt, LT U.S. equities, and short-term (ST) debt [9]. The Treasury Department estimates that, as of June 2008, China's holdings of U.S. securities totaled $1,205 billion (up from $922 billion in June 2007), making it the 2nd largest foreign holder of such securities (after Japan) [10]. Of this total, $527 billion were in LT U.S. agency securities, [11] $522 billion were in LT Treasury securities, $100 billion in LT equities, $26 billion in LT corporate securities, and $30 billion in ST debt.

If China held troubled sub-prime mortgage backed securities, they would likely be included in the corporate securities category and certain U.S. equities (which include investment company share funds, such as open-end funds, closed-end funds, money market mutual funds, and hedge funds) which may have been invested in real estate. However, these were a relatively small share of China's total U.S. securities holdings [12]. China's holdings of Fannie Mae and Freddie Mac securities (though not their stock) were likely to have been more substantial, but less risky (compared to other mortgage-backed securities), especially after these two institutions were placed in conservatorship by the Federal Government in September 2008 and thus have government backing.

The Chinese government generally does not release detailed information on the holdings of its financial entities, although some of its banks have reported on their level of exposure to sub- prime U.S. mortgages [13]. Such entities have generally reported that their exposure to troubled sub- prime U.S. mortgages has been minor relative to their total investments, that they have liquidated such assets and/or have written off losses, and that they (the banks) continue to earn high profit margins [14]. For example, the Bank of China (one of China's largest state-owned commercial banks) reported in March 2008 that its investment in asset-backed securities supported by U.S. sub-prime mortgages totaled $10.6 billion in 2006 (accounting for 3.5% of its investment securities portfolio). In October 2008, it reported that it had reduced holdings of such securities to $3.3 billion (1.4% of its total securities investments) by the end of September 2008, while its holdings of debt securities issued or backed by Freddie Mac and Fannie Mae were at $10 billion. Fitch Ratings service reported that the Bank of China's exposure to U.S. sub-prime-related investments was the largest among Asian financial institutions, and that further losses from these investments were likely, but went on to state that the Bank of China would be able to absorb any related losses "without undue strain" [15].

However, China's economy has not been immune to effects of the global financial crisis, given its heavy reliance on trade and foreign direct investment (FDI) for its economic growth. Numerous sectors have been hard hit [16]. To illustrate:

- The real estate market in several Chinese cities has exhibited signs of a bubble that is bursting, including a slowdown in construction, falling prices and growing levels of unoccupied buildings. This has increased pressure on the banks to lower interest rates further to stabilize the market.
- The value of China's main stock market index, the Shanghai Stock Exchange Composite Index, dropped by 36% from June 2, 2008 to March 18, 2009 [17]
- China's trade has plummeted in recent months (see Figure 1). For example, exports and imports in February 2009 were down 25.7% and 24.1%, respectively on a year-on-year basis. The decline in exports was the biggest monthly decline every recorded.
- The level of FDI flows to China has fallen four months in a row (November 2008-February 2009). Monthly FDI flows to China dropped by 15.8% in February 2009 and by 32.6% in January (year-on-year basis).

- Numerous press reports indicate sharp reductions of production and employment in China. The Chinese government in January 2009 estimated that 20 million migrant workers had lost their jobs in 2008 because of the global economic slowdown.
- Global Insight, an international forecasting firm, estimates that China's real GDP growth will slow to 5.7% in 2009 [18]. Some analysts contend annual economic growth of less than 8% could lead to social unrest, given that every year there are 20 million new job seekers in China [19]

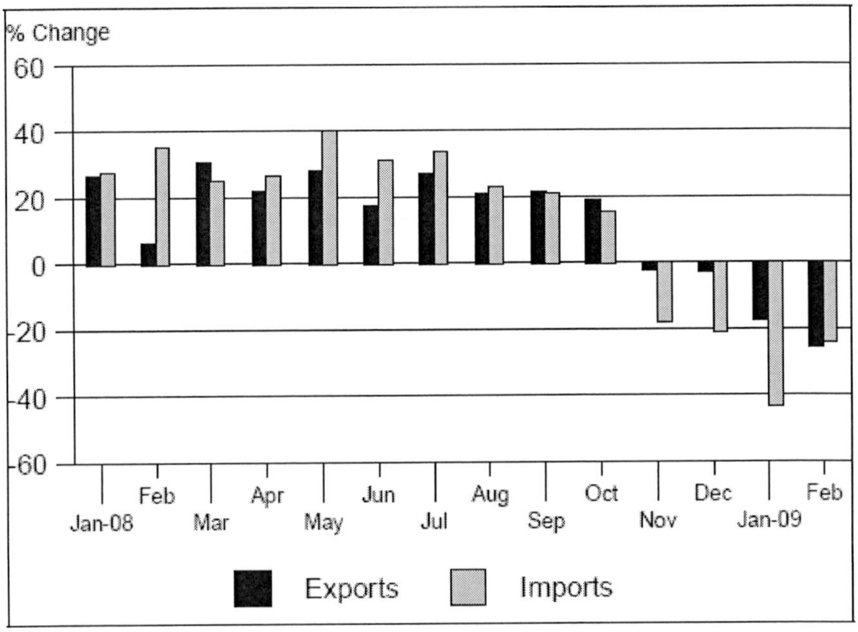

Source: Global Insight and China's Customs Administration (year-on-year basis).

Figure 1. Changes in China's Monthly Trade Data: January 2008-February 2009.

CHINA'S RESPONSE TO THE CRISIS

China has taken a number of steps to respond to the global financial crisis. On September 27, 2008, Jiabao reportedly stated that "What we can do now is to maintain the steady and fast growth of the national economy, and ensure that no major fluctuations will happen. That will be our greatest contribution to the world economy under the current circumstances." [20] On October 25, 2008, a Chinese Foreign Affairs official was reported by China's media as saying that China supported "effective and comprehensive reforms" of the global financial system. On October 30, another official stated: "In the future we are also willing, within the ambit of our abilities, to continue positively considering participating in a range of rescue plans."

On October, 8, 2008, China's central bank announced a cut (50 basis points) to its benchmark interest rate (and the reserve-requirement ratio), which coincided with rate cuts by the U.S. Federal Reserve and several other major central banks. China cut its rates again (by 27 basis points) on October 29 following the Federal Reserve's cut (by 50 basis points).

China has also indicated plans to make greater efforts to shore up its own economy to promote greater domestic demand, boost living standards in the poorer sections of the country, achieve more balanced economic growth (e.g., lowering dependency on exports), and address a number of economic and social issues, such as boosting energy efficiency, lowering pollution, narrowing income disparities, and improving the social safety net (such as health care, education, pensions, and social security). A number of initiatives were announced by the government in October 2008, including plans to: implement a new economic stimulus package, including an acceleration of construction projects, new export tax rebates; tax and interest rate cuts on housing transactions; increased agriculture subsidies and new loans for small and medium-sized enterprises; and elimination of taxes on interest income from stocks and savings [21]. On November 9, 2008, the Chinese government announced it would implement a two-year $586 billion stimulus package, mainly dedicated to infrastructure projects. The package would finance programs in 10 major areas, including affordable housing, rural infrastructure, water, electricity, transport, the environment, technological innovation and rebuilding areas hit by disasters (especially, areas that were hit by the May 12, 2008 earthquake) [22]. On April 1, 2009, Chinese President Hu Jintao stated that the economic stimulus was beginning to take effect. The Chinese government predicts that the stimulus package will add between 1.5 and 1.9 percentage points to the underlying growth rate in 2009, and that overall GDP growth will be 8.0%. [23]. An Asian Development Bank official predicted in March 2009 that China will "emerge from the crisis in better shape than it was before if it can rise to the challenge of rebalancing its economy" [24].

China's Potential Role and Implications for the United States

Analysts debate what role China might play in responding to the global financial crisis, given its huge foreign exchange reserves but its relative reluctance to become a major player in global economic affairs and its tendency to be cautious with its reserves. Some have speculated that China would, in order to help stabilize its most important trading partner (the United States), boost purchases of U.S. securities (especially Treasury securities) in order to help fund the hundreds of billions of dollars that are expected to be spent by the U.S. government to purchase troubled assets and stimulate the economy [25]. Additionally, China might try to shore up the U.S. economy by buying U.S. stocks. On September 21, 2008, the White House indicated that President Bush had called President Hu about the financial crisis and steps the Administration was planning to take. An unnamed Chinese trade official was reported as stating that "the purpose of that call was to ask for China's help to deal with this financial crisis by urging China to hold even more U.S. Treasury bonds and U.S. assets." The official was further quoted as saying that China recognized that it "has a stake" in the health of the U.S. economy, both as a major market for Chinese exports and in terms of preserving the value of U.S.-based assets held by China" and that a stabilized U.S. economy was in China's own interest [26]. During her first visit to China in February 2009, Secretary of State Clinton urged China to continue to buy U.S. Treasury securities. Some contend that taking an active role to help the United States (and other troubled economies) would boost China's image as a positive contributor to world economic stability, similar to what occurred during the 1997-1998 Asian financial crisis when it offered financial aid to Thailand and pledged not to devalue its currency.

On the other hand, there are a number of reasons why China might be reluctant to significantly increase its investments of U.S. assets. One concern could be whether increased Chinese investments in the U.S. economy would produce long-term economic benefits for China. Some Chinese investments in U.S. financial companies have fared poorly, and Chinese officials could be reluctant to put additional money into investments that were deemed to be too risky [27]. Secondly, a sharp economic downturn of the Chinese economy would likely increase pressure to invest money at home, rather than overseas. Many analysts (including some in China) have questioned the wisdom of China's policy of investing a large volume of foreign exchange reserves in U.S. government securities (which offer a relatively low rate of return) when China has such huge development needs at home [28]. China's holdings of U.S. securities at the end of 2008 are estimated to be roughly equivalent to over $1,000 per person in China, a significant figure for a country with a per capita GDP of about $3,190 (2008) [29]. On March 13, 2009, Chinese Premier Wen Jiabao at a news conference stated that he was "a little bit worried" about the safety of Chinese assets in the United States [30]. On March 24, 2009, the governor of the People's Bank of China, Zhou Xiaochuan, published a paper calling for the replacing the U.S. dollar as the international reserve currency with a new global system controlled by the International Monetary Fund [31]. Many analysts (including some in China) have questioned the wisdom of China's policy of investing a large level of foreign exchange reserves in U.S. government securities, which offer a relatively low rate of return when China has such huge development needs at home.

While additional large-scale Chinese purchases of U.S. securities might provide short-term benefits to the U.S. economy and may be welcomed by some policymakers, they could also raise a number of issues and concerns. Some U.S. policymakers have expressed concern that China might try to use its large holdings of U.S. securities as leverage against U.S. policies it opposes. For example, various Chinese government officials reportedly suggested on a number of occasions in the past that China could dump (or threaten to dump) a large share of its holdings in order to counter U.S. pressure (such as threats of trade sanctions) on various trade issues (such as China's currency policy). In exchange for new purchases of U.S. debt, China would likely want U.S. policymakers to lower expectations that China will move more rapidly to reform its financial sector and/or allow its currency to appreciate more substantially against the dollar [32]. Some analysts have suggested that China could choose to utilize its reserves to buy stakes in various distressed U.S. industries. However, this could also raise concerns in the United States that China was being allowed to buy equity or ownership in U.S. firms at rock bottom prices, that technology and intellectual property from acquired firms could be transferred to Chinese business entities (boosting their competitiveness vis-a-vis U.S. firms), and that becoming a large stakeholder in major U.S. companies would give the Chinese government enormous new political influence in the United States [33]. U.S. policymakers in the past have sometimes opposed attempts by Chinese firms to acquire shares or ownership of U.S. firms [34].

While attending the G-20 summit in London on the global financial crisis on April 1, 2009, President Obama President Hu met separately to discuss a number issues. The two sides agreed "to work together to resolutely support global trade and investment flows" and to "resist protectionism" [35]

REFERENCES

[1] *Invest in China*, September 10, 2007.

[2] Associated Press, "China's official data masks severity of slump, February 6, 2009.

[3] According to *Xinhua Net* (March 9, 2008), China's Labor and Social Security Minister Tian Chengping warned that the employment situation in China in 2008 was expected to be "very severe."

[4] *IMF Survey Magazine: What the Numbers Show*, October 17, 2007.

[5] Some analysts contend that China's policy of keeping the value of its currency low against the dollar and large purchases of U.S. debt may have been a contributing cause to the current global financial crisis.

[6] China's central bank manages its currency (the renminbi or yuan) against a basket of major currencies (largely the U.S. dollar) by heavily intervening in international currency markets to maintain targeted exchange rates. See CRS Report CRS Report RL32165, *China's Currency: Economic Issues and Options for U.S. Trade Policy*, by Wayne M. Morrison and Marc Labonte.

[7] For an overview of the China Investment Corporation, see CRS Report RL34337, *China's Sovereign Wealth Fund*, by Michael F. Martin.

[8] China's large and growing reserves are largely the result of China's currency policy (which requires the government to intervene in currency markets to prevent the renminbi from appreciating), large levels of FDI, and large trade surpluses.

[9] ST debt includes Treasury, agency, corporate, and equity debt with less than one year maturity.

[10] Although the Chinese government does not make public the dollar composition of its foreign exchange holdings, many analysts estimate this level to be around 70%. Based on this estimate, China's holdings of such securities may have risen to about $1.4 trillion through the end of 2008, and it is likely that China surpassed Japan by the end of 2008 as the largest foreign holder of U.S. securities.

[11] China was the largest foreign holder of U.S. agency debt, accounting for 36% of total as of June 2008.

[12] According to the Treasury Department, China was not among the top 10 global investors of U.S. corporate mortgage- backed securities.

[13] *Financial Times*, September 11, 2008.

[14] According to Caijing.com, Chinese banks held $670 million worth of bonds issued by U.S. investment bank Lehman Brothers when it went bankrupt in September 2008.

[15] *Fitch Ratings*, Press Release, January 24, 2008.

[16] China's economy was already slowing down before the global financial crisis hit. This was in large part the result of government efforts to slow the rate of inflation. China's real GDP growth fell from 13% in 2007 to 9% in 2008. The global financial crisis has sharply diminished economic growth. Thus, the Chinese government has abandoned its anti- inflation policies and instead has sought to stimulate the economy.

[17] However, the Shanghai Index is one of the few global indexes to experience positive growth in 2009; from January 5, 2009 to March 18, 2009, it was up 18%.

[18] Global Insight, *China*, March 18, 2009.

[19] According to Xinhua Net (March 9, 2008), China's Labor and Social Security Minister Tian Chengping warned that the employment situation in China in 2008 was expected to be "very severe," noting that towns and cities would be able to provide only 12 million new jobs.

[20] *Chinaview*, September 27, 2008.

[21] China *Xinhua News Agency*, Special Report, Financial Crisis.

[22] China *Xinhua News Agency*, November 12, 2008.

[23] Global Insight, *Country Intelligence Analysis*, March 23, 2009.

[24] Asian Development Bank, *News Release*, March 31, 2009.

[25] According to the Treasury Department, China overtook Japan in September 2008 as the largest foreign holder of U.S. Treasury securities. As of January 2009, China's holdings totaled $740 billion, accounting for 24.1% of total foreign holdings of U.S. Treasury securities. China accounted for more than one-third of total new purchases of these securities by foreign investors from January 2008 to January 2009.

[26] *Inside U.S. Trade, China Trade Extra*, September 24, 2008.

[27] For example, in June 2007, China's sovereign wealth fund bought $3 billion worth of shares from Blackstone LP (a U.S. private equity firm) at $31 each, but the value of those shares fell to $7.3 as of Aprill 1, 2009.

[28] China could use some of these reserves to purchase foreign imports, such as food, equipment, raw materials, consumer goods, etc. However, a significant sell-off of U.S. assets could destabilize the value of China's remaining U.S. assets and could weaken its ability to maintain its exchange rate goals. A similar result would occur if the government sold off its dollar holdings in China to obtain renminbi to be used to stimulate the domestic economy—it would cause the value of the renminbi to depreciate against the dollar, which could decrease exports.

[29] As long as the Chinese government continues to intervene in currency markets to keep the value of the renminbi low against the dollar, and continues to experience large trade surpluses, it will have relatively few options for dealing with additional foreign exchange reserves, other than to keep buying U.S. assets.

[30] Xinhua News Agency, March 13, 2009.

[31] *Financial Times*, "China calls for new reserve currency," March 24, 2009.

[32] China's currency has appreciated by about 19% to the dollar since reforms were made in July 2005, but many U.S. policymakers contend that it remains significantly undervalued.

[33] Most Chinese firms that have been allowed to invest overseas are state-owned enterprises.

[34] For example, efforts by a Chinese state-owned oil company (CNOOC) in 2005 to purchase a U.S. energy company (Unocal) was widely opposed in Congress and eventually led the Chinese company to drop its bid. In 2007 a Chinese firm (Huawei) attempted to buy a stake in a U.S. technology company (3Com), but dropped its bid after a number of national security concerns were raised in a review by the U.S. Committee on Foreign Investment in the United States.

[35] White House Pres Release, April 1, 2009.

In: The Global Financial Crisis: Policies and Implications
Editor: J. P. Gallagher and E. C. Wilkins
ISBN 978-1-61470-317-4
© 2012 Nova Science Publishers, Inc.

Chapter 5

THE GLOBAL FINANCIAL CRISIS: FOREIGN AND TRADE POLICY EFFECTS*

Dick K. Nanto

ABSTRACT

The global financial and economic crisis affects all three of the essential national interests of the United States: national security, economic well being, and value projection. Only occasionally does an event of this magnitude occur that generates such daunting challenges yet also opportunities for U.S. policy. The effects of the crisis on foreign policy, trade, and security are so diverse and widespread that, out of necessity, policy responses must range from the highly specific to the broad and ethereal.

This report provides an overview of the major non-financial effects of the global crisis. In some countries, incumbent governments have lost support or authoritarian governments are consolidating power. In certain countries, conditions for citizen discontent or even radicalism are being augmented and market capitalism is being questioned. On the world stage, U.S. leadership is being challenged; money to lend is becoming a critical component of soft power; budgets are tightening and threatening funds for economic assistance and national security; international financial institutions are assuming a higher profile relative to national governments; and shifts in trade flows are raising forces for protectionism. As seen in the G-20 London Summit, the financial crisis also has become a rallying point for anti-globalization groups and anti-government activists. The U.S. Director of National Intelligence, Dennis Blair, has told Congress that instability in countries around the world caused by the global economic crisis and its geopolitical implications, rather than terrorism, is the primary near-term security threat to the United States.

The political and foreign policy effects of the global financial crisis can be divided roughly into the following categories: effects on political leadership, regimes, stability, and spheres of influence; effects on economic philosophies, state capitalism, and trade protectionism; effects on U.S. international leadership and attitudes toward the United States; effects on supranational financial and economic organizations; effects on poverty; and budgetary effects on resources for aid, diplomacy, and defense.

---

* This is an edited, reformatted and augmented version of CRS Report R40496, dated April 7, 2009.

Congress has been active in recognizing and moving toward dealing with the longer-term effects of the crisis, but most of the long-term effects are just developing, and it is yet not clear whether they are temporary jogs in a path or a permanent deviation from post-World War II trends. The response to the effects depends both on "more of the same" (working through existing institutions for diplomacy, aid, trade policy, and security) with incremental changes and at a higher level of intensity, and on new and innovative approaches to cope with problems laid bare by the crisis. As the dust from the onset of the crisis has begun to clear, it is apparent that the world has become more unstable, that much of the blame for the turmoil is being aimed at the United States, that attempted solutions are taking enormous amounts of budgetary resources, and that, if the crisis worsens, it may cause wrenching changes both within the countries most vulnerable and among the big power nations of the world.

THE ISSUE AND ROLE OF CONGRESS

The world now faces the worst financial and economic crisis since the Great Depression. The bursting of the U.S. housing market bubble has sparked a ripple effect that has grown to major proportions and is wreaking havoc on market after market and country after country as it works its way around the world. The sudden loss of trillions of dollars in wealth, the addition of tens of millions of people to the ranks of the unemployed, and historic drops in economic activity have combined to create new challenges for policymakers. While the current focus is on measures to recover from the financial and economic turmoil, the uncertainty and socio-political forces being generated are creating political instability, heightening security risks, and affecting U.S. interests in ways that could hardly have been imagined just a year ago.

This report provides an overview of the major non-financial impact of the global financial and economic crisis—both actual and potential. Although the eventual effects of the crisis are yet to be determined, looking back at the Great Depression, it is clear that a prolonged and widespread economic contraction can lead to major shifts in governments and acts of desperation that can be catastrophic in nature and far reaching in effect. International Monetary Fund Managing Director Dominique Strauss-Kahn recently stated that as the crisis spills over into developing countries, millions will be pushed into poverty and unemployment, and, for many countries, this will be at the roots of social unrest, some threat to democracy, and for some cases may also end in armed conflict [1].

The forces that determine foreign policy and provide a foundation for the basic paradigms that underlie policy initiatives tend to have a long history and a momentum of their own. Therefore, the ultimate effects of the global financial crisis likely will depend on the length and severity of the global recession. If, as many economic forecasts indicate, the global downturn is U-shaped with a recession that lasts for about two years and recovery beginning in late 2009 or in 2010, the long-term effects are likely to be more of an exacerbation of previously existing trends rather than revolutionary direction-changing events except in particularly dire situations. However, if the global recession takes an L-shape with prolonged contraction and stagnation, much like the Great Depression, the probability rises that changes will be more than mere blips in a continuum but significant turns in the road.

As the crisis has progressed, policymakers have moved from rescues of financial institutions and loosened monetary measures to shoring up manufacturers in the real economy and expansionary fiscal policy. Now the crisis is extending into political and security concerns and is affecting fundamental issues such as basic economic philosophy or the underlying assumptions about the workings of market based economies. Some wonder if a statement by Albert Einstein may not apply here:

> The significant problems we face today cannot be solved at the same level of thinking we were at when we created them.

As indicated in Figure 1, the financial crisis began with a rising default level in subprime mortgages, bankruptcies, an overextension of credit and then a freezing of credit markets, and excessive financial bets on securitized debt obligations mainly in the United States but also in Europe. This has now grown into a global financial crisis with wildly diverse effects. At first, the crisis was transmitted through the globally interconnected financial system primarily among industrialized countries. As the economies of North America, Europe, and East Asia slowed or dropped into recession, the concomitant drops in commodity prices, international trade flows, and remittances along with tightening credit, and depreciating currencies (relative to the dollar and, in cases, the euro) caused similar contraction in growth in developing and emerging market countries [2]. This, in turn, has caused social and economic effects that pose the foreign policy challenges discussed in this report, and which ultimately can lead to a greater role for international financial institutions and a weakening of pro-United States and pro-Western.

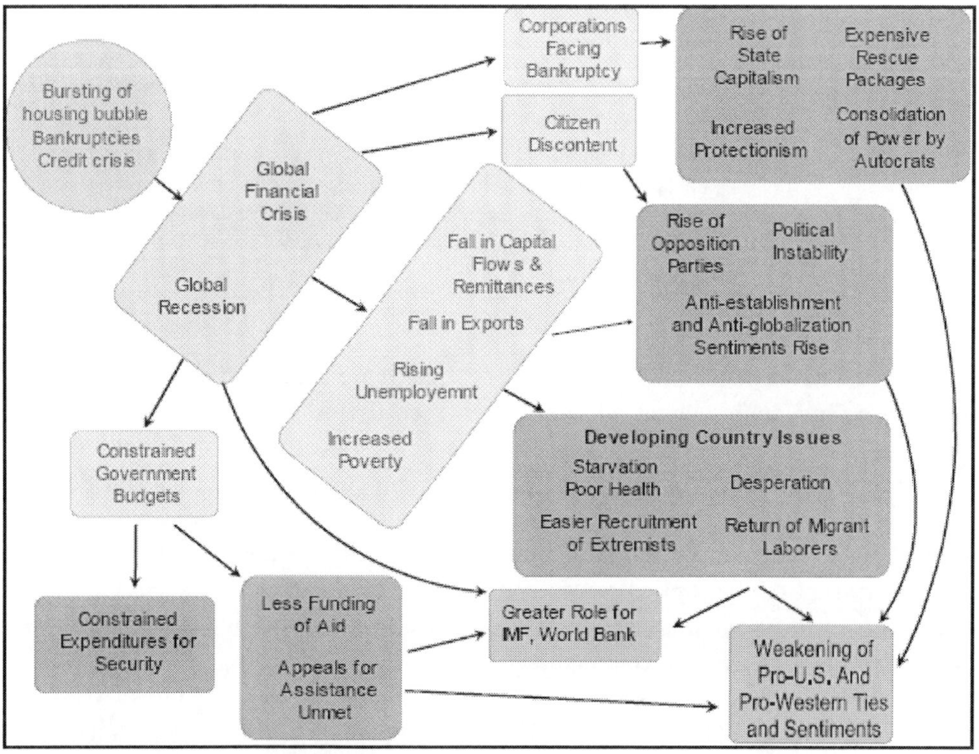

Source: Congressional Research Service.

Figure 1. Actual and Potential Foreign Policy Related Effects of the Global Financial Crisis.

Some of the specific effects being created or exacerbated by the financial crisis are shown in Table 1. These include changes in the U.S. leadership role and in international relations both among countries and between the United States and other nations. The enhanced role of the International Monetary Fund both as a lender of last resort and coordinator (along with the Financial Stability Board) of international financial regulatory reform is particularly notable.

Table 1. Actual and Potential Foreign Policy and Security Changes Caused or Exacerbated by the Global Financial Crisis

Category of Change	Actual or Potential Changes
International Relations	Potential effects on the U.S. leadership position in the world Enhanced role for the International Monetary Fund, Financial Stability Board, and Multilateral Development Banks The rise of China as a player in international financial issues and the co-mingling of U.S. and Chinese financial interests Additional pressures on European unity and policy discord between the United States and Germany/France Economic and political crises in Eastern Europe and tug-of-war for influence there between Russia and the EU/U.S.
Fundamental Philosophies	Rise of state capitalism and questioning of the Western economic model of deregulated, market-based decisionmaking Risk of rising trade protectionism and intensified anti-globalization efforts Potential for more authoritarianism in countries such as China and Russia and/or rise in authoritarian models of governance in the developing world
Security	Rising poverty and potential political instability in developing nations providing fertile ground for recruits for religious extremism
	Budgetary pressures in Western nations that could constrain international security and diplomatic efforts
Financial and Economic Fallout	Possible reduced U.S. financial primacy in the world and importance of the dollar as a reserve currency Diminished flows of economic assistance, capital, and remittances to developing nations For developing nations, declines in export earnings from low prices for commodities and from shrinking world trade

Source: Congressional Research Service.

Among the fundamental philosophies being affected are the rise of state capitalism, trade protectionism, and doubts about what has been seen as the Western economic model of market- based capitalism. Security issues include rising poverty and conditions that could provide ready recruits for religious extremism in certain countries of Africa and South Asia and budgetary pressures that could constrain security related expenditures. Among the challenges stemming from the economic and financial fallout from the crisis are questions about the primacy of the United States and the role of the dollar as a reserve currency, problems for developing nations caused by diminished inflows of capital and remittances and declining exports and prices for commodities.

The role of Congress in this aspect of the crisis is multifaceted and broad based. As of early 2009, the major policy focus has been on containing the crisis and doing what is necessary to promote recovery and reform in financial markets both in the United States and abroad. Congress has a particular role to play in protecting the national interest; informing the public and managing public expectations; budgeting for economic assistance, diplomacy, and defense; determining trade policy; providing capital for the International Monetary Fund and Multilateral Development Banks and determining their role relative to the U.S. government; and ensuring that the U.S. grand strategy in dealing with the world succeeds. Several committees in both the Senate and House already have held hearings on the foreign policy and security implications of the global financial crisis [3]

Two Indicators of the Severity of the Crisis: Growth and Trade

How severe is the global financial crisis? On March 19, 2009, the International Monetary Fund projected global economic activity to contract by 1/2 to 1% in 2009—the first such fall in 60 years. Figure 2 shows projected growth rates by quarter (annualized) by Global Insight, an econometric forecasting firm. As can be seen, countries of the world are experiencing a simultaneous downturn with the advanced industrialized countries of North America, Europe, and Japan dropping into recession and a significant slowdown in economic growth rates in both developing countries and in emerging markets in Eastern Europe. Particularly noteworthy are the growth rates for China which still is positive but down considerably, and those for Japan (the second largest economy in the world) and Ukraine (an example of a particularly hard-hit economy), both facing severe recessions.

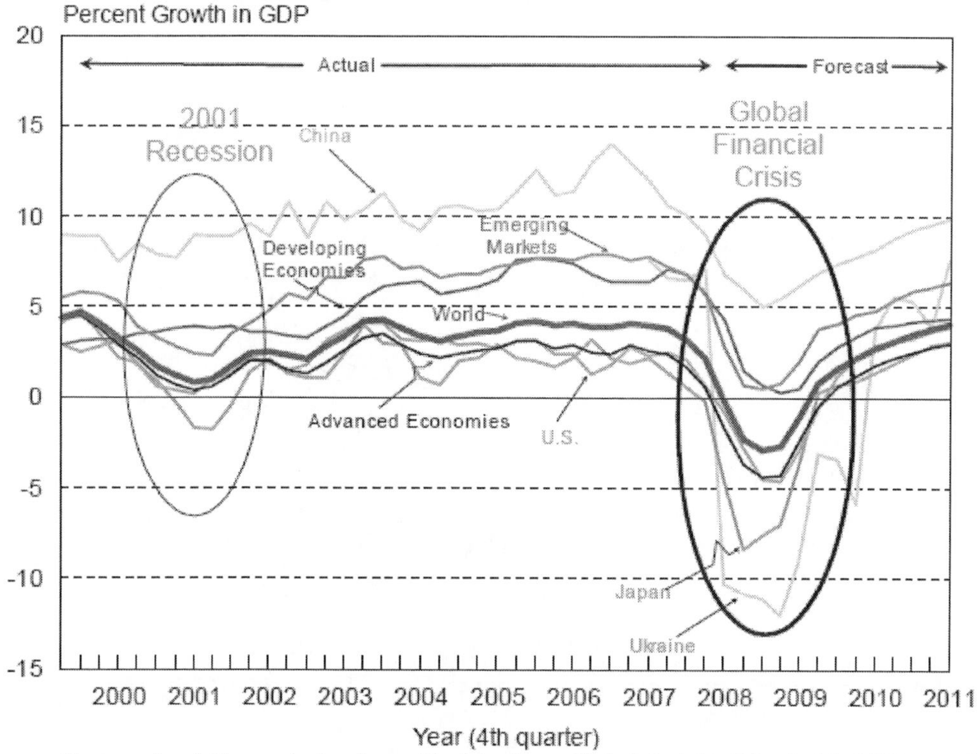

Source: Congressional Research Service with data from Global Insight (March 14, 2009, monthly forecast).

Figure 2. Actual and Forecasted Economic Growth Rates for Country Groups and the United States, Japan, and Ukraine (Annualized Quarterly Changes).

These declines in economic activity have combined with trillions of dollars lost in equity markets and a credit squeeze that not only is affecting households and businesses world wide but is putting a damper on the financing of activities such as world trade and oil exploration. The International Labor Organization has noted that after four years of consecutive declines in world unemployment, the number of unemployed persons had increased in 2008 by 14 million. As the crisis continues to spread and job losses mount, worldwide unemployment could increase by at least 38 million by the end of 2009 [4].

Exports of goods and services provide the main vehicle for countries to generate the foreign exchange necessary to pay for imports and to repay international debt. A deficit in a country's balance of trade also tends to depress the value of its currency which then raises the cost of debt service for governments, businesses, and households that have borrowed in international currencies. This is a particular problem for Eastern European nations whose public and private debt often is denominated in euros or Swiss francs. Also, in many less developed countries, the decline both in volume and price of exports of minerals and agricultural commodities undermines the basic levels of income for large segments of the working poor. Figure 3 shows estimates of the change in export levels in February 2009 compared with that a year previous.

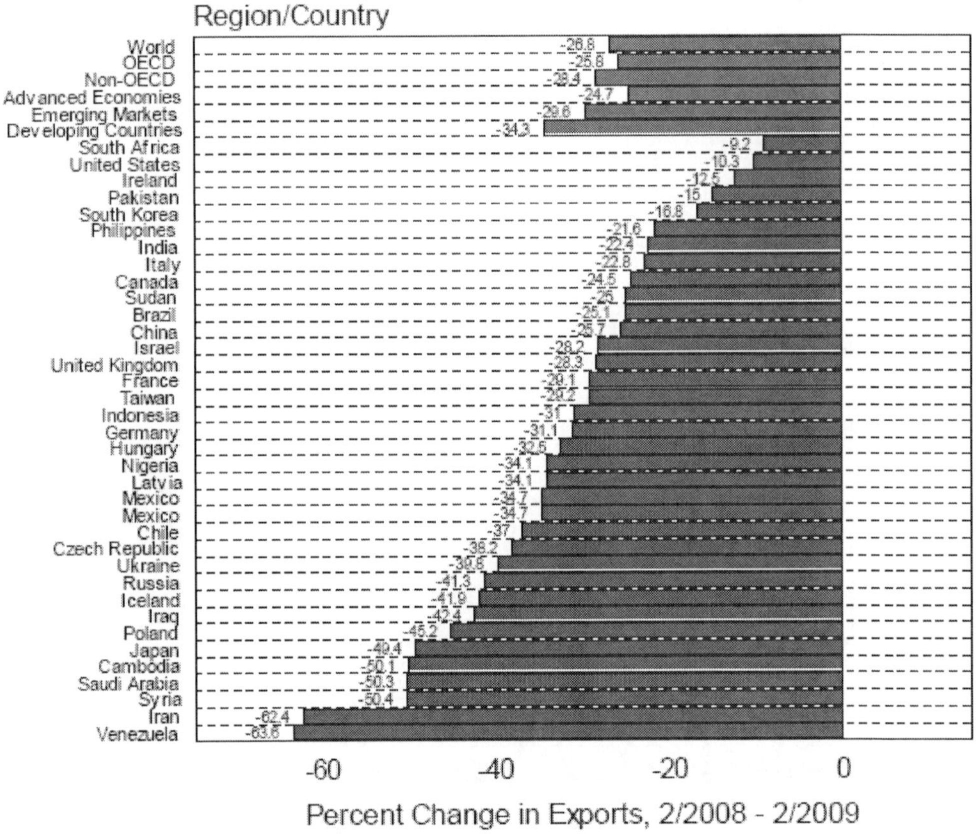

Source: CRS, Forecast data from Global Insight (March 14, 2009 forecast).

Figure 3. Change in Merchandise Export Levels for Selected Regions and Countries, February 2008-February 2009.

For the world, advanced economies, and emerging markets, exports were estimated to be down about 25% (Japan's were down 49%). For developing countries, however, exports were down by more than a third. Exports were down from 9% to 64% for the other countries indicated. These are historic drops in trade volume. Even though imports also are falling, the shrinking of international trade is adding to the contraction in global economic growth and causing unemployment rates to rise and pushing more people into poverty.

As the crisis has spread, the adverse macroeconomic effects are reverberating back to further weaken financial institutions, currencies, and equity markets. This is working to exacerbate adverse long-term effects that may affect U.S. foreign policy and, ultimately, U.S. security.

POLITICAL AND FOREIGN POLICY EFFECTS OF THE CRISIS

Any event of the magnitude of the global financial crisis generates unanticipated effects and this particular set of events seems to be driving states to adopt policies unprecedented in recent times. The financial crisis can be divided into four overlapping phases, each with a different focus. The first has been to contain the contagion and strengthen financial institutions through various financial packages aimed at restoring balance sheets of financial institutions and confidence in markets. Although the worst of the credit crunch seems to have subsided, the inventory of legacy "toxic" assets still has curtailed the ability of banks to lend and, combined with depressed equity values, is threatening insurance companies, pension funds, and investments held by a large swath of households and institutions across the world. The second phase of the crisis has been to deal with the slowdown and recession in world economies through various stimulus packages and other measures. The third phase has been to change financial regulations and build oversight and a regulatory architecture designed to prevent future crises and correct past abuses of the system. The fourth phase has been to deal with political and foreign policy effects of the crisis.

On February 12, 2009, the U.S. Director of National Intelligence, Dennis Blair, told Congress that instability in countries around the world caused by the global economic crisis and its geopolitical implications, rather than terrorism, is the primary near-term security threat to the United States. In his testimony before Congress, Blair stated that the crisis has already "increased questioning of U.S. stewardship of the global economy" and if it continued to spread and deepen, it would contribute to unrest and imperil some governments. He said that according to their statistical modeling, if economic crises persist over a one-to-two year period, they increase the risk of "regime-threatening instability" [5].

Other countries also have recognized that potential political and security effects of the crisis. On March 6, 2009, the United Kingdom established a new security committee called the National Security Forum and asked it to assess the security implications of the global financial crisis. The 12-member group is to bring together experts on policing, counter-terrorism, intelligence, finance and diplomacy to provide analysis to the UK's national security decision-makers [6].

The political and foreign policy effects of the global financial crisis can be divided roughly into the following categories:

- effects on political leadership; regimes; perceived countries of influence; and stability, violence, and terrorism;
- effects on economic philosophy, state capitalism, and protectionism;
- effects on U.S. international leadership and attitudes toward the United States;
- effects on supranational financial and economic organizations;
- effects on poverty; and
- budgetary effects on resources for aid, diplomacy, and defense.

Effects on Political Leadership; Regimes; Perceived Countries of Influence; and Stability, Violence, and Terrorism

Political Leadership

Two of the major mechanisms through which the financial crisis works on political leadership and regimes within countries are citizen discontent and the consolidation of power by governments.

Citizen Discontent

The discontent from citizens arises from those who are losing jobs, seeing businesses go bankrupt, losing wealth both in financial and real assets, and facing declining prices for their products. This discontent often results in public opposition to the existing establishment or ruling regime and, in democracies, can lead to their replacement through established electoral processes. One commentator has called this the “Axis of Upheaval” [7] referring to the concept that the substantial increase in unemployment and a painful decline in incomes are likely to cause, or contribute to, political upheavals in countries. While financial crises may not be the only cause of such political instability, they may push conditions to a “tipping point.”

For example, on January 26, 2009, in financially beleaguered Iceland, Prime Minister Geir Haarde and his cabinet resigned just three months after the collapse of the country's currency, stock market, and several major banks, and following large outbursts of public protest [8]. On February 20, 2009, Latvia's center-right coalition government collapsed, a victim of the country's growing economic and political turmoil [9]. In Hungary, the country’s economic crisis has provided an opportunity for a political comeback for Viktor Orban, the long-standing leader of Hungary’s conservative opposition [10]. A similar situation has developed in Japan where Prime Minister Taro Aso’s approval rating has dropped to about 10% (in February 2009) apparently because of public discontent with his efforts to rekindle economic growth [11]. His conservative Liberal Democratic Party could well lose control of the government in the next election to an emboldened opposition [12] Ukraine and Georgia also have been moving into a period of political uncertainty as they sink deeper into economic recession [13]. Public discontent over the adverse effects of the financial crisis also is rising in countries such as Greece, France, the United Kingdom, Ireland, Thailand, Haiti, and China. Some have called this the “European winter of discontent” [14] even though the impact extends far beyond the European continent. This illustrates how the global financial crisis can create chances for opposition leaders, regardless of political philosophy, to put pressure on incumbent governments.

In some cases public discontent may be manifest in extremist movements, particularly in poorer countries where large numbers of unemployed young people may become susceptible to religious radicalism that demonizes Western industrialized society and encourages terrorist activity. (See section on Stability and Violence below.) Although not completely related to the financial crisis, in March 2009 in El Salvador, the left-wing FMLN party of former Marxist guerrillas claimed victory in a hotly contested election [15]. If governments change, moreover, the rising new government may play on nationalistic sentiments, particularly if the previous regime is seen as having been too oriented toward international considerations.

Some members of the European Union initially viewed the financial crisis as primarily an American phenomenon. That view has changed as economic activity in the EU has declined at a faster pace than in the United States and public protests against the growing financial and economic turmoil have increased the political stakes for EU governments and their leaders. As one commentator has put it, "As panic grips Cabinet rooms across the Continent, the public is driven to fury." [16] Of growing concern is the impact the financial crisis and the economic recession are having on the economies of Eastern Europe and prospects for political instability as well as the future course for market reforms. Western European banks are heavily involved in Eastern Europe, and worsening economic conditions there could compound the current problems facing financial institutions in EU member nations [17].

Consolidating Government Power

The second way that the crisis works on ruling regimes is through the actions of existing governments both to stay in power and to deal with the adverse effects of the crisis. Any crisis generates centrifugal forces that tend to strengthen central government power. Most nations view the current financial crisis as having been created by the financial elite in New York and London in cooperation with increasingly laissez faire governments in the United States and the United Kingdom. During the January 2009 World Economic Forum in Davos, Switzerland, for example, Chinese Premier Wen Jiabao charged that America's voracious appetite for debt and "blind pursuit of profit" had led to the worst recession since the Great Depression [18]. By blaming the industrialized West, particularly the United States, for their economic woes, governments can stoke the fires of nationalism and seek support for themselves.

As nationalist sentiments rise and economic conditions worsen, citizens look to governments as a rescuer of last resort. Political authorities can take actions, ostensibly to counter the effects of the crisis, but often with the result of consolidating their power and preserving their own positions. Authoritarian regimes, in particular, can take even more extreme actions to deal with financial and economic challenges.

In Venezuela, for instance, President Hugo Chavez won a referendum on February 15, 2009, ending the two-term limit on presidential elections, a battle he had previously lost in December 2007. Although the result of a democratic process and not completely attributable to the global financial crisis, this does point to the tightening of Chavez's power in Venezuela. On February 28, he sent troops to temporarily take over rice processing plants including one owned by the American company Cargill. Falling oil prices have limited the government's ability to provide compensation for takeovers of private businesses [19].

In Russia, the impact of the financial crisis has been particularly severe as it faces a decline in global demand for its exports of oil and natural gas and a 71% drop in the price of its petroleum. The crisis has exposed Russia's significant dependence on oil, natural gas, and other commodities. In 2008, oil, natural gas, and other fuels accounted for about 65% of Russia's export revenues. In addition, the Russian government is dependent on taxes on sales of oil and natural gas for more than half of its revenues; Russia has generated budget surpluses since 1998, but it is expected to have a budget deficit in 2009, primarily because of the fall in oil prices.

The fall in world demand for oil also has hit other parts of the Russian economy. As of April 6, 2009, Russia's RTS stock market index had lost nearly 70% of its value from the peak reached on May 19, 2008. From June 2008 to the end of January 2009, the ruble had depreciated by 52% in terms of the dollar and 22% in terms of the euro. This compelled the Central Bank of Russia to intervene to bolster the value of its currency by selling foreign exchange and buying rubles. This caused Russia's official foreign exchange reserves to decline accordingly.

These increasingly difficult economic circumstances in Russia are proving to be a factor in rising nationalism and spreading state capitalism there. Some feel, for example, that Russia has taken advantage of the need to intervene in the economy to counter effects of the financial crisis to make the country a harder, more vertically managed power with state capitalism as the foundation of its industrial sector. This reversing or slowing down of many of the structural economic reforms had been pursued under then President Putin, but as the financial crisis and drop in the price of energy has hit Russia, the Kremlin and now Prime Minister Putin have increased the government's control over critical sectors such as oil, natural gas, and other commodities.

Perceived Countries of Influence

As the financial crisis spreads to emerging and developing nations, many of these countries are facing gargantuan financial problems that they are unable to resolve themselves. They have turned to outside assistance from sources such as Russia, the European Union, China, and the International Monetary Fund. Whether such assistance is extended or not may affect strategic and political relations with the nations in question. In Eastern Europe, in particular, there appears to be a tug of war developing between the European Union and Russia for the long-term allegiances of Eastern European states [20]. The situation in Ukraine illustrates the problem. After being rebuffed by the IMF for additional financing, Ukraine Prime Minister Yulia Tymoshenko said that she had sent letters requesting financial aid to the United States, the European Union, China, Japan, and Russia. She also noted that Russia had responded with a positive reply, although Moscow has yet to announce a decision [21] (Eventually, Ukraine accepted an IMF loan and has agreed to its rather stringent conditions [such as increasing its retirement age].)

In April 2009, OAO Surgutneftegaz, a Russian oil company close to the Kremlin, announced that it had acquired a 21% stake in Hungary's national energy company. This sparked criticism that Moscow was exploiting the financial crisis by parlaying its energy resources into greater economic influence in Eastern Europe [22].

In one case, the financial crisis may help in moving a country away from Russia and toward the West. On January 12, 2009, the IMF approved a 15-month Stand-By Arrangement of $2.46 billion for Belarus. Belarus also had unsuccessfully approached Russia for a $3 billion currency swap arrangement and then asked for a $2 billion bank loan guaranteed by the Russian government. Some assert that Belarus has set up a "bidding war" between the East and West for influence there [23]

"Checkbook diplomacy" (using economic assistance to gain political advantage), in many cases has returned only mixed results. However, public memories of events during times of crisis tend to linger. In Thailand and other Southeast Asian countries, perceptions persisted that the United States had been slow in lending support during the 1997-98 Asian financial crisis and were only partly assuaged years later through the outpouring of U.S. assistance to Southeast Asian nations following the 2004 Indian Ocean Tsunami [24]

A Dutch think-tank also has been following the security impact of the financial crisis. It has been particularly interested in a possible power shift from the West to the East because of China's rising financial power [25]. The London Economist puts the situation in these terms:

> China's prime minister, Wen Jiabao, no longer sticks to the script that China is a humble player in world affairs that wants to focus on it own economic development. He talks of China as a "great power" and worries about America's profligate spending endangering his $1 trillion nest egg there. ...Already a big idea has spread far beyond China: that geopolitics is now a bipolar affair, with America and China the only two that matter [26]

The financial crisis also is providing an opportunity for cash-rich China to secure critical supplies of minerals and raw materials [27]. Although China's quest for food, fuel, and ores is not new and Chinese companies are backing out of some deals, Chinese companies are among the few with cash on hand to do deals in the current recessionary economic conditions. In February 2009, China reached a long-term deal to lend $25 billion to two Russian energy companies in exchange for an expanded supply of Russian oil. China Minmetals Corporation also had offered roughly $1.7 billion to buy Australia's OZ Minerals Ltd., and Aluminum Corp. of China announced a planned $19.5 billion investment in Australia's mining giant Rio Tinto [28]. The financial crisis apparently has made companies facing falling demand eager to secure cash and more amenable to overtures by Chinese companies. While locking up such supplies of raw materials may not translate into political allegiances, they constitute a strong link in supply chain ties that tend to bind economies together [29].

China also has entered into currency swap arrangements totaling 650 billion Chinese yuan ($95 billion) with South Korea, Hong Kong, Malaysia, Indonesia, Belarus and Argentina. Under the swap arrangements, those countries could swap a foreign currency for yuan that can be used to settle trade with China [30].

The financial crisis also has been buffeting the sense of unity among the eurozone nations. There has been some speculation on a potential break-up of the eurozone, a development that could affect European security. The issue revolves around the troubles that Ireland and southern members of the single currency arrangement (Portugal, Spain, Italy, and Greece) have had in selling bonds and stabilizing their growing budget deficits [31]. At the same time, the financial crisis and the accompanying economic downturn have battered the currencies of many of the noneurozone countries, especially in Central and Eastern Europe. As a result, many of these countries have become more interested in joining the perceived safety of the eurozone and have pressed the eurozone members to relax the rules on entry into the euro area. These actions are straining relations with the larger, more prosperous economies of the eurozone and the European Union who hold a skeptical view of any rapid expansion in eurozone membership. For some of the aspiring economies, however, opposition within the euro area to their membership is especially embittering, because the recession is undermining their ability to meet the rigid requirements for membership in the eurozone set by the more prosperous economies, who, they argue, are to blame for originating the crisis.

Stability, Violence, and Terrorism

Citizen discontent, the consolidation of government power, and effects on international relations relate to economic and political stability both within and among countries. Stability, in and of itself, is not an overriding foreign policy goal, [32] but no one likes to deal with surprises, particularly those that can threaten U.S. interests. If change happens, U.S. foreign policy analysts would like to be able to predict it and prepare for the consequences. The National Intelligence Council in its November 2008 report forecasting global trends to 2025, noted that economic volatility introduces a major risk factor to political stability. Historians and social scientists have discovered a strong correlation between rapid economic change—both positive and negative— and political instability. The Council cited the massive dislocation and economic volatility introduced by the end of the "first" globalization in 1914-1918 that helped lay the groundwork for the rise of protectionism in the 1920s and 1930, and then to World War II that, in turn, unleashed a long series of national and ethnic conflicts that reverberates today [33]. One thing that could be said about stability, is that instability generally favors a rising power or opposition forces. For a dominant power, instability may pose a risk to its hegemony.

For U.S. businesses operating overseas, stability is essential for smooth operations. Obtaining government approvals, building manufacturing facilities, expanding service networks, maintaining a labor force, and shipping components and final products all are threatened by political, financial, and economic instability. Also, political instability may bring a rise in crime, traffic in illegal drugs and counterfeit products, kidnappings, and other illicit activity.

The financial crisis also may worsen problems that already have escalated in recent years. In particular, violence by drug cartels and crime syndicates seems to be on the rise in various countries. Mexico is a case in point. Rising violence in Mexico is forcing American companies to change their operating procedures and shipping routes, and to tighten security for their employees [34]. Mexican President Felipe Calderon has rejected U.S. concerns that Mexico is losing control of its territory to drug cartels and called "absolutely false" the idea that Mexico is in danger of becoming a failed state if the violence continues. However, in 2008, 6,290 people were killed in drug violence [35] and government officials say the drug war and economic crisis are starting to feed off each other. The violence discourages foreign investment and tourism while rising unemployment could nudge more youths to join the drug cartels. Lower growth also could leave Mexico with less cash to spend on the drug war, which cost $6.4 billion over 2007 and 2008 [36].

Even in China, where rates of violent crime have traditionally been low, there reportedly has been an increase in kidnappings for ransom since the onset of the economic slowdown and an overall rise in security issues for multinational companies, particularly from laid-off workers. Desperation over unemployment seems to be the primary cause of this increasing threat [37].

Political instability and poverty also can provide an incubator for extremism. The financial crisis may not be the primary cause of ideologically driven terrorism, but the worsening of economic conditions and rising joblessness among young people provide better recruitment opportunities for extremist terrorist groups. Militants thrive in places of political instability and lack of strong central governmental control. The global financial crisis threatens to create more such places. Countries of concern may include Pakistan, Bangladesh, Yemen, Nigeria, Sudan, Somalia, and Egypt. As one analyst has stated,

> No matter how cohesive and determined a terrorist organization, it needs a supportive environment in which to flourish. That means a location that provides a steady stream of funds and recruits and the support (or at least acceptance) of the local population. ... As more people lose their jobs, their homes, and opportunities for prosperity—in emerging market countries or even within minority communities inside developed states—it becomes easier for local militants to find volunteers [38].

The global financial crisis also is causing mass deportations or voluntary exodus by many immigrant workers who no longer can find employment abroad. As these workers return to their home countries, they may join the many already unemployed and become targets for recruitment by militant groups and insurgent movements. For example, most of the Gulf Cooperation Council states rely heavily on foreign labor in their construction and oil industries. Many of these workers are from Pakistan, India, Bangladesh, and the Philippines. Dubai's labor ministry reportedly has been cancelling 1,500 work permits per day since late October 2008 [39].

In February 2009, the Chairman of the Joint Chiefs of Staff, Admiral Mike Mullen outlined what he thinks about the future and evolution of the U.S. military stated that the world's financial crisis has to be taken into consideration as well. Mullen noted that poor economic states may become future targets for terrorism. He also added that U.S. defense may be affected by budget cuts, possibly shifting mission focuses [40]. As noted above, on March 23, 2009, IMF Managing Director Dominique Strauss-Kahn said the world is in a dire economic crisis that will push millions into poverty and unemployment, risking social unrest and even war and that urgent action is required [41].

The rising unemployment problem is exacerbated by declining remittances from workers overseas, a critical component of household income in many poorer countries. The global financial crisis not only has reduced export income and inflows of investment capital in many developing nations, but as demand shrinks for foreign labor in more industrialized economies, the money sent to home countries also may decline. In 2008, remittances from foreign workers accounted for an estimated $305 billion in flows to developing countries [42]. For many countries, this is greater than inflows of aid and foreign investment funds combined. The countries that rely on remittances for at least one-fifth of their income include such post-conflict and conflict-prone nations as Lebanon, Burundi, Liberia, Kyrgyzstan, Tajikistan, Afghanistan, Bosnia, Moldova and Haiti [43].

In Latin America, currencies, stock markets, and output are down broadly by one-third to one-half from a year earlier. Unemployment is also on the rise. While most countries in the region are likely to ride out the economic contraction, many are watching Argentina to see if it again ends up defaulting on its foreign debts, thereby raising the specter of a social breakdown. Financially, the country is extremely fragile and already is experiencing protests. This could present a challenge to U.S. policy and status, given that Argentines often blame the United States for many of their economic problems.

The precipitous drop in the price of oil, moreover, holds important implications for countries such as Mexico, Venezuela, and other petroleum exporters, who were counting on oil revenues to fund activities considered to be essential to their interests. The oil-producing Andean countries of Ecuador and Bolivia also tend to be financially fragile and have left-leaning governments. While moderating oil prices may be a positive development for the U.S. consumer and for the U.S. balance of trade, such price declines also may cause political instability in certain of these petroleum exporting countries. The concomitant drop in prices of commodities such as rubber, copper ore, iron ore, beef, rice, coffee, and tea also carries serious consequences for exporter countries in Africa, Latin America, and Asia [44]

The decline in oil prices may be particularly troubling in oil-dependent Yemen, a country with a large population of unemployed young people and a history of support for militant Islamic groups. Also, in Pakistan, a particular security problem exacerbated by the financial crisis could be developing. The IMF has approved a $7.6 billion loan package for Pakistan, but the country faces serious economic problems at a time when it is dealing with challenges from suspected Al Qaeda and Taliban sympathizers, when citizen objections are rising to U.S. missile strikes on suspected terrorist targets in Pakistan and the country faces a budget shortfall that may curtail the ability of the government to continue its counterterror operations.45 The Iraqi government also depends heavily on revenues from exports of oil. Such revenues finance about 95% of the government's budget.

Effects on Economic Philosophies, State Capitalism, and Protectionism

Economic Philosophies

The global financial crisis may have ended what some call the period of economic neoliberalism that began with President Ronald Reagan and British Prime Minister Margaret Thatcher. This economic philosophy already was being disparaged in many Latin American countries. Some also have asserted that the crisis has effectually ended the Washington Consensus, the economic strictures often prescribed for Latin American countries in financial trouble [46]. The Washington Consensus included fiscal discipline, liberalization of trade and direct investment flows, privatization, deregulation, and flexible exchange rates [47]. While the elements of the Washington Consensus and neoliberalism do not overlap completely, the underlying premise of each was that market-based, rather than government-based, economic decisionmaking along with fiscal discipline can lead to higher rates of economic growth and greater prosperity for nations. Budget deficits and their borrowing requirements, in particular, had to be controlled because they caused inflation and economic instability and crowded out private economic activity.

Now, however, many countries (including the United States in some respects) seem to be turning toward large budget deficits, increased trade protectionism, restrictions on capital flows, government ownership of companies, and tighter regulation of financial markets and players. After the global financial crisis has passed, the basic structure of market-based capitalism and liberalized international trade are likely to survive, but countries today seem to be turning more toward viewing economic policies through a strategic lens and some question whether the costs of neoliberal economic policies being manifest by the financial crisis are worth their benefits. Of course, coping with the crisis can be viewed as a case of expediency overriding values rather than a shift in philosophy. As one analyst has noted about financial crises: as each crisis arrives, policy makers express ritual shock, then proceed to break every rule in the book. The alternative is unthinkable. When the worst is passed, participants renounce crisis apostasy and pledge to hold firm next time [48].

At the January 2009 World Economic Forum in Davos, Switzerland, the question was raised whether the rules and values that were in place to safeguard the capitalist system have failed or whether the system itself is in need of an overhaul. Most Forum panelists agreed that, while the financial system needs to be fixed, the solution is not excessive regulation that stifles innovation and free enterprise. Former British Prime Minister Tony Blair, for example, argued that "the free enterprise system as a whole has not failed. The financial system has failed." He noted that the financial system was originally there to serve the wider economy and the wider economy to serve the wider society. According to him, the financial system was not meant to be an end in itself [49]. One commentator may have captured the essence of the issue with this comment, "Capitalism isn't the enemy, and it isn't the savior. It is simply a system fueled by human creativity but vulnerable to human weaknesses such as greed" [50].

State Capitalism

Increased government ownership and direction of enterprises and investment funds has been called state capitalism [51] or public-sector capitalism. The formal term for government takeovers of companies or assets is "nationalization," although in most cases, the current cases differ from past cases of nationalizations by communist or socialist governments. Those essentially amounted to expropriation in which governments would seize private sector assets without fully compensating owners. Most industrialized market-oriented economies of the world are taking over firms as part of rescue packages (out of expediency) with the major goal of providing support to the financial or other sectors of the economy and not to shift the basic structure of the economy away from capitalism. It is probably not the case, as some have postulated, that "we are all socialists now," [52] but increased government ownership and management of business assets brings a new dimension to the interaction between policy and business activity.

A challenge for the United States is to balance its own free-market economic philosophy with the fact that it is now a major owner or player in businesses that it has rescued because of the financial crisis. Compared with formerly socialist countries, U.S. state capitalism is small in scale, but the challenges of government management and the potential to sway business decisions because of political considerations are similar.

With respect to foreign policy, one danger of state ownership of businesses is that governments may exploit state-owned or state-invested enterprises for international political gains [53]. Nationalizations also pose risks for businesses that have invested in foreign countries. Governments could take over their operations without sufficient compensation. A related issue is that government ownership may cause companies to become less efficient and unable to compete as well in the global marketplace over the long-term. Governments may not have the expertise or manpower to successfully manage or make quick decisions at nationalized firms. Government ownership of companies, moreover, may induce companies to take actions in response to popular pressure rather than to market forces. This may lead to inefficiencies and further uncertainties about economies.

Some examples of increasing state capitalism include the following. Iceland has nationalized all its major banks, and the UK has taken a 68% share of the Royal Bank of Scotland [54]. The United States has taken control over Fannie Mae and Freddie Mac and has substantial input into the operations of AIG, Citigroup, General Motors, and Chrysler [55].

Germany has approved a law letting the government nationalize banks [56]. Loans being extended to private businesses as well as capital injections into financial institutions also are coming with strings attached. Whether the strings are limits on executive compensation, fuel economy standards, pressures on banks to lend more domestically, or other specific performance requirements, governments now have greater voice in the operation of many corporations.

In countries such as Russia, where histories of command economics predispose the government toward state ownership of the means of production, the shift toward state capitalism already was developing before the financial crisis and has continued to develop. National oil companies, other state-owned enterprises, and sovereign wealth funds have brought politicians and political bureaucrats into economic decision-making on a scale not seen since the before the market reforms that followed the end of the Cold War [57]. Although not totally attributable to the financial crisis, the line between the state-owned Gazprom and the Russian state can be quite thin. Under former President Putin, Gazprom reportedly became an instrument for centralizing authority, buying up opposition television stations and newspapers [58]. In a poll taken in Russia asking what socio-economic system the respondent favors, 58% favored the old Soviet system of state planning and distribution, while 28% favored one based on private property and market relations, and 14% responded that it was hard to say. The polling center indicated that the growth of "antibourgeois" sentiments can be explained by the financial crisis [59]

Trade Protectionism

For many, the global financial and economic crisis has confirmed existing anti-globalization sentiments and is being reflected in opposition to more liberalized trade. [60]. Under the dislocation caused by the financial crisis, many countries are attempting to curtail imports or impose other restrictions on trade. At both the G-20 Leaders' Summit and the meetings of finance ministers and central bank governors, participants agreed to fight all forms of protectionism and maintain open trade [61] However, in March 2009, World Trade Organization Director-General Pascal Lamy stated that members of the WTO were showing a "worrying tendency toward increased trade protectionism as a result of the deepening global economic crisis." He indicated that the WTO had identified 85 verified trade measures imposed by 23 countries between September 2008 and March 2009. The large majority were trade-restrictive, although some were in the direction of trade liberalization. The largest number of measures were imposed by India, most of them trade restrictive (duty hikes, import bans introduction of licensing requirements, antidumping actions, etc.) and some nonrestrictive (removal of export duties). Others that the WTO reported as having imposed a large number of new trade measures were the EU, China, Indonesia, Argentina, and Russia. The report also identified a further 14 non-verified trade measures imposed by 12 countries between September 2008 and March 2009 (with the information largely gleaned from press reports). Lamy stated that a "pattern is beginning to emerge of increases in import licensing, import tariffs and surcharges, and trade remedies to support industries that have faced difficulties early on in this crisis." There also has been an increase in initiations of antidumping investigations [62].

The overt forms of protectionism or beggar-thy-neighbor policies are limited by rules countries have agreed to as members of the WTO. However, there is ample scope for increases in trade barriers that are consistent with WTO rules and obligations, including increases in applied tariffs to higher bound levels. If all WTO members raised their currently applied tariffs to today's WTO bound rates, tariffs worldwide would double. The WTO has said that such increases in trade barriers could cause world trade to shrink by up to 8% and reduce global welfare by up to $350 billion [63]

WTO rules also allow countries to impose countervailing duties on unfairly subsidized imports or to take antidumping measures against imports being sold at less than fair value. Certain sectors also are excluded from trade agreements for national security or other reasons. Moreover, there are opportunities to favor domestic producers at the expense of foreign producers through industry-specific relief or subsidy programs, broad fiscal stimulus programs, buy-domestic provisions, or currency depreciation.

Almost any government intervention into economic activity affects international trade and capital flows. Since government intervention generally is influenced by political considerations and may involve tax dollars, it usually favors domestic constituencies at the expense of foreign constituencies. A danger in the process of recovering from the global financial crisis is that countries may try to capture a larger share of a declining volume of international trade rather than attempt to induce recovery in trade flows by helping their macroeconomies return to health. Government assistance packages also could result in a form of "creeping protectionism." At what point do government loans and assistance become an unfair subsidy under international trade rules? Also, would a government rescue a company and then stand by while it succumbs later to import competition? Governments also may turn toward "managed trade" as occurred in the 1980s in response to the oil shock of the 1970s. Managed trade was not an increase of tariff rates to reduce imports but rather the imposition of import-reducing measures such as "voluntary export restraints" or local-content requirements [64]. Imports also can be restricted through various other non-tariff measures, such as standards and technical regulations (including sanitary and phytosanitary measures).

China, for example, has announced plans to provide subsidies to various industries (such as steel and motor vehicles) and to boost export tax rebates. Also, despite calls for it to allow its currency to appreciate, the Chinese government has kept its exchange rate relatively stable since mid-2008 arguably to help its export industries. This ended a period beginning in 2005 in which China had allowed its currency to appreciate by about 20% against the dollar.

A concern among developing nations is that a type of "financial protectionism" may rise. The combination of the global economic slowdown, fragile banking and securities sectors, tighter lending standards, increased capital reserve requirements, plus government pressures on banks to lend more domestically rather than overseas may shrink the amount of capital available for emerging and developing nations. Some are wondering if the U.S. Treasury, in borrowing to finance the growing U.S. budget deficit, could crowd out borrowers from countries also seeking to cover their deficits. Also of concern to countries such as Vietnam, China, and other exporters of foreign brand name exports is that private flows of investment capital may decline as producers face rising inventories and excess production capacity. Why build another factory when existing ones sit idle?

In the United States, Members of Congress are called on to balance constituent pressures for relief from imports against the increased integration of the United States in the global economy. This has combined with increased public skepticism about the benefits of free trade and globalization. The "Buy American" provision in the February 2009 stimulus package [65] has been characterized by some as a step down the slippery slope leading to protectionism and a sign, worrying to many, that the United States may not be a leader of the free-trade initiatives in the years ahead. The European Union has raised questions about whether its provisions are compatible with U.S. international trade commitments [66] even though the provision applies only to steel, iron, and manufactured goods used in construction projects and language was included that the provision "shall be applied in a manner consistent with United States obligations under international agreements" [67]. The criticism from other nations of this provision appears to be based on both its presumed effects and the fear that even a relatively small "Buy American" provision at this time could set a precedent that could open the floodgates and provide the excuse for a cycle of "creeping protectionism" by other nations.

On March 31, 2009, just prior to the G-20 London Leaders' Summit, the Obama Administration issued an interim rule implementing the "Buy American" provisions in the economic stimulus package that was consistent with existing U.S. practice. The interim rule imposed no new restrictions in terms of the origin of products that are eligible to be purchased by the federal government for procurement projects. It upheld that the manufacturing of all iron or steel used in federal projects funded by the stimulus bill must take place in the United States, except for metallurgical processes involving refinement of steel additives. The new rule also established no requirements on the origin of components or subcomponents used in construction materials, so long as the manufacture of the construction material occurs in the United States. It also exempted from the "Buy American" provision all 38 countries that have signed the World Trade Organization's Government Procurement Agreement and 47 least-developed countries [68]

Many analysts note that the relationship between government procurement and the world trading system has always been tenuous. The national treatment provisions of the 1947 General Agreement on Tariffs and Trade (GATT)(Article III(8)) excluded government procurement from its obligations entirely. However, as the government share of GDP grew in the postwar period, especially in countries where industry sectors such as airlines and steel were nationalized, some GATT members came to believe that the trading system needed to place government procurement practices under certain disciplines. The Tokyo Round negotiations, which concluded in 1979, contained several plurilateral codes including an Agreement on Government Procurement, which members could join voluntarily. The Uruguay Round Agreements creating the WTO renegotiated these codes in areas such as antidumping and subsidies and converted them into mandatory agreements, which became prerequisites for membership in the WTO. However, the Agreement on Government Procurement (AGP) remained a plurilateral agreement open to WTO members. Many developing countries such as China, India, and Brazil have not joined the AGP [69]

For the United States to both support the inclusion of government procurement in trade negotiations yet also place certain "Buy American" restrictions on its own procurement policies illustrates the ambivalence that it, like many nations, feels toward opening government procurement policies to the same disciplines that govern other commerce. Alone among the Tokyo Round codes, the AGP was not converted into a mandatory agreement in the WTO. The political nature of government procurement may account for this ambivalence. First, the underlying rationale of the WTO system is to increase economic efficiency through freer trade. However, government procurement decisions may not depend on economic considerations. Governments use purchasing decisions to achieve domestic policy goals, such as to provide economic stimulus or the promotion of specific local industry sectors or social groups. Because taxpayer dollars are involved, however, for many there is a political imperative that money be spent locally. As one commentator summed up the dilemma, "Countries that feel themselves to be competitive in supplying goods have an incentive to improve market access, but few countries seem willing to give up the ability to discriminate in favor of either domestic providers or regional partners"[70].

Effects on U.S. Leadership and Attitudes toward the United States

Another issue raised by the global financial crisis has been the role of the United States on the world stage, the U.S. leadership position relative to other countries, and U.S. credibility. These are largely intangible qualities that depend partly on the effectiveness of current U.S. leaders but also depend on a host of other factors such as the relative military and economic might of the United States (including the role of the U.S. dollar and American market in the global economy), attitudes and perceptions abroad, actions by other nations, and the skillful use of all aspects of U.S. power. As the global financial crisis has progressed, a world-wide perception has developed that the lack of oversight and regulation by the United States was a major contributor to the crisis and has imposed huge costs both on investors and "innocent bystanders" abroad. This has been added to existing discontent in many countries with the situation in Iraq and other U.S. policies and may work to reduce the ability of Washington to lead in finding solutions to both the current financial crisis and other issues.

The financial crisis appears to have had a dual effect on perceptions of the United States as a world leader. On one hand, U.S. policy is seen as key to financial and economic recovery and in reforming the international financial system. The crisis has reminded the world that the United States is a central node in the network of financial and trade linkages that encircle the globe. Despite efforts to diversify economic and financial ties, most economies remain closely linked to the United States. Prospects for recovery from the crisis would be quite dim without U.S. policy initiatives and U.S. leadership. On the other hand, the crisis itself is perceived by some as weakening the U.S. position in the world and providing an opportunity for other nations to adjust the global balance of power away from the United States and toward Europe, China, Russia, and India. The fact that the G-20, not the G-7, [71] has become the international coordinating body for resolving the global financial crisis indicates that countries such as China, Russia, India, and Brazil have taken a seat at the head table along with the advanced industrial nations of North America, Europe, and Japan.

During the early months of the crisis, European leaders (particularly British Prime Minister Gordon Brown, French President Nicolas Sarkozy, and German Chancellor Angela Merkel) played a major leadership role in coordinating policies and convening meetings in which immediate rescue actions as well as principles for solutions and proposed policies were addressed. The end-of-term status of President George W. Bush may have contributed to this situation, and President Obama made his international debut at the April 2009 London Leader's Summit. It appears that other nations are according the Obama Administration room for a "fresh start."

The global financial crisis also has enabled countries with large currency reserves, such as China and Japan, to assume higher profiles in world financial circles. Americans are unaccustomed to being lectured to by Chinese officials, but on several occasions Chinese officials have publicly blamed the United States for causing the current crisis. Many contend that the crisis has undermined U.S. credibility on economic issues and may make it harder for

Washington to induce China to continue to reform its economy, especially its financial system. In addition, Chinese officials have expressed strong dissatisfaction over suggestions by some U.S. analysts that China's economic policies (such as its large purchases of U.S. debt securities) were a contributing factor to the U.S. subprime mortgage bubble [72]. For the Obama Administration and Congress, bilateral relations with Beijing are likely to be a challenge and require close attention and skill in managing communications and relations with the Chinese leadership. At the London Summit, President Obama accepted an invitation to visit China in the second half of 2009 [73].

China's large holdings of U.S. Treasury securities ($696 billion as of December 2008) pose a dilemma for U.S. policymakers. On one hand, Chinese purchases of U.S. debt have helped fund the U.S. budget deficit and has helped keep U.S. interest rates relatively low. However, much of the approximately $2 trillion in stimulus spending, troubled asset recovery, capital injections, mortgage restructuring and other U.S. programs will likely be financed by additional borrowing. China, which is the world's largest holder of foreign exchange reserves (at nearly $2 trillion), will likely be a major purchaser of this new debt. When Secretary of State Hillary Clinton visited China in February 2009, she expressed her appreciation for the Chinese government's continuing confidence in the U.S. Treasury securities [74]. Many analysts have warned that increased Chinese ownership of U.S. debt could enhance its political leverage over the United States. For example, China could threaten to suspend or limit future purchases of U.S. Treasury securities or threaten to liquidate its current holdings, which could further undermine the U.S. economy. Such action, however, could also reduce the value of China's investments, not only in U.S. Treasury securities, but in other financial instruments and in the U.S. economy.

China's presence at the multilateral negotiating table also could complicate the process of policymaking. China's policymakers have a strong domestic focus, and the country has a relatively short history of cooperating with international bodies in consensus decision-making. At the United Nations, China has used its Security Council veto power to block some U.S. and European initiatives. China's own financial regulatory system is still developing, and its stances on global financial oversight and regulation are only in the process of being formed. But China clearly seeks a voice in the discussion. In 2009, Zhou Xiaochuan, the governor of the People's Bank of China (China's central bank), proposed reforming the international monetary system by replacing the dollar as a reserve currency [75]. China's financial weight could provide the potential for it to play the United States off against others, including Europe and Japan, in multilateral discussions of financial regulation. This could make finding a consensus more difficult at the G20 level. China also is actively seeking to take a larger role in activities of the IMF and other multilateral financial institutions.

As for Japan, it is lending $100 billion to the International Monetary Fund and has been active in moves to create an Asian Monetary Fund and other monetary arrangements in Asia to counter the effects of currency crises [76]. This is despite the fact that the Japanese economy is in recession, the government is deeply indebted, and the country seems to be losing international financial and political clout to China.

The financial crisis and flight to dollar assets for safety also have revived discussion of the role of the U.S. dollar as a reserve currency. The international role of the dollar not only allows the United States to run trade deficits without the currency depreciation faced by most other nations, but the international role of the dollar is a factor in U.S. global influence. Russia's Prime Minister Putin has called over-reliance on the dollar "dangerous" and has proposed the development of multiple, regional reserve currencies in addition to the dollar [77]. Joseph Stiglitz, a Nobel laureate in economics, has advocated the development of a global reserve currency based on a basket of currencies to reflect the multi-polar world of today [78]. China also has joined the voices arguing for a creation of a new currency to eventually replace the dollar as the world's standard [79] Although such proposals are far from being implemented, a decline in use of the dollar as a reserve currency could make it more difficult for the United States to finance its budget and trade deficits, and if the value of the dollar fell, this would reduce the buying power of U.S. companies investing abroad and the purchasing power in other countries of U.S. budgeted funds for diplomacy, aid, security operations, and other foreign activities.

The recession in the United States and elsewhere also may hamper efforts to reach agreement on international issues such as climate change. A new climate change agreement may require sacrifice, and the willingness of either Americans or others to make sacrifices in the current environment (and our ability to convince China, India, and others to do so) may limit the range of possible outcomes.

In addition, U.S. trade and foreign investments are key components of American soft power. At a time when U.S. policymakers are turning toward the use of soft power (or what is sometimes termed "smart power" [80]), if U.S. companies are perceived as reducing their overseas business activities because of the global financial crisis, this could cause a drop in perceived U.S. importance in overseas business communities and could also lower U.S. diplomatic interest in countries of lesser importance to U.S. businesses.

Effects on Supranational Financial and Economic Organizations

The financial crisis has brought international financial organizations and institutions into the spotlight. The issue here is threefold. First is how much sovereignty to yield to the International Monetary Fund, Financial Supervisory Board, Bank for International Settlements or other such organizations in devising macroprudential regulations for the world financial system that would identify signs of problems that could engulf entire economies. For example, how much authority should the IMF have to compel countries to implement policies to reduce the risk of a systemic financial failure? A second aspect of the issue deals with how much additional capital member countries should provide to the IMF, World Bank, and other global lenders. The third aspect is governance of the institutions. Given the increasing role of China, India, and other new members of the G-20 in the financial crisis, should they also have a commensurately larger role in the governance of the international financial institutions?

The economic crisis has highlighted the inter-connected nature of the global financial system and the rapidity with which a financial crisis in one country crosses borders and spreads across manufacturing, retailing, and other sectors. It also has raised the importance of having an international early warning system and some institution that can assess systemic risk occurring across countries and across financial sectors and take measures to stem world financial problems before they become too costly and reach the catastrophic level. It has become apparent that remedial and recovery measures, both on macroeconomic and microeconomic levels, need to be coordinated. On the macroeconomic level, one country can "free ride" on a stimulus package by another economy through increased demand for its exports. On the microeconomic level, the forces of international competition drive business activity away from overregulated or high-cost financial centers. If, for example, financial institutions in New York are more restricted than those in London, financial deals may simply migrate from the United States to the U.K.

The major international organizations dealing with the financial crisis include the International Monetary Fund, the Financial Stability Forum, the Bank for International Settlements, the World Bank, and the G-20. Several other organizations also play a role in coordinating policy among nations. Some leaders have called for a Bretton Woods II agreement that would remake the international financial architecture that was created in 1944 centered around the IMF and World Bank [81]. Some of the questions being addressed include whether the major role of the IMF should be informational, advisory, and technical, or should it have enforcement authority? For example, if the IMF finds that a country is teetering on the brink of a financial crisis, what can and should it do proactively to lessen the risk that the crisis actually occurs? Any public action could be the trigger that would start such a crisis, but quietly discussing the issue with national authorities without any enforcement authority is rarely sufficient to spur corrective actions that may be politically unpopular. Also, should any enforcement be done through a dispute resolution process, through rules similar to those that the European Union requires of its members, or should the IMF or other international institution be ceded oversight and regulatory authority by national governments? [82]

The IMF, Financial Stability Forum (now Financial Stability Board), and the Bank for International Settlements already have made recommendations for changes in regulations for member nations. Each is contributing to the G-20 process to devise policies for nations to adopt. Countries, however, have been slow to implement regulatory changes previously recommended. Traditionally, the U.S. Treasury and other financial regulatory agencies, not the State Department, interface with these international financial organizations. As can be seen with the global financial crisis, however, financial foreign policy can have as large an impact on international relations and world stability as traditional political and security policies.

At the London Summit of the G-20, the leaders agreed to boost the IMF's reserves to around $500 billion through bilateral borrowing from members and also from borrowing in world financial markets (much as the World Bank already does). There appears to be consensus that the IMF lacks the necessary financial resources to tackle the problems of struggling countries, with particular concern about Eastern Europe. The G-20 leaders also agreed to provide the World Bank and other regional development banks with extra funds.

Effects on Poverty

In a February 2009 commentary, Dominique Strauss-Kahn, Managing Director of the IMF, noted that during the financial turmoil attention has been focused on the advanced and emerging-market economies that are most immediately affected, but, in his opinion, the impact on poor countries is far more severe [83]. He pointed out that weak global growth is shrinking export markets, and many commodity prices are plunging. The combination of tighter credit conditions in the advanced economies and dimmer economic prospects in low-income countries is reducing investment flows, while workers' remittances, which now eclipse aid as the largest financial flows to many low-income countries, also are falling.

Even though the poorest countries in the world, many in sub-Saharan Africa, are less integrated into global capital markets than the advanced industrial nations or emerging economies in Eastern Europe, the global economic crisis is affecting standards of living and is expected to lead to higher levels of global poverty. Many argue that the impact on poverty also may be most felt in the large, middle-income countries such as China and India, the world's two most populous nations, and not just in the least developed countries. Over the past two decades, the largest gains in raising people out of poverty have been made in these two countries. For several years China has averaged economic growth rates of 10% or higher, while India has grown at 8% or more per year. The World Bank estimates each one percentage point drop in world economic growth could trap another 20 million people in poverty [84]. In 2008, global growth was an estimated 2.5%. For 2009, growth is expected to drop by three percentage points or more.85 In February 2009, China reported that about 20 million of the nation's 130 million migrant workers already had become unemployed [86]

The impact of the global crisis is transmitted to the poorest countries through several channels. These include:

- Declining exports. In Pakistan, for example, textile exports fell by 4.1% year-onyear in December 2008. The textile sector represents approximately two-thirds of Pakistan's total export revenues.
- Declining commodity prices. Because many of the poorest countries are heavily dependent on a few primary export commodities, rapid swings in commodity prices can wreak havoc on their domestic economy. Yemen, for example, announced in January that it would have to decrease public expenditures by 50% because of the financial crisis and the lower government revenues from its oil exports.
- Migration and remittances. The combination of slow growth rates, job losses, and the rising cost of living in advanced countries has led to fewer economic migrants from developing countries and lower levels of remittances. This could have major effects in countries which provide large numbers of migrant workers, including Mexico, Guatemala, El Salvador, India, Bangladesh, and the Philippines. The volume of remittances soared over the past decade, but recent data show significant deceleration since the beginning of the current crisis, with Latin America and Caribbean the hardest hit. The Inter-American Development Bank calculates that remittances to the Latin American and Caribbean region declined by 1.7% between 2007 and 2008.
- Lower levels of foreign assistance. Research from previous incidences of economic crisis suggests that foreign aid from developed to poor countries is likely to decrease.
- Diminished capital flows. Although some progress has been made in developing capital markets in poor countries, they are still perceived as risky. Global credit has tightened across the world, especially among the developing countries. This has lead to a sharp contraction in capital flows to developing countries as well as restrictions on the availability of trade finance. The inability of developing country governments to raise money on international capital markets will likely have a sharp impact on government budgets, reducing the amount available for poverty reduction programs.

Once the global recession is past, estimates of declines in long-term poverty are encouraging. Over the medium term, economic growth rates may still be higher than they were in the 1990s due to macroeconomic policy improvements and structural reforms such as privatization and regulatory initiatives within developing countries [87]. This depends, however, on how quickly and fully the world economy can recover.

BUDGETARY EFFECTS ON RESOURCES FOR AID, DIPLOMACY, AND DEFENSE

The decline in government tax revenues caused by the slowdown in economic activity and the stimulus programs and automatic economic stabilizers (increased spending for unemployment compensation and welfare) are increasing competition within countries for scarce budget funds and affecting decisions about the allocation of national resources. Budget battles, already intense, have become even more heated as the global financial crisis has spread [88]. This could result in fewer resources available for foreign assistance, diplomacy, and defense [89]

A policy brief by the United Nations Conference on Trade and Development on flows of official development assistance (ODA) stated the following:

> The current recession, and some of the stimulus measures being introduced to combat it, is compounding budget deficits and budget reallocations in many donor countries. ODA is a soft target in such situations; during past banking crises, it has dipped anywhere from 20% to 40%. A recent study found that the crises affecting Finland, Japan, Norway and Sweden in the 1980s-1990s were all followed by a substantial decline in foreign aid, ranging from 10% in Norway to 62% in Finland. Furthermore, ODA levels tend to recover very slowly–in Sweden's and Norway's case, six-to-nine years after the trough, according to the same study. Finnish and Japanese aid flows, meanwhile, have yet to return to their pre-crisis peaks. Given the depth of today's crisis, the recovery period is likely to be similarly long [90]

In the United States, official development assistance to poorer nations and other programs aimed at alleviating poverty now are competing for funding in a budget deep in deficit [91]. The large expenditures to provide stimulus to the U.S. economy could clash with some early foreign policy priorities of the new Administration. President Obama and top officials in his Administration— including Secretary of State Clinton and Secretary of Defense Gates—have pledged to increase the capacity of civilian foreign policy institutions and levels of U.S. foreign assistance. Early pledges have included: a 25% increase in Foreign Service staffing; doubling of U.S. foreign assistance spending to $50 billion by 2012 (or slower increases if the current economic crisis continues); and increased funds for global health programs.

Although some efficiencies may be found in revamping foreign policy-related programs and/or improving policy coordination, one incoming State Department official emphasized outright that "we will need additional resources" to achieve foreign policy goals [92]. Financial constraints could impose difficult choices between foreign policy priorities—for example, between boosting levels of non-military aid to Afghanistan and increasing global health programs–or changes to planned levels of increases across the board. The global reach of the economic downturn further complicates the resource problem, as it both limits what other countries can do to address common international challenges and potentially exacerbates the scale of need in conflict areas and the developing world.

The budget constraint also could affect the resolution of issues such as the North Korean (DPRK) nuclear threat. Under agreed-upon requirements under the Six Party Talks, if the DPRK complies with its commitments, the United States is to provide more energy and other assistance. In addition, Japan and South Korea, two countries hit hard by the financial crisis, would have to budget funds for aid to North Korea [93].

U.S. defense expenditures also face similar budget debates [94]. Addressing U.S. security needs under the financial crisis is beyond the purview of this report, but one analysis indicates that the security threat from the crisis is likely to manifest itself in several distinctive ways.

- It will create major pressures on the defense budget, most notably acquisition— that is, the procurement and research and development accounts.
- It will likely result in a contraction of defense spending, and therefore operations as well and modernization, on the part of key allies and friends.
- It could prompt nations that are ambivalent about their relationship with the United States, most notably China and Russia, to act in ways that are deleterious to American interests.
- It could prompt even more hostile behavior on the part of nations such as Iran and Venezuela that already bear deep antipathy toward the United States.
- It could further destabilize states that are already vulnerable to internal unrest.
- It could spur further international criminal behavior that could undermine internal American security [95]

REFERENCES

[1] Jonathan Lynn, "IMF says clean up banks to tackle dire world crisis," Reuters, March 23, 20009, Reuters.com

[2] For details, see CRS Report RL34742, *The Global Financial Crisis: Analysis and Policy Implications*, coordinated by Dick K. Nanto.

[3] U.S. Congress, Senate Committee on Foreign Relations, *Foreign Policy Implications of the Global Economic Crisis*, Hearing, 111th Cong., 1st sess., February 11, 2009 and *Foreign Policy and the Global Economic* Crisis, March 25, 2009. U.S. Congress, Senate Committee on Armed Services, *To receive testimony on the current and future worldwide threats to the national security of the United States*, 111th Cong., 1st sess., March 10, 2009. U.S. Congress, House Committee on Armed Services, *Hearing on Security Challenges Arising from the Global Financial Crisis*, 111th Cong., 1st sess., March 11, 2009. U.S. Congress, House Committee on Foreign Affairs, *U.S. Foreign Economic Policy in the Global Crisis*, 11 1th Cong., 1st sess., March 12, 2009.

[4] International Labor Organization, International Institute for Labor Studies, *The Financial and Economic Crisis: A Decent Work Response*, Preprint edition, March 2009.

[5] Dennis C. Blair, *Annual Threat Assessment of the Intelligence Community for the Senate Select Committee on Intelligence*, Director of National Intelligence, Washington, DC, February 12, 2009. See also, U.S. Senate, Committee on Foreign Relations, "Foreign Policy Implications Of The Global Economic Crisis," Roundtable before the Committee On Foreign Relations, February 11, 2009. Mark Mazzetti, "Global Economy Top Threat to U.S., Spy Chief Says," The New York Times, February 13, 2009, Internet edition.
[6] Luke Baker, "UK forms new security body, weighs financial crisis," *Reuters*, March 9, 2009.
[7] This is a reference to G.W. Bush Administration's use of "Axis of Evil" referring to Iran, Iraq, and North Korea. Niall Ferguson, "Introducing the axis of upheaval; The financial crisis is bad enough; but combined with empires in decline and ethnic disintegration, it is a recipe for disaster," *The Times (London)*, March 14, 2009, Internet edition.
[8] "Icelandic government falls; asked to stay on," CNN.com/Europe, January 26, 2009.
[9] David L. Stern, "Latvia's government collapses," *International Herald Tribune*, February 20, Internet edition.
[10] Stefan Wagstyl, "Crisis opens door for Hungrian conservatives," *Financial Times*, February 3, 2009, p. 4.
[11] Kanoko Matsuyama and Toko Sekiguchi, "Aso Approval Plunges as Japan's Economy Shrinks 12.7%," Bloomberg.com, February 16, 2009, Internet edition.
[12] Toko Sekiguchi and Sachiko Sakamaki, "Aso's Obama Summit May Be Last as Calls to Quit Grow ," Bloomberg.com, February 23, 2009.
[13] "Eastern Europe gripped by political instability," EuActive.com, February 17, 2009.
[14] Adrian Michaels, "Europe's winter of discontent," The Telegraph, January 29, 2009, Telegraph.co.uk.
[15] Adam Thomson, "El Salvador's left claims victory in historic poll," FT.com (Financial Times), March 16, 2009, Internet edition.
[16] Peter Popham, "The Big Question: How serious is the political unrest on the Continent, and can it be calmed?," *The Independent*, January 30, 2009, Internet edition.
[17] The International Monetary Fund has issued emergency loans to Hungary and Ukraine. The World Bank in a joint effort with the European Bank for Reconstruction and Development and the European Investment Bank announced on February 27, 2009 that they were providing $31 billion over two years to assist ailing banks and businesses in Eastern and Central Europe.
[18] "Furious leaders lash US over economic crisis," *ABC News*, January 29, 2009.
[19] "Chavez orders army to seize Venezuela rice mills," Reuters as reported by MSNBC.com, February 28, 2009. Deisy Buitrago, "Venezuela sees no further Cargill takeovers," Reuters, March 6, 2009.
[20] "EU, Russia quietly battle for Eastern Europe influence," EurActiv.com, February 11, 2009.
[21] Office of mass media relations of the Cabinet of Ministers of Ukraine Secretariat , *Yulia Tymoshenko: Ukraine carries on successful negotiations with many countries of the world on giving credit to cover deficit of State Budget*, Government Portal, Riga, Ukraine, February 7, 2009. Yekaterina Trofimova, "Russia Seen as Cash Cow," Utro.ru (in Russian), March 4, 2009, Translated by Open Source Center, document

CEP20090304009003. "Ukrainian Speaker Says Borrowing From Russia Would Be Advisable," ITAR-TASS, March 11, 2009.

[22] Guy Chazan and Gregory L. White, "Russian oil company buys stake in Hungary's MOL—Purchase reinforces concerns Kremlin is extending reach," *The Wall Street Journal Asia*, April 1, 2009, p. M2.

[23] Yuriy Humber, "Lukashenko Eases Grip on Belarus Amid Crisis," *The St. Petersburg Times (Russia)*, April 3, 2009, Reproduced in Dow Jones Factiva.

[24] Meetings with opinion leaders in Indonesia by Dick Nanto in February 2008.

[25] Valentina Pop, "European NATO members at odds over strategic priorities," EUuobserver.com, March 27, 2009.

[26] How China sees the world," *The Economist*, March 21, 2009, pp. 13, 27-29.

[27] For an analysis of China's trade and investments as part of its soft power, see CRS Report RL34620, *Comparing Global Influence: China's and U.S. Diplomacy, Foreign Aid, Trade, and Investment in the Developing World*, coordinated by Thomas Lum.

[28] David Winning, Shai Oster, and Alex Wilson, "China, Russia Strike $25 Billion Oil Pact ," *The Wall Street Journal, Asia*, Internet Edition, February 18, 2009.

[29] Valentina Pop, "European NATO members at odds over strategic priorities," Euobserver.com , March 27, 2009, Open Source Center article No. EUP200903273 19002.

[30] Denis McMahon and Aaron Back, "PBOC Eyes More Currency Swaps To Up Trade In Crisis," *Wall Street Journal*, March 31, 2009, Mobile edition.

[31] Valentina Pop, "European NATO members at odds over strategic priorities," Euobserver.com , March 27, 2009, Open Source Center article No. EUP200903273 19002.

[32] For a discussion of stability as a goal, see Ralph Peters, "Stability, America's Enemy," *Parameters*, 2001/2002, Winter, pp. 5-20.

[33] National Intelligence Council, *Global Trends 2025: A Transformed World*, NIC 2008-003, Washington, DC, November 2008, p. 5.

[34] "Foreign Companies React To Mexico Violence," *Associated Press, reported by CBS News*, February 24, 2009, Internet edition.

[35] "Mexico Drug Violence May Be Reaching Peak," *CBS/Associated Press*, February 26, 2009, Internet edition.

[36] Catherine Bremer, "ANALYSIS-Mexico drug war, economy hobble Calderon's ambitions," *Reuters*, April 6, 2009.

[37] Stratfor Global Intelligence, *An Uptick in Violent Crime*, China Security Memo, February 19, 2009.

[38] Ian Bremmer, "Call: Global recession = more terrorism," *Foreign Policy*, March 4, 2009, pp. Internet edition, ForeignPolicy.com.

[39] Stratfor, *Gulf States: Labor Policies, Financial Crisis and Security Concerns*, Analysis, February 24, 2009.

[40] Michael J. Carden, *Military Adapts to Special Operations Mission, Mullen Says* , American Forces Press Service, February 12, 2009.

[41] *IMF says clean up banks to tackle dire world crisis*, Reuters, March 23, 2009.

[42] "Remittances, Trickle-down economics," *The Economist (London)*, February 21, 2009, p. 76.

[43] Donald Steinberg, "First Lehman Brothers, Next Liberia?," *The Globalist*, by the International Crisis Group, January 26, 2009. Stratfor, *Watch List for Remittance Flows*, Analysis, February 4, 2009.

[44] Johnston, Tim. "Asia Nations Join to Prop Up Prices," *Washington Post*, November 1, 2008, p. A10. "Record Fall in NZ Commodity Price Gauge," *The National Business Review*, November 5, 2008.

[45] Joby Warrick, "Experts See Security Risks in Downturn, Global Financial Crisis May Fuel Instability and Weaken U.S. Defenses," *Washington Post*, November 15, 2008. p. A01. Bokhari, Farhan, "Pakistan's War On Terror Hits Roadblock, Global Economic Crisis Prompts Military To Consider Spending Cutbacks," CBS News (online version), October 28, 2008.

[46] Kevin Gallagher , "The death of the Washington consensus?," Guardian.co.uk, October 13, 2008.

[47] Center for International Development at Harvard University, Global Trade Negotiations Home Page, *Washington Consensus*, Updated April 2003.

[48] Gelpern, Anna. "Emergency Rules," *The Record* (Bergen-Hackensack, NJ), September 26, 2008.

[49] Tony Blair , Stephen Green , Indra Nooyi , and Shimon Peres , *The Values behind Market Capitalism*, The World Economic Forum, January 28, 2009.

[50] Cynthia Tucker, "Capitalism no foe; just keep an eye on it," *Atlanta Journal Constitution*, March 29, 2009, Internet edition.

[51] State capitalism also may refer to economic activities by states (e.g., New York) within the United States. Most state investment, however, tends to be unrelated to foreign policy (except for state pension funds that may eschew investing in certain countries because of human rights considerations).

[52] E.J. Dionne, Jr, "Stuck Between Stations," *The New Republic*, March 30, 2009, Internet edition.

[53] Douglas Rediker and Heidi Crebo-Rediker, "Don't Pick on Sovereign Wealth," *The Wall Street Journal Europe*, July 17, 2008, p. 12.

[54] Landon Thomas Jr., "Nationalized in all but name: U.S. move echoes U.K. share of RBS," *International Herald Tribune*, February 24, 2009, Internet edition.

[55] CRS Report RS22950, *Fannie Mae and Freddie Mac in Conservatorship*, by Mark Jickling; CRS Report RL34730, *Troubled Asset Relief Program: Legislation and Treasury Implementation*, by Baird Webel and Edward V. Murphy; Binyamin Appelbaum, "Government to Take Bigger Stake in Citigroup," *Washington Post*, February 27, 2009.

[56] "Germany approves law on bank nationalization," *Welt Online*, February 18, 2009.

[57] Ian Bremmer and Nouriel Roubini, "Expect the World Economy to Suffer Through 2009 ," *The Wall Street Journal*, January 23, 2009, p. A15.

[58] Andrew E. Kramer, "Gazprom," *The New York Times*, January 20, 2009.

[59] "Russians reject American-style capitalism more than ever," *Washington Post paid supplement, Russia Now*, March 25, 2009, p. H4.

[60] See CRS Report R40461, *The Global Economic Downturn and Protectionism*, by Raymond J. Ahearn.

[61] The Group of Twenty (G-20) Finance Ministers and Central Bank Governors , *Declaration and action plan from the Washington Summit*, November 15, 2009,

http://www.g20.org. G-20, Meeting of Finance Ministers and Central Bank Governors, United Kingdom, 14 March 2009, Communiqué, March 14, 2009.

[62] "WTO Chief Cites 'Significant Slippage' Toward Protectionism Since Late January," *International Trade Daily (The Bureau of National Affairs, Inc.)*, March 30, 2009.

[63] Pascal Lamy, *Protectionism cannot be 'smart', Lamy tells Australian think-tank*, World Trade Organization, WTO NEWS: SPEECHES—DG PASCAL LAMY, March 2, 2009.

[64] Fredrik Erixon and Razeen Sally, Protectionism is on the rise, European Centre for International Political Economy, Brussels, Belgium, February 16, 2009, posted on VoxEU.org.

[65] H.R. 1 (P.L. 111-5) Sec. 1605 provides that none of the funds appropriated or otherwise made available by the act may be used for a project for the construction, alteration, maintenance, or repair of a public building or public work unless all of the iron, steel, and manufactured goods used in the project are produced in the United States provided that such action would not be inconsistent with the public interest, such products are not produced in the United States, and would not increase the cost of the overall project by more than 25%.

[66] "EU Raises New Questions on Compatibility of U.S. 'Buy America' Provisions with GPA," *International Trade Daily (Bureau of National Affairs, Inc.)*, March 30, 2009.

[67] "Europe Warns against 'Buy American' Clause," *Spiegel Online International*, February 3, 2009, Internet edition.

[68] Department of Defense (DoD), General Services Administration, "Federal Acquisition Regulation; FAR Case 2009- 008, American Recovery and Reinvestment Act of 2009 (the Recovery Act)—Buy American Requirements for Construction Material," 74 *Federal Register* , March 31, 2009, pp. 14623-14633.

[69] The Agreement on Government Procurement (AGP) commits signatories to practice the principles of national treatment and non-discrimination in the laws, regulations, practices, and procedures concerning government procurement. The agreement provides procedures to ensure transparency, including detailed operating rules on the procurement process of the signatory, a challenge procedure by which a rejected bid can be independently and impartially reviewed, and recourse to the World Trade Organization dispute settlement provisions. However, AGP only applies to the sectors and the procurement agencies that the government includes in its schedule of national commitments. This schedule lists the national and sub-national agencies as well as other entities that will participate, exceptions within those units, and the threshold- value for including contracts.

[70] John H. Barton, et. al., *Evolution of the Trade Regime* (Princeton, NJ: Princeton University Press, c2006), p. 119.

[71] The G-7 includes Canada, France, Germany, Italy, Japan, United Kingdom, and the United States. The G-8 is the G-7 plus Russia. The G-20 adds Argentina, Australia, Brazil, China, India, Indonesia, Mexico, Saudi Arabia, South Africa, South Korea, and Turkey.

[72] U.S. Joint Economic Committee, "Chinese FX Interventions Caused international Imbalances, Contributed to U.S. Housing Bubble," by Robert O'Quinn. March 2008; Wang Yu, The U.S. is the Cause of the Financial Crisis. China Cannot Be Blamed , Xinhuanet, China, translated By Eugene Tan, and Edited by Louis Standish, printed in

Watching America, http://watchingamerica.com/News/18092/zhang-jianhua-us-is-cause-of-financial-crisis-putting-responsibilityon-china-cannot-be-justified/.

[73] "Obama accepts invitations to visit China, Russia," *Associated Press*, April 1, 2009.

[74] Hillary Rodham Clinton, *Toward a Deeper and Broader Relationship With China, Remarks With Chinese Foreign Minister Yang Jiechi* , Beijing, China, U.S. Department of State, February 21, 2009.

[75] Zhou Xiaochuan, *Reform the International Monetary System*, Peoples' Bank of China, March 26, 2009, pbc.gov.cn available at [http://news.xinhuanet.com/english/2009-03/26/content_1 1074507.htm].

[76] Ulrich Volz, "Asian Monetary Fund, Take Two," *Far Eastern Economic Review*, June 18, 2008, Internet edition; "IMF close to finalizing $100 bil. loan from Japan: Strauss-Kahn ," *Kyodo News*, February 2, 2009.

[77] "Putin Speaks at Davos," *The Wall Street Journal*, January 28, 20009, online version.

[78] Joseph Stiglitz, "Europe's leaders can seize this opportunity to fill the leadership gap," *The Daily Telegraph*, November 11, 2008, p. 7.

[79] Andrew Batson, "China Takes Aim at Dollar ," *The Wall Street Journal*, March 29, 2009, Internet edition.

[80] Luigi R. Einaudi, *U.S. Smart Power in the Americas: 2009 and Beyond*, Institute for National Strategic Studies, National Defense University, Presented at a conference U.S. Smart Power In The Americas: 2009 And Beyond at the Center for Strategic and International Studies, Washington, DC, February 11, 2008.

[81] Gerstenzang, James. "Bush will Meet with G-20 After Election," *Los Angeles Times*, October 23, 2008.

[82] For further information on the IMF, see CRS Report RS22976, *The Global Financial Crisis: The Role of the International Monetary Fund (IMF)*, by Martin A. Weiss.

[83] Dominique Strauss-Kahn, *The World Must Not Forget Africa During This Crisis*, A Commentary by Dominique Strauss-Kahn, Managing Director, International Monetary Fund, February 10, 2009.

[84] "Global Financial Crisis: Responding Today, Securing Tomorrow," Background Paper prepared by the World Bank Group, G20 Summit on Financial Markets and the World Economy Washington, D.C., November 15, 2008. http://web.worldbank.org/WBSITE/EXTERNAL/NEWS/0,,contentMDK:21972885~pagePK:64257043~piPK:437376~theSitePK:4607,00.html

[85] International Monetary Fund, *Global Economic Slump Challenges Policies*, World Economic Outlook Update, January 28, 2009.

[86] Keith Bradsher, "China's Unemployment Swells as Exports Falter," *The New York Times*, February 6, 2009, Internet edition.

[87] Ibid, p. 49.

[88] Jim Snyder, "Budget battles loom as Obama team heads to Hill," *The Hill*, March 1, 2009.

[89] See, for example, Richard Haass, *Statement of Richard N. Haass, President of the Council on Foreign Relations, Before the Committee on Armed Services, U.S. House of Representatives*, Washington, DC, March 11, 2009.

[90] United Nations Conference on Trade and Development, *Keeping ODA afloat: no stone unturned*, UNCTAD Policy Brief, No. 7, March 2009.

[91] For details of the FY2009 appropriation, see CRS Report RL34552, *State, Foreign Operations, and Related Programs: FY2009 Appropriations*, by Susan B. Epstein and Kennon H. Nakamura.

[92] Testimony of Jacob Lew, U.S. Deputy Secretary of State nominee, U.S. Senate Committee on Foreign Relations, January 22, 2009.

[93] See CRS Report R40095, *Assistance to North Korea*, by Mark E. Manyin and Mary Beth Nikitin; CRS Report RL33567, Korea-U.S. Relations: Issues for Congress, by Larry A. Niksch.

[94] For information on the FY2009 defense authorization, see CRS Report RL34473, *Defense: FY2009 Authorization and Appropriations*, by Pat Towell, Stephen Daggett, and Amy Belasco.

[95] U.S. Congress, House Committee on Armed Services, *Hearing on Security Challenges Arising from the Global Financial Crisis*, Statement by Dov S. Zakheim, "Security Challenges Arising From the Global Economic Crisis," 111th Cong., 1st sess., March 11, 2009.

INDEX

A

B

C

D

E

F

G

H

I

J

K

L

M

N

O

P

Q

R

S

T

U

V

W

Y

Z